THE ROYAL NAVY

by

William Laird Clowes

From Earliest Times to 1900

VOLUME 4B

From 1793 to 1802
Minor Operations and Exploration

ISBN 9798387644832

2023

INTRODUCTION TO THE CHRONICON EDITION

William Laird Clowes (1 February 1856 — 14 August 1905) was a British journalist and historian. He wrote numerous technical pieces on naval technology and strategy and was also noted for his articles concerning racial politics in the southern United States. Despite having trained as a lawyer, Clowes had always preferred literature and writing, publishing his first work in 1876 and becoming a full-time journalist in 1879. For the services rendered in his career, Clowes was knighted, awarded the gold medal of the United States Naval Institute and given a civil list pension.

In 1897, Clowes gave up his journalistic career to focus on naval history, spending the next six years compiling his best known work, *The Royal Navy, A History from the Earliest Times to 1900*. This publication was well received at the time and remains a standard reference text and in print. During the last years of his life he was also a contributor to Traill and Mann's six-volume series *Social England* and author of *Four Modern Naval Campaigns* (1902). Much of his research into naval history was carried out abroad, especially in Davos, Switzerland, due to repeated bouts of ill health. For his services to journalism and naval history, he was knighted in the 1902 Coronation Honours, receiving the accolade from King Edward VII at Buckingham Palace on 24 October that year. He was further given a civil list pension of £150, invited to join the Institute of Naval Architects and the Royal United Service Institution and presented with the gold medal of the United States Naval Institute. He also became a Fellow of King's College London. He died in August 1905 at his home in St Leonards, East Sussex.

THE ROYAL NAVY

His history of the Royal Navy was originally intended to be in five volumes but became seven volumes by the time he finished. This Chronicon edition is expected to be in fourteen volumes. The series will be a faithful version of his work as originally published, the only significant changes being the clarification and expansion of his citations. Discovered typographic errors will have been corrected.

David Mignery
Editor

William Laird Clowes

THE ROYAL NAVY

A History
From the Earliest Times to the Present

By

William Laird Clowes

Fellow of King's College, London; Gold Medallist U.S. Naval Institute; Honourable Member of the R.U.S. Institution

Assisted by

Sir Clements Markham, K.C.B, P.R.G.S.
Captain A.T. Mahan, U.S.N.
H. W. Wilson
Theodore Roosevelt
Mr. L. Carr Laughton
et cetera

Twenty-Five Photogravures and Hundreds of Full Page and Other Illustrations, Maps, Charts, et cetera.

In Seven Volumes

Vol. IV

LONDON

Sampson Low, Marston and Company
Limited
Saint Dunstan's House, Fetter Lane, E.C.
1899

LONDON:

Printed by
WILLIAM CLOWES AND SONS, LIMITED
Stamford Street and Charing Cross

THE ROYAL NAVY

CONTENTS

VOLUME 4B

Chapter XXXVI Minor Operations, 1793-1802	8
Appendix to Chapters XXXV and XXXVI	98
Chapter XXXVII Voyages and Discoveries, 1793-1802:	151
Index of Citations	162
General Index	166

LIST OF ILLUSTRATIONS

Capture of the *Cleopatre* by the *Nymphe,* June 18th 1793	12
Captain Robert Faulknor (3rd), R.N.	28
Admiral Sir Henry Trollope, Knight	43
Signature of Captain Edward Pakenham, R.N., Who Perished in H.M.S. *Resistance*, 1798	57
Admiral Sir Edward Hamilton, Baronet	75
Captain Matthew Flinders, R.N.	155

CHAPTER XXXVI

MINOR OPERATIONS OF THE ROYAL NAVY, 1793-1802

H.W. WILSON.

Beginning of hostilities — Capture of privateers — The Iris and Citoyenne Francaise — Loss of the Hyaena — The Venus and the Semillante — The Nymphe takes the Cleopatre — The Boston and the Embuscade — The Crescent takes the Reunion — Nelson and a French squadron — The Thames and the Uranie — Loss of the Thames — Capture of the Inconstant — The Antelope takes the Atalante — Escape of the Juno — Defence of the Pigot — Capture of the Pomone and Engageante — The Orpheus takes the Duguay Trouin — The Swiftsure takes the Atalante — Loss of the Castor — Her recapture — Escape of the Crescent, Druid, and Eurydice — The Romney takes the Sibylle — Loss of the Hound — Destruction of the Volontaire — Saumarez frightens Weymouth — Capture of the Revolutionnaire — Captain Matthew Smith's action — Loss of the Daphne — Faulknor at Desirade — The Blanche takes the Pique — Loss of the Esperance and capture of the Requin — The Lively takes the Espion and the Tourterelle — The Coureuse and Jean Bart taken — The Astraea takes the Gloire — The Hannibal takes the Gentille — Blowing up of the Boyne — French convoy destroyed in Camaret Bay — Capture of French storeships — The Courier National, Prompte, and Liberte taken — Capture of the Minerve — The Alliantie taken — The Southampton and the Vestale — Capture of the Superbe, Brutus, Republicaine, Bonne Citoyenne, Aspic, and Mutine — Sidney Smith at Erqui — Warren's action with a convoy — The Revolutionnaire takes the Unite — Smith taken prisoner — Fremantle at Bona — Capture of the Virginie — The Ecureuil burnt —

THE ROYAL NAVY

The Spencer takes the Volcan — The Argo taken — The Santa Margarita takes the Tamise, and the Unicorn the Tribune — Cutting out of the Utile — The Dryad captures the Proserpine — Capture of the Legere and Renommee — The Glatton and French frigates — Indecisive actions — The Andromaque destroyed — Escape of the Raison — The Topaze takes the Elisabeth — Frigate action off Sumatra — Blowing up of the Amphion — Defence of the Pelican — The Terpsichore captures the Mahonesa — The Lapwing at Anguilla — The Terpsichore and the Vestale — Capture and recapture of the Sabina — The Blanche and the Ceres — Capture of the Tartu — Escape of Indiamen — An Algerine pirate taken — Landing of French criminals at Fishguard — Capture of the Resistance and Constance — The Ninfa and Santa Elena taken — Destruction of the Calliope — Capture of the Gaite — Action with the Reolaise, et cetera — The Ranger and the Hyene taken — The Phoebe takes the Nereide — Capture of the Daphne — The Sibylle and Fox at Manilla — The Speedy and the Papillon — Action with the Charente — Escape of the Pearl — Taking of the Corcyre and Mondovi — The Seahorse takes the Sensible — Capture of the Seine — Capture of the Santa Dorotea — Blowing up of the Resistance — Escape of the Brilliant — Cutting out of the Aventurier — The Espoir takes the Liguria — Capture of the Vaillante and of the Neptune — Loss of the Leander — Capture of the Decade — Taking of the Furie and Waakzaamheid — Dickson at Margarita — Loss of the Ambuscade — Defence of the Wolverine — Wreck of the Proserpine — The Argo taken — The Daedalus takes the Prudente — The Espoir takes the Africa — The Sibylle captures the Forte — Frigate action off Hoedic — Loss of the Fortune — Cutting out affair at La Selva — Recapture of the Crash — The Clyde takes the Vestale — The Tamar captures the Republicaine — Taking of the Draak and Gier — Action in Algoa Bay — Escape of the Preneuse — Taking of the Arethuse and Bordelaise — Blowing up of the Trincomale — Capture of the Thetis and Santa Brigida — The Cerberus and Spanish frigates — Cutting out of the Hermione — The Speedy off Gibraltar Capture of the Galgo — The Solebay off San Domingo — Burning of the Preneuse — Action off Madeira — Capture of the Pallas — The Petrel takes the Ligurienne — Capture of the Carmen and Florentina — Taking of the Albanaise — Affairs off Saint Croix and Noirmoutier — Cutting out of the Desiree — Cutting out of the Cerbere — Capture of the Concorde and Medee — The Seine takes the Vengeance — Cutting out of the Esmeralda and Paz — Taking of the East Indiaman Kent — Capture of the Venus — Cutting out of the San Josef — The Milbrook and the Bellone — Destruction of the Reolaise — Cutting out of the Senegal — Capture of the Eclair and of the

Sanspareille — Gallant action of the N.S. de los Dolores — Capture of the Dedaigneuse — Taking of the Curieux — Action of the Penguin — The Phoebe takes the Africaine — Lord Cochrane in the Speedy — The Mercury at Ancona — Affair off Oropesa — Cutting out of the Chevrette — Gallant action of the Pasley — Mysterious engagements of the Sylph — Capture of the Chiffonne — The Victor and the Fleche — Recapture of the Bulldog — Unsatisfactory nature of ships' logs — Criticism of French tactics — Influence of chance — Effects of weight of metal upon the results of actions — Value of the carronade — Various categories of actions — British promptitude in refitting — Successes of merchantmen — Distribution of British cruisers.

On January 2nd, 1793, the first act of hostility between France and England in Europe occurred, the *Childers*, sloop, being fired upon by the Brest forts whilst standing in towards the harbour.

On May 13th occurred the first naval action of the war, (1) though previously, on March 13th, the British sloop, *Scourge*, Commander George Brisac, had captured one French privateer, and on April 14th a British squadron had taken another. The *Iris*, 32, Captain George Lumsdaine, sighted a strange sail in the Bay of Biscay, early in the morning, and gave chase. The stranger was closed at about 6.30 a.m., and engaged, but after an hour and a half of sharp fighting made off; and the *Iris*, having lost her foremast, main topmast, and mizenmast, was unable to overhaul her. The stranger was at the time supposed to be the French *Medee* but has been proved by James to have been the *Citoyenne Francaise*, 32.

(1)   James, *Naval History of Great Britain*, Volume I page. No notice in Troude.

Name of Ship	Tons	Guns	Broadside (pounds)	Men (nominal)	Killed	Wounded (3)	Total
Iris	688	40 (1)	246 (2)	217	4	32	36
Citoyenne Francais	800?	36	270?	275	16	37	53

(1)   Carronades, which are not counted in the rating, are always included in these comparisons.

THE ROYAL NAVY

(2)   Allowance has been made for the greater weight of the French pound in these tables. See James, *Naval History of Great Britain*, Volume I page 45.

(3)   Slightly wounded men were rarely included in the returns.

On May 27th, in the West Indies, the *Hyaena*, 24, Captain William Hargood (1), was seen and chased by the *Concorde*, 40, Captain Vandongen and by several other French vessels. (1) She was quickly overhauled and after a few shots, struck her colours.

Concorde	44 guns	broadside 410 pounds.
Hyaena	30 guns	broadside 153 pounds.

(1)   James, *Naval History of Great Britain*, Volume I page 105; Troude, *Batailles Navales de la France*, Tome II page 302.

On the same day, to the west of Cape Finisterre, (1) the British *Venus*, 32, Captain Jonathan Faulknor (2nd) sighted the *Semillante*, 32, Captain Gaillard. The two closed, the *Venus* being to windward, and began a warm fire at about 8 a.m. After two hours' fighting the *Semillante*'s guns seemed to be silenced; and the *Venus* was bearing down to take possession, when another ship under French colours hove in sight, and the *Venus* retired. The *Semillante* lost her captain and first lieutenant killed, and had her masts, sails, and hull badly injured, and five feet of water in her hold. The *Venus* was much damaged in her masts, sails, and rigging. She was fortunate in escaping the strange ship, which was the *Cleopatre*, 36, and in rejoining the British *Nymphe*, 36, from which she had parted two days before.

(1)   James, *Naval History of Great Britain*, Volume I page 103; Troude, *Batailles Navales de la France*, Tome II page 302; Williams, *History of the Liverpool Privateers and Letters of Marque with an Account of the Liverpool Slave Trade*, page 314.

Name of Ship	Tons	Guns	Broadside (pounds)	Men	Killed	Wounded (2)	Total
Venus	722(1)	38	233	192	2	20	22
Semillante	940	36	270 (2)	300?	12	20	32

(1) Charnock (*History of Marine Architecture*) gives a *Venus*, 36, of this tonnage, built in 1758. She is the same ship.
(2) James credits the *Semillante* with ten 6-pounders; Troude, with only four. See note in James, *Naval History of Great Britain*, Volume I page 103. I have followed Troude.

CAPTURE OF THE *CLEOPATRE* BY THE *NYMPHE*
JUNE 18TH 1793

(from T. Medland's engraving after the drawing by N. Pockock)

On June 18th, the British frigate, *Nymphe*, 36, Captain Edward Pellew, whilst cruising in the Channel, sighted the *Cleopatre*, 36, Captain Mullon, and bore down upon her. (1) The French ship shortened sail and waited for the British attack. The two vessels were within hail before a shot had been fired. The *Nymphe*'s men gave three cheers for the King; the French replied and Captain Mullon, standing in the gangway, waved his hat and shouted, "*Vive la nation!*"

(1) Troude, *Batailles Navales de la France*, Tome II page 303; James, *Naval History of Great Britain*, Volume I page 106; Osler, *The Life of Admiral Viscount Exmouth*, page 54.

At 6.15 a.m., Pellew, who had been standing with his hat in his hand, put it on his head, as the concerted signal for opening fire. About seven, the *Cleopatre*'s mizenmast fell, masking some of her guns on the engaged

THE ROYAL NAVY

side; and just at the same time Israel Pellew, the captain's brother, who was on board as a volunteer, succeeded in shooting away the *Cleopatre*'s wheel, on which she fell on board the *Nymphe* with her other broadside bearing, her jib boom striking the *Nymphe*'s mainmast. The jib boom broke, but one of the *Cleopatre*'s studding sail boom-irons hooked the *Nymphe*'s main topsail leech-rope, and the latter had to be cut away to save the mast. The *Nymphe* anchored that the French ship might clear her, but before this could happen the *Cleopatre* had fallen. Pellew noticed that the French were gathering to board and ordered his men to prepare to repel them; on which the British seamen swept on board the enemy and carried the ship. The heroic Mullon was discovered in the agony of death, striving to bite to pieces a paper which, he thought, contained the French secret coast signals. (1) His failing consciousness did not reveal to him that he was destroying the paper containing his commission.

(1)   As a trait of chivalrous generosity, it should be recorded that Pellew sent pecuniary aid to Captain Mullon's widow.

For this action Captain Pellew was knighted, and his brother, Israel, was promoted to post rank.

Name of Ship	Tons	Guns	Broadside (pounds)	Men	Killed	Wounded	Total
Nymphe	938	40	322	240	23	27	50
Cleopatre (2)	913	40 (1)	290 (1)	320			63

55 minutes.

(1)   Troude (*Batailles Navales de la France*) differs from James as to the armament, giving *Cleopatre* thirty-six guns with a broadside of 204 pounds; but, as *Cleopatre* was captured, it may be assumed that the English figures are the more correct. Also, Pellew in Osler, *The Life of Admiral Viscount Exmouth*, page 59, who gives her forty guns, some 18s.

(2)   The *Cleopatre* was purchased for the British Navy, and re-named *Oiseau*.

In July, Captain George William Augustus Courtenay of the British frigate *Boston*, 32, cruising off New York, sent in a challenge to Captain Jean Baptiste Francois Bompard of the French frigate *Embuscade*, 34, having first captured by an adroit stratagem the *Embuscade*'s first lieutenant with a boat's crew. (1) Courtenay offered to wait for three days off Sandy Hook and had a written copy of the challenge posted up in one of the New York coffee-rooms. On July 30th, a considerable French fleet passed, but the *Boston* kept her station, and in the night of the 31st saw a large ship standing towards her. The *Embuscade* had come out to fight. Both ships hoisted their colours at about dawn, and, soon after five, closed and began action, the *Boston* with her larboard and the *Embuscade* with her starboard broadside. Their evolutions were watched by a great crowd on the New Jersey beach, twelve miles away. In less than an hour the *Boston*'s rigging was so injured that she lost command of her sails, and a little later her main topmast went overboard. By 6.20 Captain Courtenay and the lieutenant of marines were killed; the two lieutenants borne on the ship's books were both severely wounded; and the mizenmast was tottering. The crew fell into confusion, but the wounded first lieutenant, John Edwards, took command and fought the ship.

(1)   James, *Naval History of Great Britain*, Volume I page 110; Brenton, *Naval History of Great Britain from the Year 1783 to 1822*, Volume I page 263; Troude, *Batailles Navales de la France*, Tome II page 304.

With difficulty the *Boston* avoided an attempt of the *Embuscade* to rake her. Her condition was desperate, as the wreck of the main topmast hampered the service of her guns, and all her chief officers were killed and wounded. She turned and fled before the wind, followed for some distance by the *Embuscade*, which had, however, been too much injured in masts, sails, and rigging to overtake her.

After an hour's chase, the Frenchman put about and returned to New York. The *Boston* was much the weaker and smaller ship; and at that time indiscipline had not destroyed the moral of the French Navy. On her return to New York the *Embuscade* had to remove her masts. Captain Bompard was presented with a gold medal, and Captain Courtenay's widow and children were pensioned by the King. Brenton accuses Lieutenant Edwards of cowardice, but, it would appear, on quite insufficient evidence.

THE ROYAL NAVY

Name of Ship	Tons	Guns (1)	Broadside (ponds)	Men	Killed	Wounded	Total
Embuscade	906	34 (1)	280 (1)	327			50
Boston	676	38	210	210	10	24	34

About 1 hour 40 minutes.

(1)   So Troude (*Batailles Navales de la France*). James (*Naval History of Great Britain*) differs, giving *Embuscade* thirty-eight guns and 240-pound broadsides. Brenton (*Naval History of Great Britain from the Year 1783 to 1822*) calls her an 18-pounder frigate.

The battery of the *Boston* included six very indifferent 12-pounder carronades, which, James states, were of the "useless monkey tailed" type.

On October 20th, the *Crescent*, 36, Captain James Saumarez, sighted the French *Reunion*, 36, Captain Francois A. Deniau, and a cutter, at daylight, off Cherbourg. (1) Saumarez had been informed that there was a French frigate at Cherbourg, which left that port at nightfall, cruised during the night, and returned early in the morning. This was in fact the procedure of the *Reunion*. The *Crescent* was on her way with dispatches from Portsmouth to the Channel Islands. She had just been docked and sailed very fast.

(1)   James, *Naval History of Great Britain*, Volume I page 114; Troude, *Batailles Navales de la France*, Tome II page 309; Ross, *Memoires and Correspondence of Admiral Lord de Saumarez*, Volume I page 101.

At 10.30 a.m., the *Crescent* was close enough to the enemy to open fire, both ships being on the larboard tack. The cutter had made off. In three-quarters of an hour the *Reunion* lost her foreyard and mizen-topmast, and was in consequence exposed to the raking fire of the *Crescent*, which ship, by a singularly adroit manoeuvre of Saumarez, had wore round on her heel. Keeping under the enemy's stern, the *Crescent* was able to use her larboard broadside, receiving scarcely a shot from the *Reunion*. After a brave resistance which had lasted over two hours, the *Reunion* struck, as the British *Circe*, 28, was approaching in the distance. She had lost her main top gallant mast, in addition to her mizen-topmast, and was a good deal damaged. The *Crescent*'s only loss was one man wounded by the recoil of a gun.

Name of Ship	Tons	Guns	Broadside (ponds)	Men	Killed	Wounded	Total
Crescent	888	36	315	257	0	0	0
Reunion	951	40	310 (1)	320	33	48	81

2 hours 10 minutes.

(1)   Saumarez makes her weight of metal 330 pounds, which is a slight exaggeration.

Captain Saumarez was knighted for this action. The *Reunion* was purchased for the Navy and retained her French name.

On October 22nd, the *Agamemnon*, 64, Captain Horatio Nelson, cruising off Sardinia, sighted a French squadron composed as follows: (1)

Melpomene	40	Captain Gay.
Minerve	38	Captain Z.J.T. Allemand?
Fortunee	36	Captain Maistral.
Mignonne	28.	
Hasard?	14.	

and made sail in chase. (2) By 4 a.m. he was close enough to one of the hostile frigates to speak her, and, as she did not answer his hail but fired her stern-chasers at him, opened on her. She constantly yawed and fired at the *Agamemnon*'s rigging, whilst the slower sailing British ship could make but little reply. At first the *Agamemnon* and her enemy had far outdistanced the other French ships, but at about nine the *Agamemnon* ran into a calm, and her enemy, hauling up, joined her French consorts. The *Agamemnon* was too crippled to pursue, and the frigates were very satisfied to get away. The British loss was one killed and six wounded. The frigate engaged was apparently in a sinking state, but her loss is unknown.

THE ROYAL NAVY

(1) Nelson, *The Dispatches and Letters of Vice Admiral Lord Viscount Nelson*, Volume I page 334; Troude, *Batailles Navales de la France*, Tome II page 313; James, *Naval History of Great Britain*, Volume I page 117.

(2) So James (*Naval History of Great Britain*). Nelson (*The Dispatches and Letters of Vice Admiral Lord Viscount Nelson*) speaks of four frigates one looking like a ship of the line and a brig; he omits the *Fleche*, and gives the *Fouchet*, 24, and an unknown brig. Troude (*Batailles Navales de la France*) gives the *Fleche*, 18, and omits *Mignonne* and *Hasard*. But as he makes Z.J.T. Allemand the captain of the *Minerve*, when his own and other accounts show Z. Allemand, at about this very time, to have been commanding the *Carmagnole* in the Bay, his authority cannot be accepted. It is much to be regretted that there is no really trustworthy French history of this war. The *Gazette de France* ceases to afford valuable information; and deliberate falsification of facts, which is not noticeable in 1778-1783, becomes too common. Chevalier (*Histoire de la Marine Francaise dans la Guerre de 1778*) omits minor actions with some rare exceptions. Troude misdates this action.

On October 24th, the *Thames*, 32, Captain James Cotes, sighted the *Uranie*, 36, Captain Tartu, in the Bay of Biscay. (1) The two closed at once, and in thick weather began action at a little before 11 a.m., the *Thames* passing and repassing the *Uranie* on the opposite tack, the ships each time exchanging fire. At 2.20 the *Uranie* succeeded in raking the *Thames,* and tried to board, but was raked in turn and driven off. She dropped to the south, and the British crew hailed her retreat with cheers. She finally spread all sail and retired, the *Thames* being too badly damaged to pursue her.

(1) Troude, *Batailles Navales de la France*, Tome II page 310; James, *Naval History of Great Britain*, Volume I page 113; Marshall, *Royal Navy Biography*, Part III Volume II page 252; (compilation), *Public Record Office, Minutes of Courts Martial*, Volume 72 June 11th.

The *Thames* had suffered very severely in masts and rigging. Her hull was terribly shattered, three guns were dismounted, and almost all the gun-tackles and breechings had been carried away. The *Uranie*'s rigging was very much cut up, and her captain wounded. Having on board many

18 William Laird Clowes

Spanish prisoners from the *Alcudia*, 16, which she had captured some days before, she made for Rochefort.

Name of Ship	Tons	Guns (1)	Broadside (pounds) (1)	Men	Killed	Wounded	Total
Uranie	1100	40	280	260 (1)	?	?	?
Thames	656	32	174	187 (2)	11	23	34

3 hours

(1)   *Uranie* per Troude (*Batailles Navales de la France*). James (*Naval History of Great Britain*) says forty-four guns, 403 pounds broadside.
(2)   Captain Cotes's letter, 134 men and boys.

Whilst the battered *Thames* was refitting, at about 4 p.m., four sail came in sight. Escape was out of the question for her, and one of the strangers drew up under her stern and fired a broadside, when she struck. Her captor was the *Carmagnole*, 40, Captain Zacharie Jacques Theodore Allemand. The British crew were treated with great severity and rigidly imprisoned. Captain Cotes's official letter did not reach the Admiralty till May 7th, 1795, as the French intercepted all correspondence. The *Uranie*'s name was changed to *Tartu*, (1) after the battle, in memory of her captain.

(1)   English authorities say *Tortue*, and that the change was made to hide the discreditable "defeat" of the French. But *Tartu* seems to have been the name, see Troude, *Batailles Navales de la France*. When in 1796 she entered the British service, she was renamed *Urania*.

On November 25th, the British frigates *Penelope*, 32, Captain Bartholomew Samuel Rowley, and *Iphigenia*, 32, Captain Patrick Sinclair, fell in off San Domingo with the French *Inconstante*, 36, Captain Riouffe. (1) The *Penelope* began the action at about 1.30 a.m. The hammock cloths on her engaged side soon took fire, but this did not compel her to haul off. At two the *Iphigenia* came up, and the *Inconstante* struck. The French captain was caught by a superior force

THE ROYAL NAVY

with his ship unprepared for action and could do little. The *Inconstante* was purchased for the Navy.

(1)   James, *Naval History of Great Britain*, Volume I page 122; Troude, *Batailles Navales de la France*, Tome II page 313.

Name of Ship	Tons	Guns	Broadside (pounds)	Men (nominal)	Killed	Wounded	Total
Penelope	720	40	246	217	1	7	8
Iphigenia	681	40	246	217	0	0	0
Inconstante		40	270	300	7	21	28

30 minutes.

On November 30th, the French brig *Espiegle*, 16, was captured off Ushant by the British frigates *Nymphe* and *Circe*. (1)

(1)   Troude, *Batailles Navales de la France*, Tome II page 293; Log of *Nymphe*.

On December 2nd, the diminutive West India packet *Antelope*, 6 (3-pounders) with an effective crew of twenty-one, fought and captured a French privateer, the *Atalante*, 8, fitted out at Charleston, South Carolina, and manned with a crew of sixty-five men, many of whom were Americans. The *Antelope* lost three killed and four wounded. Of her crew a French Royalist, named Nodin, distinguished himself most.

On January 8th, 1794, the *Hind*, 28, Captain Philip Charles Durham, was chased by five French frigates and a brig. (1) She escaped with the loss of twelve men killed or wounded. The British ships of the line, *Impregnable*, 90, and *Majestic*, 74, were close at hand, but at first would give no aid, because they were weakly manned, fresh from port, and took the *Hind* for a decoy.

(1)   Murray, *Memoir of the Naval Life and Service of Admiral Sir Philip C.H.C. Durham*, page 27.

On January 11th, 1794, after the evacuation of Toulon, the British frigate *Juno*, 32, Captain Samuel Hood (2nd), arrived from Malta at that place. (1) Hood was not aware that the British had abandoned it, and could exchange no signals, as it was night when he neared the port. He entered the inner harbour unchallenged, but took the ground slightly, in attempting to pass a brig. That vessel hailed him and was answered by his informing her of his ship's name and nationality. The *Juno* anchored with her stern on the shoal and hoisted out a launch to warp off. Whilst she was thus engaged, a boat rowed alongside, and from it two officers came up the ship's side and directed Hood to go to another part of the harbour. Something in their words attracted attention, and a midshipman, looking carefully at them in the dim light, saw that they wore tri-coloured cockades. They were seized, the cable was cut, and the *Juno*'s sails were set, whereupon the stern came off the ground and the ship stood down the harbour. All the forts fired at her, but she escaped without the loss of a man. Some damage to sail and rigging was the only result of the brush with the formidable works of Toulon. This incident shows the ease with which the forts of those days could be passed at night, even by a sailing ship.

(1)   James, *Naval History of Great Britain*, Volume I page 216.

On January 17th, two large French privateers, the *Resolue*, 26, and *Vengeur*, 34, attacked the *Pigot*, East Indiaman, George Ballantyne, master, near Bencoolen, and were ignominiously beaten off. Though the action lasted for nearly two hours the *Pigot* only lost one man. Five days later the privateers were attacked by five British East Indiamen (1) and captured. Their loss was heavy: the British loss trifling.

(1)   *William Pitt, Britannia, Nonsuch, Houghton*, and brig *Nautilus*.

On April 23rd, the British frigates *Flora*, 36, Commodore Sir John Borlase Warren; *Arethusa*, 38, Captain Sir Edward Pellew; *Melampus*, 36, (1) Captain Thomas Wells; *Concorde*, 36, Captain Sir Richard John Strachan; and *Nymphe*, 36, Captain George Murray (3rd), whilst cruising off the Channel Islands, sighted the French ships *Engageante*, 36, Commodore Desgarceaux; *Resolue*, 36, Captain P. Villeon; *Pomone*, 44, Captain Etienne Pevrieu; and *Babet*, 20, Lieutenant P.J.P. Belhomme. (2) The French formed in line of battle: the British came up one by one to windward of them. The *Flora* began the action at 6.30 a.m., but lost her main topmast, had her rigging cut to pieces, and dropped behind. The *Arethusa*, after engaging the *Babet*, took the *Flora*'s place, whilst both sides crowded all sail the French to escape, the British to pursue. The *Arethusa* and *Melampus* captured the *Babet* at 8.30: the *Engageante* and *Resolue* had left the *Pomone* behind, and on that ship next fell the brunt

THE ROYAL NAVY

of the British onset. Already the *Pomone* had been much damaged by the *Flora*'s fire. The *Arethusa* completed her discomfiture by shooting away her main and mizen-masts and setting her on fire. She struck at 9.30.

(1)   In the (compilation), *Navy List of the Royal Navy*, page a 38.

(2)   James, *Naval History of Great Britain*, Volume I page 222; Troude, *Batailles Navales de la France*, Tome II page 323; Osler, *The Life of Admiral Viscount Exmouth*, page 64; Brenton, *Naval History of Great Britain from the Year 1783 to 1822*, Volume I page 122. The British cruiser squadron was to protect trade. Its cruising ground extended from Cape Finisterre to Cherbourg. It was found so useful that other light squadrons of three or four frigates were sent out to scour the same waters.

The *Concorde* and *Melampus* then pushed on after the *Resolue* and *Engageante* but could not separate the pair nor delay them both enough to enable the other ships to come up. The *Concorde* accordingly decided to secure one and closed the *Engageante*. The two fought side by side almost uninterrupted, as the *Resolue* quickly retired, and the other British ships were too far astern to give help. At 1.45 p.m. the *Engageante* struck. In comparative force the British had a great superiority — 210 guns to 144: (l) 40 of those in the *Resolue* were scarcely engaged, as against as many in the *Nymphe* which were not in action, owing to that ship being left behind. None of the British ships were very severely damaged. Their loss is stated as follows:

(1)   Troude, *Batailles Navales de la France*, Tome II page 136.

Name of Ship	Men	Killed	Wounded	Total
Flora	267	1	3	4
Arethusa	277	3	5	8
Melampus	267	5	5	10
Concorde	257	1	12	13

French losses were as follows:

Name of Ship	Men	Loss

Engageante	?	?
Pomone	341	80-100
Babet	178	30-40

The *Pomone* was of 1239 tons, of unusual beam, and an excellent sailer. (1) She was purchased for the Navy.

(1)   According to Osler (*The Life of Admiral Viscount Exmouth*) and James (*Naval History of Great Britain*) she carried 24-pounders on her main deck; according to Brenton, 18-pounders.

On May 5th, in East Indian waters, the *Orpheus*, 32, Captain Henry Newcome; *Centurion*, 50, and *Resistance*, 44, chased the French *Duguay Trouin*, 34, and another ship. (1) The *Orpheus* closed the *Duguay Trouin* and began action before noon. In little more than an hour the Frenchman struck. She had been an East Indiaman and was probably weakly built.

(1)   James, *Naval History of Great Britain*, Volume I page 226. Not in Troude. Possibly the *Duguay Trouin* was a privateer.

Name of Ship	Tons	Guns	Broadside (pounds)	Men	Killed	Wounded	Total
Orpheus	708	40	246	194	1	9	10
Duguay Trouin		34	194?	?	21	60	81

The *Centurion* and *Resistance* were coming up fast when the enemy surrendered.

On the same day, the *Swiftsure*, 74, Captain Charles Boyles, and *Saint Albans*, 64 with a convoy out from Cork, saw and chased the French frigate *Atalante*, 36, Captain Charles Alexandre Leon Durand Linois, and the corvette *Levrette*. (1) The *Swiftsure* chose the former as her quarry, and after a long chase, in which the two exchanged fire more than once, brought her to close action on the 7th at 2.30 a.m. The *Levrette* seems to have escaped. After fifty-five minutes fighting the *Atalante* struck. Her masts and rigging were in bad order before the action, and were now disabled. Her crew was weak, and had been for two whole days and nights at quarters.

THE ROYAL NAVY

(1)   James, *Naval History of Great Britain*, Volume I page 227; Troude, *Batailles Navales de la France*, Tome II page 376; Hennequin, *Biographie Maritime*, Tome I page 320.

Name of Ship	Tons	Guns	Broadside (pounds)	Men	Killed	Wounded	Total
Swiftsure	1612	82	928?	644	1	0	1
Atalante	951	40?	280?	274	10	32	42

55 minutes.

The *Swiftsure* and her prize were seen and unsuccessfully chased by three 74s of M. Nielly's squadron. The *Atalante* was purchased for the Navy and renamed *Espion*.

On May 10th, the *Castor*, 32, Captain Thomas Troubridge, was captured on her way to Newfoundland without any resistance, (1) by the French *Patriote*, 74, one of Admiral Nielly's squadron. On the 29th she was sighted by the *Carysfort*, 28, Captain Francis Laforey, and, after seventy-five minutes' action, recaptured. On board were twenty of the *Castor*'s British crew.

(1)   James, *Naval History of Great Britain*, Volume I page 228; Troude, *Batailles Navales de la France*, Tome II page 379; (compilation), *Public Record Office, Minutes of Courts Martial*, Volume 71, June 24th.

Name of Ship	Tons	Guns	Broadside (pounds)	Men	Killed	Wounded	Total
Carysfort	599	32	156	180	1	4	5
Castor	678	36	200	274	16	9?	25?

75 minutes.

On May 25th, Lord Howe's fleet captured and destroyed the French *Republicaine*, 20, and *Inconnue*, 12. (1)

(1)   Logs of *Audacious* and *Niger*.

On June 8th, the *Crescent*, 36, Captain Sir James Saumarez; *Druid*, 32, Captain Joseph Ellison; and *Eurydice*, 24, Captain Francis Cole, fell in with the French cut-down 74s, *Scevola*, 50, and *Brutus*, 50, two 36-gun frigates and a brig, but succeeded in making their escape. The *Crescent* drew off the French pursuit, from the slower ships, heading into Guernsey Road by a channel till then unused by warships. Captain Saumarez was a Channel Islander, and his local knowledge stood him in good stead. This was an achievement as brilliant as it was gallant and skillful.

On June 17th, Captain the Honourable William Paget in the *Romney*, 50, with a convoy, discovered the French *Sibylle*, 40, Captain J.M. Rondeau, at anchor in the harbour of Mykonos. (1) Three other British vessels were in sight from the *Romney*'s masthead, and, as her convoy would for that reason be safe, she went into the harbour, anchored close to the *Sibylle*, and summoned her to surrender. The *Sibylle*'s captain refused, and the *Romney* opened fire. After seventy minutes' fighting most of the French crew fled ashore, and Captain Rondeau struck his colours. The *Sibylle* fought 14 instead of 13 guns on her main-deck engaged broadside.

(1)   James, *Naval History of Great Britain*, Volume I page 231; Troude, *Batailles Navales de la France*, Tome II page 381.

Name of Ship	Tons	Guns	Broadside (pounds)	Men	Killed	Wounded	Total
Romney	1046	54 (1)	462	266	8	30	38
Sibylle	1091	44	380	380	44	112	156

70 minutes.

(1)   James (*Naval History of Great Britain*) gives her no carronades, but I have allowed her four. Troude (*Batailles Navales de la France*) gives her ten and reduces the *Sibylle*'s battery to thirty-two guns.

The *Sibylle* was purchased into the British Navy.

THE ROYAL NAVY

On July 14th, the sloop *Hound*, 16, Commander Richard Piercy, on her way home from the West Indies, was captured, thirty miles to the west of the Scillies, by the French frigates *Seine*, 40, and *Galatee*, 36. (1) To a force so superior she offered no resistance.

(1)   (compilation), *Public Record Office, Minutes of Courts Martial*, Volume 72, June 29th.

On August 23rd, early in the morning, the British frigates *Flora*, Captain Sir John Warren; *Arethusa*, 38, Captain Sir Edward Pellew; *Diamond*, 38, Captain Sir William Sidney Smith; *Artois*, 38, Captain Edmund Nagle; *Diana*, 38, Captain Jonathan Faulknor (2nd); and *Santa Margarita*, 36, Captain Eliab Harvey, discovered the French frigate *Volontaire*, 36, Captain Papin, off Brest, and compelled her to anchor off the Penmarcks. (1) There she was vigorously attacked by four of the British ships and, cutting her cables to take up a better position, was driven ashore. Her pumps could not keep the water down, and therefore Captain Papin abandoned her. At the same time the French corvettes *Alerte*, 12, and *Espion*, 18, were driven ashore in Audierne Bay and boarded by British boats. Fifty-two French prisoners were brought off, but the vessels, as they had many wounded on board, could not be destroyed. The *Espion* was got off by the French (2) in the night. The *Alerte* was lost.

(1)   James, *Naval History of Great Britain*, Volume I page 233; Troude, *Batailles Navales de la France*, Tome II page 383; Osler, *The Life of Admiral Viscount Exmouth*, page 67.
(2)   The *Espion* was finally taken, however, by the *Lively*, in 1795.

On September 14th, an amusing incident happened. Captain Saumarez's squadron of four frigates was sighted off Weymouth, where at that time was the Royal family, and failed to answer the guardship *Trusty*'s private signal. It was immediately supposed that the French were making an attempt to carry off the King, and the troops at Weymouth stood to arms, the batteries were manned, and carriages for the Royal household were got ready. The misunderstanding was, however, cleared up after dark, when Saumarez entered the road.

On October 21st, the *Arethusa*, 38, Captain Sir Edward Pellew; *Diamond*, 38, Captain Sir William Sidney Smith; *Artois*, 38, Captain Edmund Nagle, and *Galatea*, 32, Captain Richard Goodwin Keats, (1) off Ushant, saw and chased a French frigate, the *Revolutionnaire*, 44,

26 William Laird Clowes

Captain H.A. Thevenard. The French ship was with some difficulty cut off from the land and brought to action by the *Artois*, 38, Captain Edmund Nagle, which had outsailed the other British ships. A warm action of forty minutes' duration followed before the *Diamond* came up astern of the Frenchman, though Smith would not spoil the *Artois'* game by firing. Then, after a gallant and creditable defence in the face of a greatly superior force, Captain Thevenard struck his colours, as his men would no longer fight the ship. He was but just out from port with a raw crew.

(1)   James, *Naval History of Great Britain*, Volume I page 235; Troude, *Batailles Navales de la France*, Tome II page 384; Osler, *The Life of Admiral Viscount Exmouth*, page 68.

Name of Ship	Tons	Guns	Broadside (pounds)	Men	Killed	Wounded	Total
Artois	996	44	370	281 (1)	3	5	8
Revolutionnaire	1148	44	403	351	8	5	13

40 minutes.

(1)   Nominal.

Captain Nagle was knighted, and his capture purchased for the Navy.

On October 22nd, whilst cruising off Mauritius, the *Centurion*, 50, Captain Samuel Osborn, and *Diomede*, 44, Captain Matthew Smith, (1) saw and chased four French ships, the *Cybele*, 40, Captain Trehouart; *Prudente*, 36, Commodore, (2) Jean Marie Benaud; *Jean Bart*, 20, and *Courier*, 14, which had put to sea with the express purpose of fighting the British squadron. The *Centurion* and *Diomede* placed themselves opposite the French frigates and opened action at about 3.30 p.m. The *Centurion* was soon so much cut up in her rigging that she dropped behind, and the *Prudente*, leaving the French line, was able to get away from her. The *Cybele*, passing the *Centurion*, brought down the latter's mizen and fore-topgallant-mast, but, on the wind dropping, was engaged by the powerful British ship and roughly handled. The *Diomede* did little or nothing, except fire from a distance at the French. Soon after five the wind again freshened, and the *Cybele* got away with her main-topgallant-

THE ROYAL NAVY

mast gone. Though both British ships pursued her they could not prevent the *Prudente* from taking her in tow, and with her escaping.

(1)   James, *Naval History of Great Britain*, Volume I page 236; Troude, *Batailles Navales de la France*, Tome II page 370.

(2)   *Chef de division.*

Name of Ship	Tons	Guns	Broadside (pounds)	Men (1)	Killed	Wounded	Total
Centurion	1044	54	462	345	3	24	27
Diomede	891	54	408	297	0	0	0
Prudente	897	40	280	300	15	20	35
Cybele		44	410	330	22	62	84
Jean Bart		20	?	?	1	5	6
Courier		14	?	?	0	0	0

(1)   Nominal

Captain Smith for his behaviour was court-martialled and dismissed the service, but the sentence was quashed in 1798. He retired, however, in 1806.

On December 22nd, the *Daphne*, 20, Captain William Edward Cracraft, was captured by Admiral Villaret's fleet in the Bay. She made no resistance.

On December 30th, the boats of the *Blanche*, 32, Captain Robert Faulknor (3rd), cut out a French armed schooner at Desirade, Guadeloupe with the loss of only six men. (1)

(1)   James, *Naval History of Great Britain*, Volume I page 308.

On January 5th, 1795, the *Blanche*, 32, whilst cruising off Guadeloupe, encountered the French *Pique*, 36, Captain Conseil. (1) The action began soon after midnight, when the *Blanche* passed the *Pique* on the opposite tack, exchanging broadsides with her. Then, as the *Blanche* tacked and came up in the wake of the *Pique*, the French ship, having the weather

28   William Laird Clowes

gage, wore to rake her; but Captain Robert Faulknor (3rd) was able to defeat the manoeuvre by also wearing.

(1)   James, *Naval History of Great Britain*, Volume I page 309; Troude, *Batailles Navales de la France*, Tome II page 439; Brenton, *Naval History of Great Britain from the Year 1783 to 1822*, Volume I page 247; (compilation), *Naval Chronicle*, Volume XVI page 40.

The ships fought broadside to broadside till 2.30 a.m., when the *Blanche* shot ahead. At that moment, just as the *Blanche* was preparing to rake the *Pique*, the *Blanche*'s mizen and main masts fell, and the *Pique* ran foul of her, receiving a terrible raking fire. An attempt on the part of the French to board was repulsed with heavy loss. At about 3 a.m. the heroic Captain Faulknor was shot dead as he was endeavouring to lash the *Pique*'s bowsprit to the *Blanche*. The lashing parted, and the two ships first drifted clear of each other, and then fouled again, the *Pique* falling on the *Blanche*'s starboard quarter. The *Pique*'s bowsprit was promptly lashed to the stump of the *Blanche*'s mainmast.

CAPTAIN ROBERT FAULKNOR (3RD), R.N.
Killed in command of H.M.S. *Blanche*, January, 1795.

(from the portrait by Holt)

It was at that time that the top-fire of the *Pique*'s sharpshooters began to trouble the *Blanche*'s seamen, whilst the British frigate, having no stern ports on her main deck, could not bring her guns to bear astern on the Frenchman. In this difficulty it was decided to make ports in the ship's stern, by the simple expedient of firing two shotted 12-pounders through it, leaving firemen with buckets of water to put out the flames caused by such an heroic measure. The 12-pounders thereafter maintained a most effective fire, until the *Pique* was dismasted; but she did not strike for another two hours. At 5.15 a.m., she hauled down her flag. She had fought most gallantly and had lost more than two-thirds of her crew.

Name of Ship	Tons	Guns	Broadside (pounds)	Men	Killed	Wounded	Total
Blanche	710	38	228	198	8	21	29
Pique	906	38	273	279	76	110	186

5 hours

The *Pique* was purchased for the British Navy.

On January 8th, the French *Esperance*, 22, was captured off the Chesapeake by the British *Argonaut*, 64, and *Oiseau*, 36. (1) On February 20th, the *Requin*, 12, was taken off Dunkirk by the British *Thalia*.

(1)   Troude, *Batailles Navales de la France*, Tome II page 441.

On March 2nd, the British *Lively*, 32, Commander George Burlton (acting captain), (1) captured the French corvette *Espion*, 18, Captain Magendie, off Brest, after a two hours' action. (2)

(1)   The *Lively*'s captain, Lord Garlies, was sick on shore at the time.
(2)   Troude, *Batailles Navales de la France*, Tome II page 441.

On March 13th, the *Lively*, 32, Commander George Burlton (acting captain), sighted the French *Tourterelle*, 28, Captain G.S.A. Montalan, in the Channel. (1) The French vessel did not decline the unequal battle but stood to meet the *Lively*. Both opened fire soon after 10 a.m., when Captain Montalan, discovering the great superiority of his opponent, turned and attempted to retreat. In this he was unsuccessful, and the *Lively* closing the *Tourterelle* fought her till she struck at 1.30 p.m., in a very shattered state. The *Tourterelle* carried a furnace for heating shot, and had made use of it against the *Lively*, burning the latter's sails badly. The furnace was thrown overboard just before the French flag was lowered. At that time the use of hot shot was, perhaps rather foolishly, considered a breach of the tacit conventions of war.

(1)   James, *Naval History of Great Britain*, Volume I page 313. Troude (*Batailles Navales de la France*, Tome II page 445) dates the action May 15th, an evident mistake.

THE ROYAL NAVY

Name of Ship	Tons	Guns	Broadside (pounds)	Men	Killed	Wounded	Total
Lively	806	38	324	251	0	2	2
Tourterelle	581	30	188	230	16	25	41

2 hours

On March 25th, the French *Coureuse*, 18, was captured by a squadron of British frigates off Lorient, (1) and the *Jean Bart*, 18, on her way from the West Indies to France, was taken by the British ships *Santa Margarita* and *Cerberus*.

(1)   Troude, *Batailles Navales de la France*, Tome II page 442, 443.

On April 10th, a British fleet under Rear-Admiral John Colpoys was cruising off Brest, when three sail were seen. (1) The fleet scattered in chase, and the *Astraea*, 32, Captain Lord Henry Paulet, outsailing the ships of the line, came up with one of the three, the French *Gloire*, 36, Captain Beens. The action between the two opened at 6 p.m. At 10.30 the *Astraea* closed her adversary, and after an hour's fight made her strike her flag. The *Astraea*'s main topmast went overboard just after the close of the action, and her other topmasts were so wounded that they had to be removed.

(1)   James, *Naval History of Great Britain*, Volume I page 315; Troude, *Batailles Navales de la France*, Tome II page 443.

Name of Ship	Tons	Guns	Broadside (pounds)	Men	Killed	Wounded	Total
Astraea	703	32 (1)	174	212	0	8	8
Gloire	877	42	286	275	?	?	40

4-1/2 hours

(1)   James (*Naval History of Great Britain*) gives her no carronades; but this must be doubtful. Possibly eight 18s should be added to her battery.

The *Gloire* was purchased for the Navy but did not long remain in the service. Of the other French vessels, the *Gentille,* 36, Captain Canon, was taken on the 11th by the *Hannibal*, 74. The third escaped. The easy capture of the *Gloire* should probably be ascribed to the presence of one or two British ships of the line at no great distance.

On May 1st, the *Boyne*, 98, Captain the Honourable George Grey, took fire at Spithead, and blew up. All her crew, except eleven men, were saved, but her shotted guns, discharged by the heat, killed or wounded three men in the fleet. (1)

(1)　　(compilation), *Public Record Office, Minutes of Courts Martial*, Volume 72, May 19th.

On May 9th, Captain Sir Richard John Strachan, in the *Melampus*, 36 with the frigates *Diamond, Hebe, Niger*, and *Siren*, whilst at anchor off Jersey, saw a French convoy running along the enemy's coast. (1) Giving chase, he drove the convoy into Carteret Bay, where the boats of his squadron attacked it and captured or burnt every vessel but one with the loss of two killed and seventeen wounded.

(1)　　James, *Naval History of Great Britain*, Volume I page 318.

On May 15th, the French corvette *Hirondelle*, 18, was attacked in the Bay of Frenay, near Saint Malo, by a British squadron, but, being supported by the fire of a small fort, repulsed the ships. (1)

(1)　　Troude, *Batailles Navales de la France*, Tome II page 445.

On May 17th, the *Thetis*, 36, Captain the Honourable Alexander Forester Inglis Cochrane, and *Hussar*, 28, Captain John Poo Beresford, captured off Cape Henry two large French storeships of a squadron of five. (1) The names of the prizes were the *Prevoyante* and *Raison*. The British loss was eleven wounded. On the 28th, the *Thorn*, 16, Commander Robert Waller Otway, captured the French corvette, *Courier National*, 18, in the West Indies with a loss of six wounded; the French ship having seven killed and twenty wounded. (2) On the 28th, the French corvette *Prompte*, 28, was captured; and, on the 30th, the French *Liberte*, 20, was attacked and sunk off San Domingo by the *Alarm*, 32, Captain David Milne (3) (acting).

(1)　　James, *Naval History of Great Britain*, Volume I page 319.

THE ROYAL NAVY   33

(2)   Marshall, *Royal Navy Biography*, Part III Volume page 693.

(3)   Captain Milne was posted on October 2nd following. Troude, *Batailles Navales de la France*, Tome II page 447. *Alarm*'s log missing. According to the *Navy List of the Royal Navy*, the British captain was the Honourable Charles Carpenter, but this is an error. (compilation), *Naval Chronicle*, Volume XXXIX Appendix. W.L.C.

In June, almost at the same time, the admirals commanding the French and British fleets in the Mediterranean despatched each two frigates to ascertain one another's movements. (1) The British pair were the *Dido*, 28, Captain George Henry Towry, and *Lowestoft*, 32, Captain Robert Gambier Middleton; the French, the *Minerve*, 40, Captain Delorme, and *Artemise*, 36, Captain Decasse. The enemies sighted each other to the north of Minorca on June 24th, early in the morning. The French retired and meanwhile cleared for action. Having first drawn far ahead, they turned and stood to meet the *Dido* and *Lowestoft*. The *Minerve* was in advance, and engaged the *Dido* at 8.30 a.m. The *Minerve* attempted to run down her opponent, but, owing to the *Dido* porting her helm, only struck an oblique blow, and entangled her bowsprit in her enemy's rigging. The French endeavoured to board, but were beaten off, and in the heavy swell the *Minerve*'s bowsprit snapped and went overboard, carrying with it the *Dido*'s mizen-mast. The *Minerve* passed along the *Dido*'s larboard side, carrying away sails and rigging, but, as soon as she was clear, was attacked by the *Lowestoft*, and had her foremast, main and mizen topmast shot away.

(1)   James, *Naval History of Great Britain*, Volume I page 321; Troude, *Batailles Navales de la France*, Tome II page 448.

The *Artemise*, instead of helping her consort, only fired a broadside at each of the British ships, and retreated, pursued by the *Lowestoft*. Left to themselves, the *Minerve* and *Dido* repaired damage and cleared their decks. At 10.30 the *Lowestoft* was recalled by signal. At 11.30 she placed herself on the *Minerve*'s quarter and opened a heavy fire, whilst the *Dido* made sail to renew the attack. At 11.45 the *Minerve* hailed to say that she surrendered. The action reflects great credit upon the senior British officer, Captain Towry, (1) who had so boldly engaged a far superior force.

(1)   After serving as a Commissioner of the Navy, Captain George Henry Towry died in 1809.

Name of Ship	Tons	Guns	Broadside (pounds)	Men	Killed	Wounded	Total
Astraea	595	32	156	193	8	15	21
Lowestoft	717	36	210	212	0	3	3
Minerve	1102	42	370	318	?	?	28
Artemise		40	283	300 (1)	?	?	?

3-1/4 hours

(1)   Nominal.

The *Artemise*'s captain was tried by jury for his conduct but acquitted. The *Minerve* was purchased for the Navy.

On August 22nd, the British ships *Isis*, 50, Captain Robert Watson; *Reunion*, 36, Captain James Alms (2nd); *Stag*, 32, Captain Joseph Sydney Yorke; and *Vestal*, 28, Captain Charles White, captured the Dutch frigate *Alliantie*, 36, after an hour's fight. (1) The Dutch vessels *Argo*, 36, and *Vlugheid*, 16, which were with her, escaped into the Norwegian harbour of Egero. The British loss was 5 killed and 17 wounded. The *Argo* lost 2 killed and 15 wounded. The *Alliantie*'s (2) loss is unknown.

(1)   James, *Naval History of Great Britain*, Volume I page 324; Log of *Stag*.
(2)   Added to the Navy as *Alliance*.

On August 31st, the two French corvettes, *Suffisante*, 14, and *Victorieuse*, 14, were captured off the Texel by Admiral Duncan's squadron. (1) They were on a cruise against the British whale fisheries.

(1)   Brenton, *Naval History of Great Britain from the Year 1783 to 1822*, Volume I page 92; Troude, *Batailles Navales de la France*, Tome II page 453.

On September 2nd, the *Diamond*, 38, Captain Sir William Sidney Smith, chased and drove on the rocks of the Breton coast the French *Assemblee Nationale*, 14.

THE ROYAL NAVY

On September 29th, the *Southampton*, 32, Captain James Macnamara (2nd), cruising off Genoa, chased the French vessels *Vestale*, 36, Captain Foucaud, *Brune*, 24, *Alceste*, 14, and *Scout*, 14. (1) Selecting the *Vestale* as his quarry, Captain Macnamara opened on her at 10 p.m., and maintained a running action with her whilst she crowded all sail to get away. At about 10.30 the *Southampton*'s rigging was so damaged that she fell astern, but she effected repairs and came up again at about 11, only to lose her mizen-mast. Profiting by this incident, the *Vestale* escaped, but was chased in the course of the night by the British sloop *Moselle*, 18, Commander Charles Brisbane. The French ships had a convoy under their charge, a fact which explains their strange conduct in retiring with so superior force on their side.

(1)   James, *Naval History of Great Britain*, Volume I page 325; Marshall, *Royal Navy Biography*, Part III Volume I page 636; Troude, *Batailles Navales de la France*, Tome II page 454; Log of *Southampton*.

Name of Ship	Tons	Guns	Broadside (pounds)	Men (1)	Killed	Wounded	Total
Southampton	671	40?	246	217	?	?	?
Vestale		40	280	300	8	9	17

1/2 hour

(1)   Nominal.

On October 1st, the *Vanguard*, 74, Captain Charles Sawyer, captured the French *Superbe*, 24, Captain Doudoux, in the West Indies. (1)

(1)   James, *Naval History of Great Britain*, Volume I page 328; Troude, *Batailles Navales de la France*, Tome II page 455.

On October 10th, the *Mermaid*, 32, Captain Henry Warre, captured off Grenada the French *Brutus*, 10, and, four days later, the French *Republicaine*, 18. The British loss was only 4; the French 20. One of the prizes had a French general and troops on board, destined for Grenada, where a savage war between the British, on the one hand, and the French and Caribs, on the other, was then raging.

On March 10th, 1796, the *Bonne Citoyenne*, 20, Captain la Bourdonnais, was chased by three British frigates, and captured in the Bay by the *Phaeton*, 38, after the exchange of a few shots. (1) The *Bonne Citoyenne* was one of Rear-Admiral Sercey's squadron on her way to Mauritius. On the same day the French cutter, *Aspic*, was captured in Saint George's Channel by the *Quebec*, 32. The French brig, *Mutine*, fell to the British frigates in the Bay a few days later.

(1)   James, *Naval History of Great Britain*, Volume I page 387; Troude, *Batailles Navales de la France*, Tome III page 21.

On March 18th, Captain Sir William Sidney Smith in the *Diamond*, 38 with the *Liberty*, 14, Lieutenant George M'Kinley, and *Aristocrat*, Lieutenant Abraham Gossett, made a dash at a French corvette and some smaller vessels lying in the Breton port of Erqui. (1) Three guns, mounted in commanding positions on the cliffs, were stormed by a party of seamen and marines. The French corvette, *Etourdie*, 16, four brigs, two sloops, and a lugger were then set on fire and destroyed. In this dashing operation the British loss was only 2 killed and 7 amongst whom were two lieutenants wounded.

(1)   James, *Naval History of Great Britain*, Volume I page 355; Troude, *Batailles Navales de la France*, Tome III page 22.

On March 20th, off Pointe du Raz, the British frigates, *Pomone*, 40, Captain Sir John Borlase Warren; *Anson*, 44, Captain Philip Charles Durham; *Artois*, 38, Captain Sir Edmund Nagle, and *Galatea*, 32, Captain Richard Goodwin Keats, saw and chased a large French convoy under the charge of the frigates *Proserpine*, 40, *Unite*, *Coquille*, and *Tamise*, all of 36, and the corvette *Cigogne*, 20. (1)

(1)   James, *Naval History of Great Britain*, Volume I page 356; Troude, *Batailles Navales de la France*, Tome III page 24.

After taking several prizes from the convoy, the British squadron passed the French on the opposite tack, exchanging fire. The *Galatea* was roughly handled. Tacking, the British stood after the French, who steered for Pointe du Raz and Brest, whither they succeeded in effecting their escape. A French armed storeship, the *Etoile*, 28, was, however, added to the list of British prizes. The force of the British was superior in this affair, and it is not obvious why the French escaped so easily. Warren, the British senior officer, absurdly exaggerated the strength of his enemy

THE ROYAL NAVY
37

in his report of the business. Of the convoy six ships in all were taken. The British loss was 2 killed and 6 wounded.

On April 12th, Sir Edward Pellew's squadron of five frigates, whilst cruising off Brest, saw and chased the French *Unite*, 36, Captain C.A.L. Durand Linois. (1) The British *Revolutionnaire*, 38, Captain Francis Cole, closed her late in the evening at 11.30, and called upon Captain Linois to surrender to such a superior force. Linois refused, and a hot action began. The French crew, however, composed mostly of conscripts and not of seamen, fought badly. Thirty men fled below and pretended that they were wounded. Eighteen Vendeens refused to fight. Captain Linois, in these circumstances, struck at 11.50, just as the British *Concorde*, 36, came up. The *Revolutionnaire* by herself was far more than a match for the *Unite* in weight of metal, as she carried, besides her thirty-eight guns, eight 32-pounder carronades. Captain Linois had several passengers on board, who were transferred to a neutral ship by Sir E. Pellew.

(1)   Osler, *The Life of Admiral Viscount Exmouth*, page 80; James, *Naval History of Great Britain*, Volume I page. Troude (*Batailles Navales de la France*, Tome III page 23) calls the French ship the *Variante*, Captain Durand, and gives the date as the 11th. Pellew in a letter to the Admiralty speaks of her as "*l'Unite alias la Variante*." The Log of the *Revolutionnaire* fixes the date as the 12th.

Name of Ship	Tons	Guns	Broadside (pounds)	Men	Killed	Wounded	Total
Revolutionnaire	1148	46	425	287	0	0	0
Unite	893	38	240	255	9	11	20

20 minutes.

On April 17th, Captain Sir William Sidney Smith of the *Diamond*, 38, was captured. (1) He led a boat attack upon a privateer, the *Vengeur*, at Havre, and carried her. The privateersmen, however, had cut their cable, and, as the tide was rising, the *Vengeur* was swept up the river, two miles above Havre. Smith attempted to escape with the boats, but, as there were French ships on the move at the river's mouth, that was impossible. The intrepid officer and his men had not long to wait before they were

38 William Laird Clowes

attacked. They were surrounded by small craft and compelled to surrender with the loss of 4 killed and 7 wounded. Smith and Midshipman John Wesley Wright were considered state prisoners and shut up in the Temple. They escaped, however, in May 1798.

(1)   James, *Naval History of Great Britain*, Volume I page 359; Troude, *Batailles Navales de la France*, Tome III page 28.

On April 20th, the French corvette *Unite*, 24, was carried off from the neutral harbour of Bona by the British frigate *Inconstant*, 36, Captain Thomas Francis Fremantle. (1) The *Unite* offered no resistance. She was purchased for the Navy and renamed *Surprise*.

(1)   Troude, *Batailles Navales de la France*, Tome III page 28; Schomberg, *Naval Chronology*, Volume II page 431; James, *Naval History of Great Britain*, Volume II page 405. Log of *Inconstant* gives the *Unite* 34 guns and 318 men.

On the same day Sir Edward Pellew, in the *Indefatigable*, 44 with the *Amazon*, 36, Captain Robert Carthew Reynolds, and *Concorde*, 36, Captain Anthony Hunt (2nd), sighted the French *Virginie*, 40, Captain Bergeret, off the Lizard. (1) The three British ships at once crowded all sail and stood after the enemy. The wind was south-east and prevented the *Virginie* from retreating to Brest. After a fifteen hours chase the *Indefatigable* got close enough to begin a running fight. At about midnight the action commenced. After an hour and three-quarters firing the *Virginie* lost her mizen-mast and main topmast, and the *Indefatigable* her mizen-topmast and gaff. By reason of these injuries the British ship shot ahead and was all but raked. She was repairing damages when the *Concorde* came up astern of the *Virginie*, whereupon the latter struck in a very crippled condition with four feet of water in her hold. The *Virginie* had been bravely fought against a very superior force.

(1)   James, *Naval History of Great Britain*, Volume I page 361; Troude, *Batailles Navales de la France*, Tome III page 29; Log of *Indefatigable*.

Name of Ship	Tons	Guns	Broadside (pounds)	Men	Killed	Wounded	Total

THE ROYAL NAVY 39

| *Indefatigable* | 1384 | 46 | 702 | 327 | 0 | 0 | 0 |
| *Virginie* | 1066 | 44 | 342 | 339 | 15 | 27 | 42 |

1 hour 20 minutes.

The presence of the *Concorde* and *Amazon* at the close of the action must also be taken into account. The *Virginie* was purchased for the Navy.

On April 27th, the British frigate *Niger*, 32, Captain Edward James Foote, drove the French armed lugger, *Ecureuil*, ashore on the Penmarck rocks. (1) After cannonading her, Captain Foote sent in his boats, which, in spite of a desperate resistance on the part of the French, burnt her. The British loss was seven wounded.

(1)   Troude, *Batailles Navales de la France*, Tome III page 32.

On April 21st, the French corvette *Percante*, 26, Captain Tourtelet, was chased ashore on the San Domingo coast by the British *Irresistible*, 74, a frigate, and two smaller vessels. (1)

(1)   James, *Naval History of Great Britain*, Volume I page 362.

On May 4th, the *Spencer*, 16, Commander Andrew Fitzherbert Evans, brought the French gun-brig *Volcan*, 12, to action, after a long chase, south of Bermuda. (1) The *Spencer* was armed almost entirely with carronades, having only two long guns. Her broadside threw 88 pounds, against the French vessel's 26 pounds The *Volcan*, before she struck, had her topmasts shot away, and lost many men, some of whom were killed by the explosion of hand-grenades which had been prepared by her crew for use against the British sloop. The *Spencer* sustained a loss of one killed and one wounded, and much injury to her rigging. Three of her carronades upset in the action, which lasted for seventy-five minutes.

(1)   James, *Naval History of Great Britain*, Volume I page 363; Troude, *Batailles Navales de la France*, Tome III page 33.

On May 12th, Admiral Adam Duncan's squadron, cruising off the Texel, chased the Dutch frigate *Argo*, 36, three brigs and a cutter. (1) The *Argo* was quickly overhauled by the *Phoenix*, 36, Captain Lawrence William Halsted, and brought to action, when, after twenty minutes fighting, seeing British ships on all sides of her, the Dutchman struck. Two of the Dutch brigs were chased on shore; the third was captured, and the cutter

40 William Laird Clowes

shared her fate on May 13th. The *Argo* was purchased for the Navy, and renamed *Juno*, there being already an *Argo* in the service.

(1)   James, *Naval History of Great Britain*, Volume I page 363; Schomberg, *Naval Chronology*, Volume II page 421.

On May 2nd, (1) the British *Dryad*, 36, Captain Lord Amelius Beauclerk, for whom Commander John King Pulling was acting, captured the French corvette *Abeille*. (2)

(1)   Log of *Dryad*.
(2)   James (*Naval History of Great Britain*, Volume I page 364) gives the capture by the *Suffisante,* 14, of the French *Revanche*, 12, on May 27th without stating that the letter was a privateer. Troude (*Batailles Navales de la France*, Tome III page 34) omits this action.

On June 8th, the British frigates *Santa Margarita*, 36, Captain Thomas Byam Martin, and *Unicorn*, 32, Captain Thomas Williams (4th), sighted in the Channel the French *Tribune*, 36, Captain Jean Moultson, *Tamise*, 36, Captain J.B.A. Fradin, and *Legere*, 18, Lieutenant J.M.M. Carpentier. (1) As the British ships approached, the *Legere* drew away from her two consorts. A running fight began at 1 p.m., as the result of which the British vessels suffered much in their masts and rigging. At 4 p.m., however, the *Santa Margarita* closed the *Tamise*, and fought her broadside to broadside, whilst the *Unicorn* continued the pursuit of the *Tribune*. After twenty minutes fighting, the *Tamise* struck.

(1)   James, *Naval History of Great Britain*, Volume I page 365; Troude, *Batailles Navales de la France*, Tome III page 36.

Name of Ship	Tons	Guns	Broadside (pounds)	Men	Killed	Wounded	Total
Santa Margarita	993	40	250	237	2	3	5
Tamise	656	40	279	306	32	19	51

3 hours 20 minutes.

The *Tamise* was restored to the Navy under her original name, *Thames*.

THE ROYAL NAVY

The *Unicorn* after a long chase closed the *Tribune* at 10.30 p.m., and fought her for thirty-five minutes, when the Frenchman dropped astern. The *Unicorn*, backing her sails, followed her adroitly, placed herself on the *Tribune*'s weather bow, brought down her foremast, mainmast and mizen-topmast, and compelled her to strike.

Name of Ship	Tons	Guns	Broadside (pounds)	Men	Killed	Wounded	Total
Unicorn	791	44	348	240	0	0	0
Tribune	916	38	260	339	37	14	51

It is, as James comments, extraordinary that the *Unicorn* should have suffered no loss; and the only conclusion is that the French gunnery was exceedingly bad. This was the third frigate action within a few months in which the same phenomenon occurred.

On June 9th, the British Mediterranean Fleet was cruising off Toulon when a French corvette was noticed in Hyeres Roads. (1) Sir John Jervis, the British admiral, summoned Captain James Macnamara (2nd) of the *Southampton*, 32, on board the flagship and pointed out "this eyesore." Macnamara accepted the hint; stood in under easy sail past the French batteries, which took his ship for a neutral, dashed at the corvette, *Utile*, 24, boarded and carried her, and then, taking her in tow, repassed the forts under a heavy fire. Lieutenant Charles Lydiard, who led the *Southampton*'s boarders, was promoted by Jervis on the spot to the command of the *Utile*. (2) The British loss was one killed; the French, eight killed and seventeen wounded.

(1)   Tucker, *Memoirs of Admiral the Right Hon. the Earl of St. Vincent*, Volume I page 185; James, *Naval History of Great Britain*, Volume I page 370; Troude, *Batailles Navales de la France*, Tome III page 38.

(2)   Lydiard, who was further promoted on January 1st, 1801, to the rank of Captain, was drowned in the *Anson* in 1807. W.L.C.

On June 11th, the French corvettes *Trois Couleurs*, 14, and *Betsy*, (1) 18, were taken off Brest by the *Amazon*, 38, and other British frigates. (2)

(1)   The *Betsy* appears in the prize lists as the *Blonde*. W.L.C.

(2)   Troude, *Batailles Navales de la France*, Tome III page 38; Log
           of *Amazon*.

On June 13th, to the south of Cape Clear, the *Dryad*, 36, Captain Lord
Amelius Beauclerk, brought the French frigate *Proserpine*, 40, Captain
Pevrieu, to action at about 8 a.m. (1) For an hour the engagement was a
running one. Then the *Dryad* came up on the Frenchman's larboard
quarter and began a close action. After forty-five minutes of this the
French ship struck. Neither vessel lost a spar, and neither was much
damaged in sails or rigging.

(1)   Troude, *Batailles Navales de la France*, Tome III page 39; Log
           of *Dryad*.

Name of Ship	Tons	Guns	Broadside (pounds)	Men	Killed	Wounded	Total
Dryad	924	44	407	254	2	7	9
Proserpine	1059	42	366	346	30	45	75

1-3/4 hours.

The *Proserpine* was purchased for the Navy and re-named *Amelia*.

On June 22nd, the French corvette *Legere*, 18, was captured off Brest by
the British frigates *Apollo,* 38, and *Doris*, 36. (1)

(1)   James, *Naval History of Great Britain*, Volume I page 370.

On July 12th, the French frigate *Renommee*, 36, Captain Pitot, was
overtaken by the British *Alfred*, 74, Captain Thomas Drury, off San
Domingo. (1) Two broadsides from the *Alfred* disabled the French
frigate, several shots striking the latter below the water-line, and flooding
the magazines in a moment.

(1)   Troude, *Batailles Navales de la France*, Tome III page 41.

Late in the evening of July 15th, the *Glatton*, 56 with twenty-eight 68-
pounder carronades on her lower deck, and as many 32-pounder
carronades on her upper deck, under Captain Henry Trollope, met a
French squadron of seven or eight ships in the North Sea. These were

THE ROYAL NAVY

probably the *Brutus*, (1) 46 or 50, *Incorruptible*, 38, *Rassurante*, 36, *Republicaine*, 28, and four small corvettes. The French formed in line ahead. The *Glatton* stood past the small ships and attacked the largest of her enemies. Two of the other French frigates hung about her, but all three were very roughly handled and beaten off. The *Glatton*, however, was so wounded in her masts and rigging, at which the enemy fired, and was withal so slow a sailer, that she could not take possession of any of her opponents. It is astonishing to record that only two men were wounded in her. Her 68-pounder carronades were very effective at close quarters, but she had not enough men to fight both broadsides at once. It is said that one of the French ships foundered on the squadron taking refuge in Flushing, whither it was chased by the *Glatton*.

(1)   James, *Naval History of Great Britain*, Volume I page 372. Troude (*Batailles Navales de la France*, Tome III page 41) does not mention the *Brutus*. The *Glatton*'s carronades appear to have been mounted on the non-recoil principle.

ADMIRAL SIR HENRY TROLLOPE, KNIGHT

(from H.B. Cook's engraving, after the portrait by Bowyer, painted when Sir Henry was a vice-admiral, 1805-1812)

On July 22nd, off Guadeloupe, the British *Aimable*, 32, Captain Jemmett Mainwaring, chased the French *Pensee*, 36, Captain Valteau. (1) After exchanging fire in the evening, the *Pensee* fled and drew ahead during the night. At about 7 a.m., however, she shortened sail; the *Aimable* closed; and the two captains saluted one another. Then, as the *Pensee* was again retreating, the *Aimable* bore up at about 8.40 a.m. and fired into her, but, after a running engagement, dropped astern out of range.

(1)   James, *Naval History of Great Britain*, Volume I page 377.

THE ROYAL NAVY

Name of Ship	Tons	Guns	Broadside (pounds)	Men (1)	Killed	Wounded	Total
Aimable	782	40	246	217	0	2	2
Pensee		40	289 (2)	300	?	?	?

(1)   Nominal.
(2)   Troude, *Batailles Navales de la France*, Tome III page 43, forty-two guns, 320-pounds broadside.

On August 8th, in the same waters, the *Mermaid*, 32, Captain Robert Waller Otway, engaged the French *Vengeance*, 40, at 11.50 a.m. (1) A prolonged but indecisive action followed, until, on the British *Beaulieu*, 40, Captain Francis Laforey, coming up, the *Vengeance* retired, under shelter of the Basseterre batteries. The French ship sustained most of her loss when twice missing stays.

(1)   James, *Naval History of Great Britain*, Volume I page 379; Ralfe, *The Naval Biography of Great Britain*, Volume IV page 7.

Name of Ship	Tons	Guns	Broadside (pounds)	Men (1)	Killed	Wounded	Total
Mermaid	689	40	246	217	0	0	0
Vengeance	1180	44 (2)	410	330	12	26	38

(1)   Nominal.
(2)   James (*Naval History of Great Britain*) says fifty-two.

On August 22nd, Commodore Sir John Borlase Warren's squadron of four frigates and a sloop, cruising off the mouth of the Gironde, chased the French frigate *Andromaque*, 36. (1) She was cut off from the Gironde by the *Galatea*, 32, Captain Richard Goodwin Keats, and *Sylph*, 18, Commander John Chambers White, and, after she had several times been lost sight of through the darkness of the night, was driven ashore on the morning of the 23rd. The *Sylph* proceeded to fire into her bottom, and in the afternoon sent in her boats and burnt her.

(1)   James, *Naval History of Great Britain*, Volume I page 383.

On August 25th, the *Raison*, 20, Captain John Poo Beresford, was chased by the French *Vengeance*, 40, to the west of the Gulf of Maine. (1) The British vessel, however, after a running action of two hours, escaped from her powerful antagonist with the loss of three killed and six wounded, whilst the French lost six killed and an unknown number of wounded. The *Raison* was helped in her escape by the very foggy weather.

(1)   James, *Naval History of Great Britain*, Volume I page 384.

On August 28th, the French *Elisabeth*, 36, was captured by the *Topaze*, 36, Captain Stephen George Church, off Cape Henry, after a broadside had been exchanged. (1) A large British squadron was coming up behind the *Topaze*.

(1)   James, *Naval History of Great Britain*, Volume I page 385; Troude, *Batailles Navales de la France*, Tome III page 43.

On September 9th, off the coast of Sumatra, Rear-Admiral Sercey's squadron, composed of the *Forte* and *Regeneree*, 38, *Vertu* and *Cybele*, 36, *Prudente*, 32, and the armed ship *Seine*, was attacked by the *Arrogant*, 74, Captain Richard Lucas, and *Victorious*, 74, Captain William Clark, which had been following since the previous day. (1) The enemies passed on opposite tacks, exchanging fire, but the *Arrogant* was very soon so much damaged in her rigging that she fell behind and ceased firing, having, however, almost crippled the *Vertu*. Four of the British ship's guns were disabled or dismounted. The *Victorious* continued the action, but without great success. She was outmanoeuvred by the French frigates, which kept as far as possible outside the field of fire commanded by her broadside and attempted to rake her. Sercey retired at 10.55, and at 11.15 a.m. the *Victorious* ceased her fire.

(1)   James, *Naval History of Great Britain*, Volume I page 391; Troude, *Batailles Navales de la France*, Tome III page 18; Chevalier, *Histoire de la Marine Francaise sous la Première République*, page 245.

THE ROYAL NAVY

Navy	Tons	Guns	Broadside (pounds)	Men (1)	Killed	Wounded	Total
British		164	1676	1200?	24	84	108
French (1)		220?	1700?	1400?	42	104	146

(1)   The *Seine*'s armament being uncertain, a minimum of force has been allowed her.

Sercey appears to have had the undoubted advantage, and this though he was engaging ships of the line with stouter sides than his frigates. His orders to avoid fighting and attack commerce probably prevented him from obtaining a more significant success.

On September 22nd, the *Amphion*, 32, Captain Israel Pellew, blew up at Plymouth from some unexplained cause. Captain Pellew was saved with ten out of 312 officers and men or visitors on board.

On September 23rd, the *Pelican*, 18, (1) Captain John Clarke Searle, (2) attacked the French *Medee*, 36, in the West Indies, and fought with her a close action of two hours' duration, when the Frenchman retired. The *Pelican* was so cut up that she could not pursue. After such an astounding action the value of the carronade, in certain cases, seems self-evident.

(1)   James, *Naval History of Great Britain*, Volume I page 396, sixteen 32-pounder carronades, two long 6s.
(2)   Searle had been posted on the previous 13th of July, but still retained his commander's command.

Name of Ship	Tons	Guns	Broadside (pounds)	Men	Killed	Wounded	Total
Pelican		18	262	97		1	1
Medee		40	410	300 (1)	?	?	33

2 hours.

(1)   Nominal.

48 William Laird Clowes

It appears that the *Medee*'s captain imagined that the *Pelican* was a frigate "with her mizen-mast out."

On October 13th, off Cartagena, the *Terpsichore*, 32, Captain Richard Bowen with a weak and sickly crew, engaged the Spanish *Mahonesa*, 34, Captain Don T. Ayaldi. (1) After a two hours' warm action the *Terpsichore* dropped astern with serious injuries to masts and rigging. Refitting in twenty minutes, she came up again, when the *Mahonesa* struck her colours.

(1)   James, *Naval History of Great Britain*, Volume I page 399; Log of *Terpsichore*.

Name of Ship	Tons	Guns	Broadside (pounds)	Men	Killed	Wounded	Total
Terpsichore	682	40	276	182	0	4	4
Mahonesa	921	34?	180?	275	30	30	60

120 minutes.

The *Terpsichore* had her three masts wounded, and shots through her spars and boats: otherwise she was little the worse. The *Mahonesa* was added to the Navy.

On November 25th, the *Lapwing*, 28, Captain Robert Barton, was summoned from Saint Kitts to the aid of Anguilla, in the West Indies, where a French force had disembarked. (1) She arrived on the 26th, and immediately the French re-embarked in the *Decius*, 20, and *Vaillante*, 10; but the *Decius* was captured after an hour's action, in which she lost 120 killed and wounded out of 336 on board. The *Lapwing* had one killed and six wounded. The *Vaillante*, to avoid capture, ran ashore, and was destroyed by the *Lapwing*'s guns.

(1)   James, *Naval History of Great Britain*, Volume I page 401.

On December 12th, the *Terpsichore*, Captain Richard Bowen, chased the French *Vestale*, 36, Captain Fourcaud, off Cadiz. (1) On the 13th the Frenchman hove to, and waited for the *Terpsichore*, which came up at 11.30 p.m. and began a hot action in stormy weather. At 1.20 a.m. the

THE ROYAL NAVY

Vestale with all her masts and her bowsprit tottering, struck. Her mizenmast fell just after her surrender; and, before the British boats could reach her, her main mast, foremast and bowsprit followed.

(1)   James, *Naval History of Great Britain*, Volume I page 402; Troude, *Batailles Navales de la France*, Tome III page 45; Chevalier, *Histoire de la Marine Francaise sous la Première République,* page 261; Log of *Terpsichore*.

Name of Ship	Tons	Guns	Broadside (pounds)	Men	Killed	Wounded	Total
Terpsichore	682	40	276	166	4	18	22
Vestale		40	286	300?	30	37	67

1 hour 40 minutes.

The high sea and strong wind prevented the *Terpsichore* from placing an adequate crew on board the prize, or transferring the prisoners, and, on the 14th, the *Vestale*'s men rose on the British party, recaptured the ship, and reached Cadiz. For this action the gallant Bowen received no warm commendation from Sir John Jervis, and no reward from the country. The merchants of London gave him, however, a piece of plate.

On December 19th, Commodore Horatio Nelson in the *Minerve*, 38, Captain George Cockburn with the *Blanche*, 32, Captain d'Arcy Preston, fell in with two Spanish frigates, *Sabina*, 40, Captain Don Jacob Steuart, and *Ceres*, 40, off Cartagena. At 10.40 the *Minerve* engaged the *Sabina*. (1) In fifty minutes, the Spanish ship's mizenmast went overboard, and at 1.20 a.m. she struck.

(1)   Nelson, *The Dispatches and Letters of Vice Admiral Lord Viscount Nelson*, Volume II page 312; James, *Naval History of Great Britain*, Volume I page 406.

Name of Ship	Tons	Guns	Broadside (pounds)	Men	Killed	Wounded	Total
Minerve	1102	42	370	286	7	34	41
Sabina		40	300	286	?	?	164

2 hours 40 minutes.

Lieutenants John Culverhouse and Thomas Masterman Hardy with a prize crew, were placed on board the *Sabina*; but at 4 a.m. of the 20th the *Minerve* had to cast off the tow-rope and engage a second Spanish frigate, the *Matilda*, 34, which she drove off with the loss of ten wounded. As a Spanish 112-gun ship and two more frigates were coming up, the *Minerve* was then obliged to look to her own safety. She owed her escape to the fact that Hardy and Culverhouse hoisted the British colours above the Spanish in the *Sabina*, and thereby drew off the enemy's attention. The *Sabina* was recaptured.

The *Blanche* meanwhile engaged the *Ceres* and quickly brought her colours down, but could not take possession owing to the arrival of the other Spanish ships. The *Blanche* lost no one; the *Ceres*, seven killed and fifteen wounded.

On December 30th, the *Polyphemus*, 64, Captain George Lumsdaine, captured the French *Tartu*, (1) 40, after a running fight of four hours. (2) The *Tartu* had formed part of the ill-fated expedition to Ireland. She was purchased for the Navy, in which she figured under her old name, *Urania*.

(1) Or *Tortue*. See page 18, antea.
(2) James (*Naval History of Great Britain*, Volume II page 11) gives the date as January 5th, 1797. Log of *Polyphemus*: which ship had one wounded.

On January 28th, 1797, five large East Indiamen, under Charles Lennox, master of the *Woodford*, met Rear-Admiral Sercey's squadron of six French frigates off Java. (1) Lennox with remarkable judgment, hoisted a British admiral's flag and made signals, so that the French, convinced that they saw before them Rear-Admiral Peter Rainier's squadron, were only too pleased to retire.

THE ROYAL NAVY

(1)   James, *Naval History of Great Britain*, Volume II page 89.

On January 31st, an Algerine corsair of twenty-four guns, mistook the British *Andromache*, 32, Captain Charles John Moore Mansfield, cruising on the Mediterranean station, for a Portuguese frigate, and found that she had caught a tartar. (1) The Algerine lost sixty-six killed and fifty wounded, to the *Andromache*'s two killed and four wounded, and struck her colours.

(1)   James, *Naval History of Great Britain*, Volume II page 90; Log of *Andromache*.

On February 22nd, the French vessels *Resistance, Vengeance*, 40, *Constance*, 22, and *Vautour*, lugger, landed in Fisgard (1) Bay, Pembroke, a nondescript force of 1500 criminals, armed and dressed as soldiers. The instructions to the French captains were to destroy Bristol and then attack Liverpool, but their hearts failed them. The criminals were captured with ridiculous ease by Welsh yeomanry, militia, and fencibles.

(1)   Guillon, *La France et l'Irlande Pendant la Revolution*, page 297. The name is now spelt Fishguard. Barras, *Memoires de Barras*, Tome II page 345.

On March 9th, the British frigates *San Fiorenzo*, 36, Captain Sir Harry Burrard Neale, and *Nymphe,* 36, Captain John Cooke (2nd), discovered two of the French ships engaged in this expedition, the *Resistance*, 40, Captain J.B.M. Laroque, and *Constance*, 22, Captain Purchet, approaching Brest. The British frigates at once bore down, though the Brest fleet of twenty sail could be made out from the masthead, and attacked. The *Resistance* struck after twenty minutes' fight. She had lost her rudder and steered badly. The *Constance* offered a stouter resistance but ended by hauling down her flag ten minutes later. The British *Robust*, 74, and *Triton*, 28, came in sight at the close of the action. The British ships suffered no loss. The French had eighteen killed and fifteen wounded. The *Resistance* mounted 48 guns and measured 1182 tons. She was purchased for the Navy and renamed the *Fishguard*, after the place where she had landed the invading force. (1)

(1)   James, *Naval History of Great Britain*, Volume II page 91; Troude, *Batailles Navales de la France*, Tome III page 61.

On April 26th, the British *Irresistible*, 74, Captain George Martin (2nd), and *Emerald*, 36, Captain Velters Cornwall Berkeley, forming part of the squadron blockading Cadiz, chased the Spanish frigates, *Ninfa*, 34, and *Santa Elena*, 34, (1) into Conil Bay, near Cadiz, attacked them at 2.30 p.m., and compelled them to strike ninety minutes later. The *Santa Elena*, however, after striking, cut her cable and went ashore, when her crew escaped. She sank after being got off. The *Ninfa*, purchased for the Navy, was renamed the *Hamadryad*. The Spanish loss was eighteen killed and thirty wounded; the British, one killed and one wounded. The Spanish frigates had treasure on board, but unloaded it into fishing boats, and despatched it ashore before they were attacked.

(1)   James, *Naval History of Great Britain*, Volume II page 93; Brenton, *Naval History of Great Britain from the Year 1783 to 1822*, Volume I page 494.

On July 16th, Sir John Borlase Warren's frigate squadron, composed of the *Pomone*, 40, *Anson*, 44, *Artois,* 38, *Sylph*, 18, (1) and a cutter, chased a French convoy in charge of the *Calliope*, 28, and two corvettes. The corvettes escaped into Audierne Bay, but the *Calliope* was driven upon the Penmarcks early on the 17th. To prevent the French crew from removing her stores and guns, she was cannonaded, first by the *Anson* and then at close quarters by the *Sylph*. The *Calliope* went to pieces on the 18th. The loss of the *Sylph* in her gallant attack was six wounded.

(1)   James, *Naval History of Great Britain*, Volume II page 95; Troude, *Batailles Navales de la France*, Tome III page 70.

On August 10th, the *Arethusa*, 38, Captain Thomas Wolley, cruising in the latitude of the Bermudas, fell in with the French corvette *Gaite*, 20, Enseigne J.F. Guine. (1) The latter did not attempt to escape but fought the heavy British frigate for half an hour and then struck. For his recklessness Guine was court martialled and censured.

(1)   Troude, *Batailles Navales de la France*, Tome III page 71; James, *Naval History of Great Britain*, Volume II page 98.

THE ROYAL NAVY

Name of Ship	Tons	Guns	Broadside (pounds)	Men	Killed	Wounded	Total
Arethusa	938	44	393?	277	1	3	4
Gaite	544	20	88	186	2	8	10

30 minutes.

On August 11th, Warren's squadron of three frigates (*Pomone, Jason,* and *Triton*) and one brig-sloop, the *Sylph,* 18, Commander John Chambers White, attacked a French convoy, under the charge of the corvette *Reolaise,* 20, a gunboat and a lugger. (1) The gunboat was destroyed and the corvette a good deal cut up with a loss to the British ships of three killed and five wounded.

(1)   James, *Naval History of Great Britain,* Volume II page 96; Troude, *Batailles Navales de la France,* Tome III page 72.

On October 14th, near the Canaries, the French *Ranger,* 12, Captain Hullin, was captured by the *Indefatigable,* 44, Captain Sir Edward Pellew. (1) On the 25th, in the same waters, the same British ship was mistaken by a French privateer for an East Indiaman. The capture of the Frenchman was the result. The vessel proved to be the *Hyene,* 24, a ship taken from Britain by the French in 1793 and commissioned as a privateer.

(1)   Troude, 73. Log of *Indefatigable.* Osler, 116.
(1)   Troude, *Batailles Navales de la France,* Tome III page 73; Log of *Indefatigable*; Osler, *The Life of Admiral Viscount Exmouth,* page 116.

On December 20th, the *Phoebe,* 36, Captain Robert Barlow, gave chase in the Bay to the French *Nereide,* 36, Captain A. Canon. (1) At 9 p.m. the two were near enough for the *Nereide* to open with her stern-chasers, which inflicted much damage on the *Phoebe*'s masts, sails, and rigging. The *Nereide* then suddenly tacked, and the *Phoebe* shot ahead. The *Phoebe,* however, tacked as soon as she could, and seemingly the *Nereide* tacked again, for the two passed on opposite courses exchanging fire. Finally, they closed and fought at three hundred yards for three-quarters of an hour. The *Nereide* once fell on board the *Phoebe,* but the latter easily got clear. At 10.45 p.m. the French ship struck, being in a very battered condition.

(1) James, *Naval History of Great Britain*, Volume II page 103; Troude, *Batailles Navales de la France*, Tome III page 73.

Name of Ship	Tons	Guns	Broadside (pounds)	Men	Killed	Wounded	Total
Phoebe	926	44	407	261	3	10	13
Nereide	892	40	278	330	20	55	75

1-3/4 hours

On December 29th, the British frigate *Anson*, 44, Captain Philip Charles Durham, captured without much difficulty the French corvette *Daphne*, 24, Captain Latreyte. (1) The two ships exchanged broadsides with the result that the *Daphne* lost two killed and five wounded. She was bound for Guadeloupe with dispatches but had not been able to get clear of the French coast. She was very much inferior in force to the *Anson*.

(1) James, *Naval History of Great Britain*, Volume II page 105; Troude, *Batailles Navales de la France*, Tome III page 74. Murray (*Memoir of the Naval Life and Service of Admiral Sir Philip C.H.C. Durham*, page 42) gives the date as the 23rd.

In January 1798, the British frigates *Sibylle*, 38, Captain Edward Cook, and *Fox*, 32, Captain Pulteney Malcolm, entered the bay of Manilla, disguised as French frigates, and succeeded in making two hundred prisoners and in capturing seven boats. (1)

(1) James, *Naval History of Great Britain*, Volume II page 237.

On the 22nd, they attacked the Spanish fort of Samboangon in the Philippines, but after a sharp action were repulsed with the loss of four killed and fifteen wounded. Visiting Pullock Harbour on the 31st, two seamen were killed by the natives and nine carried off. The latter were afterwards restored.

In the same month a number of Swedish merchantmen, freighted with contraband of war, were seized, though under convoy of a Swedish

THE ROYAL NAVY 55

warship, and condemned by the British prize-courts an act which led to great soreness in Sweden. (1) The value of the property in them was £600,000.

(1)   (compilation), *Annual Register*, 1801 page 36.

On February 3rd and 4th, the British brig *Speedy*, 14, Commander Hugh Downman, fought a protracted action with a French privateer, the *Papillon*, 14, of very superior metal. She succeeded in driving her enemy off with the loss of four killed and four wounded, but, owing to the failure of her ammunition, could not capture her.

On March 22nd, 1798, the *Canada*, 74, Captain Sir John Borlase Warren, *Anson*, 44, Captain Philip Charles Durham, and *Phaeton*, 38, Captain the Honourable Robert Stopford, chased, off the Isle of Aix, the French *Charente*, 36, Captain A.A.M. Bruillac with a number of French political prisoners on board, destined for Cayenne. (1) Early in the morning of the 23rd the *Phaeton* got within long range of the *Charente*, whereupon the latter turned and ran for the Gironde, exchanging broadsides with the *Canada* in passing. A little later, both the *Charente* and *Canada* ran aground. The former, after throwing her guns overboard, escaped up the river to Bordeaux in a damaged condition. The latter was got off without, much difficulty a little later.

(1)   Troude, *Batailles Navales de la France*, Tome III page 124; James, *Naval History of Great Britain*, Volume II page 228.

On April 23rd, the French gunboat *Arrogante*, 6, was captured off Brest by the British frigates *Jason* and *Naiad*.

On April 24th, the *Pearl*, 32, Captain Samuel James Ballard, found the French frigate *Regeneree*, 36, at anchor at Factory Island in the Loss Archipelago on the west coast of Africa and attacked her. (1) On this a second French frigate, the *Vertu*, 40, came up to the help of the *Regeneree*, and the latter weighed, and with her companion gave chase to the *Pearl*. The British frigate, though hotly pursued for twenty-four hours, made good her escape to Sierra Leone with one man mortally wounded.

(1)   James, *Naval History of Great Britain*, Volume II page 246; Troude, *Batailles Navales de la France*, Tome III page 139.

On May 2nd, the *Flora*, 36, Captain Robert Gambier Middleton, captured the French brig *Corcyre*, 12, off Sardinia. (1) On the 13th, she drove the French brig *Mondovi*, 18, into Cerigo, where late in the night her boats boarded and carried off the enemy with the loss of only one killed and eight wounded.

(1)   James, *Naval History of Great Britain*, Volume II page 250; Troude, *Batailles Navales de la France*, Tome III page 131; Log of *Flora*.

After the capture of Malta by the French, the frigate *Sensible*, 36, Captain Bourde, was sent with dispatches and valuables to Toulon, and when on her way thither off Marittimo, was chased by the British *Seahorse*, 38, Captain Edward James Foote. (1) The French ship turned and ran towards Malta, as she had but a very weak crew on board and was not properly equipped. In the night of the 26th-27th, the *Seahorse* gained upon her, and, after a running fight, brought her to close action at 4 a.m. Many of the Maltese galley slaves, who had been placed on board the *Sensible*, deserted their guns at the first broadside, and at the end of eight minutes action the French captain, having made a vain attempt to board his enemy, hauled down his flag. He was censured by the French Directory for not having offered a more stubborn resistance, but, as a matter of fact, the force opposed to him was very superior, and he was acquitted with honour by a French court-martial on his return to Toulon.

(1)   James, *Naval History of Great Britain*, Volume II page 234; Troude, *Batailles Navales de la France*, Tome III page 134.

Name of Ship	Tons	Guns	Broadside (pounds)	Men	Killed	Wounded	Total
Seahorse	984	46	494	292	2	16	18
Sensible	946	40	280	300	25	55	80

1 hour?

The *Sensible* was purchased for the Navy.

On June 29th, the British frigates *Jason*, 38, Captain Charles Stirling, *Pique*, 36, Captain David Milne, and *Mermaid*, 32, Captain James Newman Newman, whilst cruising off the Penmarcks, sighted the French

THE ROYAL NAVY

frigate *Seine*, 38, Lieutenant J.G. Bigot, on her way home from Mauritius, (1) with four hundred soldiers on board, in addition to her crew. She was making her landfall, but, when she saw the British ships, turned south for La Rochelle, hotly pursued. The *Mermaid* and *Jason* stretched inshore to cut her off from Lorient. The *Pique* followed her, and, at 9 p.m., began a running fight, ranging alongside at 11 p.m. The two fought broadside to broadside under sail till, two and a half hours later, the *Pique*'s main topmast was shot away. Then the *Jason* came up, and Captain Stirling ordered the *Pique* to anchor, as the land was very close. Instead of so doing she pressed on and ran aground. A very little later the *Jason* shared her fate. The *Seine* drove ashore almost at the same moment. The *Jason*'s stern floated, and, as the tide rose, the ship swung round, offering her stern to the *Seine*'s raking broadsides. The *Pique* managed to bring some of her guns to bear on the French ship, and then, as the *Mermaid* was coming up fast, the *Seine* struck her colours.

(1)   James, *Naval History of Great Britain*, Volume II page 247; Troude, *Batailles Navales de la France*, Tome III page 136; Brenton, *Naval History of Great Britain from the Year 1783 to 1822*, Volume I page 389.

Name of Ship	Tons	Guns	Broadside (pounds)	Men	Killed	Wounded	Total
Pique	906	44?	314?	247 (1)	2	6	8
Jason	984	46?	494?	277 (1)	7	12	19
Seine	1146	42	390	610	170?	170?	270?

(1)   Nominal.

The *Seine* was got afloat, but the *Pique* had to be abandoned, after being rendered unserviceable.

On July 15th, to the south-east of Cartagena, the *Lion*, 64, Captain Manley Dixon, engaged four Spanish frigates, the *Pomona, Proserpina, Santa Cazilda*, and *Santa Dorotea*, each of thirty-four guns. (1) The Spaniards formed in a line of battle, the *Lion* holding the weather gage. The *Santa Dorotea* dropped astern in the line and was attacked by the British ship, whereupon the other frigates tacked to her support, and, passing the *Lion*, each gave and received a broadside twice. The *Lion*, however, closed her opponent, and the other three Spanish ships, after a third attempt to give help, stood away for Cartagena. The *Santa Dorotea*, being very much cut up and quite unable by herself to resist the battleship's crushing fire, struck her colours.

(1)   James, *Naval History of Great Britain*, Volume II page 254.

Name of Ship	Tons	Guns	Broadside (pounds)	Men	Killed	Wounded	Total
Lion	1374	72?	678?	485 (1)	0	2	2
Santa Dorotea	958	34	180?	371	20	32	52

(1)   Nominal.

The *Santa Dorotea* was purchased for the Navy.

On July 23rd, the *Resistance*, 44, Captain Edward Pakenham, whilst at anchor in the Strait of Banca, blew up from some unexplained cause. (1) Of the people on board her, 332 were killed and only thirteen survived. These clung to her wreckage, constructed a raft, and set sail for Sumatra, but a sudden storm arising, all but five perished. These five reached Sumatra and were imprisoned by the Malays. Eventually, only one man escaped.

(1)   James, *Naval History of Great Britain*, Volume II page 245.

SIGNATURE OF CAPTAIN EDWARD PAKENHAM, R.N., WHO PERISHED IN H.M.S. *RESISTANCE*, 1798.

On July 26th, the British *Brilliant*, 28, Captain the Honourable Henry Blackwood, was chased by the French *Vertu*, 36, and *Regeneree*, 36, which she had found at anchor at Tenerife. (1) They slipped, and stood

THE ROYAL NAVY

after her. In the evening, though the *Brilliant* cut away boats and anchors, the *Regeneree* came up fast and began a running fight. To extricate herself the *Brilliant* suddenly bore up, and, crossing the hawse of the *Regeneree*, which was to leeward of her, gave her a raking broadside, and, bringing her main top-sail down, ran off on the starboard tack. The *Vertu* took up the chase and opened with her bow-guns. At midnight the wind fell and the *Regeneree* was able to come up again. Matters were looking very bad for the small British frigate when a fresh breeze sprang up and the *Brilliant* drew away, covered by darkness. She suffered no loss and little damage. She was very much the weakest ship, as, allowing her six 24-pounder carronades, her broadside did not exceed 198 pounds The broadside of the two French ships was 670 pounds at least.

(1)   James, *Naval History of Great Britain*, Volume II page 250; Troude, *Batailles Navales de la France*, Tome III page 130.

On the night of August 3rd-4th, the British vessels *Melpomene*, 38, Captain Sir Charles Hamilton, and *Childers*, 14, Commander James O'Bryen, (1) sent in their boats to the harbour of Correjou, in the Isle de Bas, to cut out the French brig *Aventurier*, 12, Lieutenant R.G. Raffy. (2) The night was dark, stormy, and rainy, and this covered the British approach. At three in the morning the *Aventurier* was surprised and captured after a sharp scuffle, in which the British loss was two killed and four wounded. In spite of the fire of a fort commanding the inlet, the *Aventurier* was carried out of the port.

(1)   Nephew of Murrough, first Marquis of Thomond, and later known as Lord James O'Bryen. He succeeded his eldest brother, as third Marquis, in 1846, and died, a full Admiral, in 1855. W.L.C.

(2)   James, *Naval History of Great Britain*, Volume II page 255; Troude, *Batailles Navales de la France*, Tome III page 140.

On August 7th, the British brig-sloop *Espoir*, 14, Commander Loftus Otway Bland, (1) whilst in charge of a convoy in the Mediterranean, was attacked by a large Genoese pirate, the *Liguria*, 26. (2) The two ships began their battle at about 7 p.m. and fought till 11, when the *Liguria* struck. The indiscipline of the pirate's crew is probably the explanation of her easy defeat by a vessel so much her inferior in armament.

60 William Laird Clowes

(1)   A Commander of October 1, 1797. For this action he was posted
       on September 25, 1798 W.L.C.
(2)   James, *Naval History of Great Britain*, Volume II page 256.

Name of Ship	Tons	Guns	Broadside (pounds)	Men	Killed	Wounded	Total
Espoir	215	14	42	80	1	6	7
Liguria		26	162	120	7	14	21

4 hours

On the same day, Captain Sir Edward Pellew, in the *Indefatigable*, 44,
cruising in the Bay, fell in with and captured, after a few shots, the
French corvette *Vaillante*, 20, Lieutenant la Porte, on her way to
Cayenne with political prisoners. (1) The prize was purchased for the
Navy and equipped with thirty-four carronades and long guns. She was
renamed *Danae*.

(1)   James, *Naval History of Great Britain*, Volume II page 258;
       Osler, *The Life of Admiral Viscount Exmouth*, page 116.

On August 12th, the British sloop *Hazard*, 18, Commander William
Butterfield, chased and captured the French armed ship *Neptune*, 10, in
the North Atlantic. (1)

(1)   James, *Naval History of Great Britain*, Volume II page 259.

On August 18th, the British 50-gun ship *Leander*, Captain Thomas
Boulden Thompson, on her way from Alexandria with Nelson's
dispatches announcing the victory of the Nile, was sighted by the French
Genereux, 74, Captain Lejoille, one of the two French vessels of the line
that had escaped with Villeneuve. (1) The *Leander* was short of her
proper complement by not fewer than eighty men, had no marine officer
on board, and had had one of her two 12-pounder carronades dismounted
at the Nile. She was off the western end of Candia when she was seen.
She at once made sail to escape, being vastly inferior in force to the
French vessel which was chasing her. A breeze, however, brought up the
enemy without reaching the *Leander*, and, at 8 a.m., the *Genereux* was
within random shot. Seeing that escape was hopeless, Captain Thompson
shortened sail and waited for his powerful antagonist. Soon after nine,

THE ROYAL NAVY

the *Genereux* was close enough to the *Leander*'s larboard quarter to open fire. A furious action began, the two ships moving slowly before the wind, broadside to broadside. The *Leander* was terribly shattered in her rigging, sails, and yards, of which fact the *Genereux* took advantage by running on board the *Leander*'s larboard bow and falling alongside at 10.30. The French then made a determined attempt to board. They were repulsed by the valour and resolution of the *Leander*'s marines, who, though they had no officer to lead or encourage them, poured in a terrible fire upon the French boarding parties. Below, the great guns continued the battle.

(1)   James, *Naval History of Great Britain*, Volume II page 259; Troude, *Batailles Navales de la France*, Tome III page 140; Clarke & M'Arthur, *The Life of Admiral Lord Nelson, K.B*, Volume II page 175; Hennequin, *Biographie Maritime*, Tome III page 293.

A breeze at length sprang up and carried the *Genereux* clear. The *Leander* had been still more crippled by the fall of her mizen-mast, which covered her starboard quarter, of her fore topmast, which had gone over the larboard bow, and of her yards, which were lying on the booms. Yet, as the *Genereux* took the starboard tack, Captain Thompson managed to place his ship under his enemy's stern, where he delivered a deliberate raking broadside.

The two closed once more at the shortest range with the sea "smooth as glass," and fought thus till 3.30 p.m. Then the *Genereux* paid off and came round across the *Leander*'s bow, raking her, whilst the *Leander*'s forward guns, masked by the wreck of the fore top-mast, could not fire. In that position, the *Leander* being quite unmanageable with every mast gone and much shattered in hull, the *Genereux* hailed to know if her enemy had struck. The *Leander* seems to have had no colours flying, and thence the question. A reply was made in the affirmative by waving a French ensign on a pike; and two French officers swam on board, the *Genereux* having no boat that would float. The *Leander* was thus taken possession of, after a six and a half hours resistance, famous in history for its gallantry.

In the *Leander* the loss was heavy. Nelson's flag-captain, the gallant Edward Berry, hero of innumerable pitched battles, who was on board as the bearer of dispatches, was wounded by a piece of a man's skull being driven into his arm. Captain Thompson had three serious wounds; three midshipmen were killed and a fourth with two lieutenants, (1) the master, and a master's mate, was wounded. In all, 35 were killed and 57 wounded out of a crew of 282 men, amongst whom were included 14 men wounded at the Nile.

(1)   Bridges Watkinson Taylor and William Swiney (2nd). The former, a commander of 1799 and a captain of 1802, was drowned in the *Apollo* in 1814. The latter retired with the rank of Commander in 1830 and died in 1841. W.L.C.

The *Genereux* suffered far more heavily in spite of her thicker and stronger sides. She is said to have had 100 killed besides 188 wounded, out of a crew of 936. Thus each ship lost about one-third of her crew. The moral of the *Leander* had doubtless been raised by the great victory of the Nile, or she might have been expected to strike sooner to force so overpowering.

Name of Ship	Tons	Guns	Broadside (pounds)	Men	Killed	Wounded	Total
Genereux	1926	80	1024	936	100?	188	288
Leander	1052	51	432	282	35	57	92

6-1/2 hours

Troude describes the *Leander* as a 64 and gives her eight 32-pounder carronades. His account is apparently based upon the official letter of Captain Lejoille, who willfully misrepresented the force of the ship which he had conquered and pretended that she was a 74. It is, of course, well known and ascertained that the *Leander* carried only fifty-one effective carriage-guns in all, and therefore twenty-three guns must have been added by Lejoille's exuberant imagination.

The behaviour of the captors was disgraceful. (1) They plundered the ship and plundered the prisoners. Captain Thompson had his kit, and Captain Berry a valuable pair of pistols, taken from him. The *Leander*'s surgeon was robbed even of his instruments and was not allowed to attend upon Captain Thompson. The wounded seamen were treated with great barbarity; and the prisoners were compelled to aid in refitting the ship, a breach of the established usages of war.

(1)   Troude (*Batailles Navales de la France*) cites evidence to the contrary, but it is far from convincing. The statements of the British consul at Trieste ((compilation), *Naval Chronicle*, Volume XIV page 10) are unimpeachable, though I cannot find that either Berry or Thompson complained.

On the way to Corfu, on August 28th, the *Genereux* and her prize were sighted by the British sloop *Mutine*, 16, Captain the Honourable Thomas Bladen Capell, carrying Nelson's duplicate dispatches; and the French made preparations to cast off the prize and abandon her, but, discovering the *Mutine*'s real force, did not carry out this intention. At Corfu, after much more ill-usage, the *Leander*'s officers were released on parole. Her seamen were detained prisoners, and at a later date an attempt was made by Captain Lejoille to persuade or compel some of them to join the French Navy. The reply of a gallant main top-man, George Bannister, has come down to us over the sea of time: "No, you damned French rascal; give us back our little ship and we'll fight you again till we sink."

On the capture of Corfu by the Russians and Turks on March 3rd, 1799, the *Leander* was restored to England. Captain Thompson was most honourably acquitted by court-martial for the loss of his ship, and, going ashore after the verdict, was cheered by every vessel at Sheerness. He and Berry were knighted for their gallantry.

On August 22nd, the British *Naiad*, 38, Captain William Pierrepont, saw the French *Decade*, 36, Captain Villeneuve, making her landfall off Finisterre, and chased her during the night. (1) Next day the *Magnanime*, 44, Captain the Honourable Michael de Courcy, joined the *Naiad* in her pursuit. At 5 p.m., the *Decade* opened on the leading British ship, the *Naiad*, and the latter, a little more than an hour later, replied. The two fought for about sixty minutes, when, seeing no chance of escape from so superior a force, Captain Villeneuve hauled down his flag. The *Decade* was from Cayenne, where she had left ten of her guns; she was no match for the *Naiad* alone, which mounted forty-six guns, much less for the *Magnanime*, which carried 24-pounders, and was a cut-down 64-gun ship.

(1)   James, *Naval History of Great Britain*, Volume II page 269; Troude, *Batailles Navales de la France*, Tome III page 144.

On October 24th, off the Texel, the British *Sirius*, 36, Captain Richard King (2nd), fell in with the Dutch vessels *Furie*, 36, Captain

Bartholomeus Pletsz, and *Waakzaamheid*, 24, Captain Meindert van Neirop. (1) As these two were some distance apart, the *Sirius* was able to isolate the *Waakzaamheid* and attack her, when at the first shot she struck. A prize crew was placed on board her, and then the *Sirius* made sail after the *Furie*, which had taken to her heels. At 5 p.m., the British frigate was close enough to her enemy to open fire, and a running fight ensued. The *Furie* continued a very ill-directed fire for an hour, doing little damage to the *Sirius*, while sustaining serious injury herself. Then the Dutch colours were hauled down. In this action the two Dutch captains displayed singular incapacity, allowing their ships to be separated and beaten in detail.

(1)   James, *Naval History of Great Britain*, Volume II page 270.

Name of Ship	Tons	Guns	Broadside (pounds)	Men	Killed	Wounded	Total
Sirius	1049	44	407	251 (1)	0	1	1
Furie	827	36	202	328	8	14	22
Waakzaamheid	504	26	111	222	0	0	0

(1)   Nominal.

Both prizes were purchased for the Navy, the *Furie* being renamed the *Wilhelmina*, which had been her original appellation.

On December 3rd, the British brig-sloops *Victorieuse*, 14, Commander Edward Stirling Dickson, and *Zephyr*, 14, Commander William Champain, landed a small force in the West Indian island of Margarita to attack a fort on the River Caribe. (1) This surrendered without any ado, and the brigs sailed for Gurupano, another port in the island. Seventy soldiers and marines were landed there and stormed two forts with a loss of two killed and two wounded. A privateer in the harbour was captured.

(1)   James, *Naval History of Great Britain*, Volume II page 230.

On December 14th occurred one of the very few actions in this war which are disgraceful to the British arms. (1) The *Ambuscade*, 32, Captain Henry Jenkins, whilst cruising off the Gironde, expecting to be joined by the *Stag*, 32, sighted a sail approaching. No private signals

THE ROYAL NAVY

were made or asked for; a discreditable degree of carelessness prevailed on board, and the men went to breakfast. Suddenly, at about 9 a.m., the stranger, having approached almost within gunshot, went about under a press of sail. She was the French corvette *Bayonnaise*, 24, Lieutenant J.B.E. Richer. The *Ambuscade*, when Captain Jenkins discovered his mistake, hurried in pursuit, and towards noon was near enough to the chase to open fire. The *Bayonnaise* shortened sail and courted battle. The two fought for an hour, when one of the *Ambuscade*'s 12-pounders burst, doing much damage to the ship and wounding eleven men. (2)

(1)   James, *Naval History of Great Britain*, Volume II page 273; Troude, *Batailles Navales de la France*, Tome III page 145; (compilation), *Public Record Office, Minutes of Courts Martial*, Volume 90 August 26th.

(2)   Nine men, according to a witness at the court-martial.

Such an incident, as a study of the minor actions proves, has a disastrous effect on the moral of the ship wherein it occurs. The only exception to this is in the case of the action between the *Serapis* and *Bonhomme Richard*. The *Bayonnaise* seized the opportunity of the confusion which this occurrence caused in the *Ambuscade* to make off. She was pursued by the *Ambuscade*, which came up to leeward, and shot a little ahead under a press of sail. The French had so far suffered severely. At that juncture they determined to board. They had a much larger crew than had the *Ambuscade*; and serving in the *Bayonnaise* were thirty veteran soldiers of the Alsace Regiment. The French ship ran on board the *Ambuscade*, which was becalmed as the French ship wore under her stem, carrying away the tiller ropes, starboard quarter-deck bulwarks, mizen shrouds and mizen-mast, and locking the wheel with her sprit-sail yard, and then dropped under the British vessel's stern, but did not clear her. The French soldiers from the *Bayonnaise*'s bowsprit swept the *Ambuscade*'s deck, which was not barricaded with hammocks with a deadly fire. In a few minutes five officers (1) were killed or wounded in quick succession, and the command devolved upon the purser, Mr. William Bowman Murray. An explosion of cartridges, left on the rudderhead, blew out a portion of the *Ambuscade*'s stern, and caused panic amongst her men. Most of the British crew left their quarters. At that moment the French boarders rushed on to the *Ambuscade*'s deck and carried it.

(1)   Lieutenant Dawson Main, mortally wounded; Captain Jenkins, wounded; Lieutenant of Marines, James Sinclair, wounded; Mr.

Brown, Master, killed; Lieutenant Joseph Briggs, wounded. W.L.C.

The British crew was, according to James, an ill-disciplined one, and Captain Jenkins a most indiscreet and incompetent officer. The management of the *Ambuscade* left much to be desired, and, as often is the case, bad management was attended by bad luck. The two explosions, and the great weakness of the British crew, from which not less than thirty-one officers and men had been detached and placed on board a prize, must be taken into account. All the French officers except two were wounded; all the British executive officers killed or wounded. The action shows clearly that superiority of force is useless with a bad or weak captain and an ill-disciplined crew. The French may none the less be proud of their victory.

Name of Ship	Tons	Guns	Broadside (pounds)	Men	Killed	Wounded	Total
Bayonnaise	580?	32	123 (1)	250?	30?	30?	60?
Ambuscade	684	40	268	190	11	39	50

4 hours?

(1)   Troude, *Batailles Navales de la France*. According to James, (*Naval History of Great Britain*) her broadside was 156 pounds or thereabouts, as he credits her with two 36-pounder carronades and gives good reasons for his statement. Of the *Ambuscade*'s 24-pounder carronades some, if not all, were disabled in the action.

Captain Jenkins, whilst still suffering from his wound, was tried and acquitted for the loss of his ship. This fact may explain the verdict. His officers and his crew were likewise acquitted, though the opinion was expressed that all had not behaved with the accustomed courage of British seamen. Lieutenant Richer was promoted two steps for his brilliant success.

On January 4th, 1799, the *Wolverine*, 12, Commander Lewis Mortlock, cruising off Boulogne, was attacked by two strongly manned French privateers, the *Ruse*, 8, and the *Furet*, 4, but succeeded in repulsing them. (1) The *Wolverine*, though she carried only seventy men, could fight on

THE ROYAL NAVY

each side two 18-pounders, six 24-pounder carronades, and two, if not three, 12-pounder carronades. She was, therefore, a more formidable ship at close quarters than her rating seemed to show.

(1)   James, *Naval History of Great Britain*, Volume II page 353.

On February 1st, the British 28-gun frigate *Proserpine*, Captain James Wallis, struck on the Scharhorn Eiff, below Neuwerk, at the mouth of the Elbe, in stormy weather, and had to be abandoned. (1) Her crew escaped ashore on the ice with the loss of fourteen frozen to death in the bitterly cold weather.

(1)   James, *Naval History of Great Britain*, Volume II page 354.

On February 6th, the British ships *Leviathan*, 74, Captain John Buchanan, and *Argo*, 44, Captain James Bowen, discovered off Majorca two Spanish frigates, the *Santa Teresa*, 34, and *Proserpina*, 34. (1) The two latter separated and took different courses. The *Santa Teresa* was pursued by the *Argo*, but the *Leviathan*, which had dropped behind, did not alter course and chase the *Proserpina*. At midnight the *Argo* closed the *Santa Teresa* after a running fight, and a broadside brought down the Spanish flag. The Spaniard was no match for the *Argo* alone, much less for the *Argo* and *Leviathan* combined. The prize was purchased for the Navy.

(1)   James, *Naval History of Great Britain*, Volume II page 359.

On February 9th, the British *Daedalus*, 32, Captain Henry Lidgbird Ball, cruising in the Indian Ocean, sighted the French *Prudente*, 36, Captain Joliff with a prize. (1) The *Prudente* had only thirty guns on board, having left eight at Mauritius, and she had already detached seventeen of her officers and men to form the prize crew. She separated from her prize and was soon closed by the *Daedalus*, which engaged her hotly just after noon. The British ship crossed her stern, raked her and luffed, bringing the two broadside to broadside. At 1.21 p.m., the *Prudente* struck in a very shattered condition. According to Troude, she was a privateer and not a warship.

(1)   James, *Naval History of Great Britain*, Volume II page 357;
         Troude, *Batailles Navales de la France*, Tome III page 170.

Name of Ship	Tons	Guns	Broadside (pounds)	Men	Killed	Wounded	Total
Daedalus	703	38	246	212	2	12	14
Prudente	920	30	214	301	27	22	49

1 hour 20 minutes.

The *Prudente* was too much damaged to be purchased for the Navy.

On February 22nd, off the Spanish coast, (1) the British sloop *Espoir*, 14, Commander James Sanders, captured the Spanish xebec *Africa*, 14 with a loss of four killed and wounded. The Spanish loss was thirty-seven killed and wounded.

(1)   James, *Naval History of Great Britain*, Volume II page 364.

Late in February, the French frigate *Forte*, 40, Captain Beaulieu, arrived in the Bay of Bengal and began to harass British commerce. (1) She was in bad order; the discipline of her crew was not good; and her captain, according to Rear-Admiral Sercey, was too old and feeble for his work. The British cruiser *Sibylle*, 40, Captain Edward Cook, a very fine and powerful vessel, went to look for her to stop her depredations. In the evening of the 28th, whilst the *Sibylle* was on this quest, vivid flashes were seen to the north-west, and supposed to be lightning. As, however, the flashes went on continuously till nine, and then stopped altogether, Captain Cook began to suspect that they were from guns, and stood towards them with all lights out, to make certain. At 9.30 he sighted the *Forte* and two prizes lying side by side. Captain Cook manoeuvred to gain the weather gage, untroubled by the *Forte*. The French captain saw the *Sibylle*, but was obstinately persuaded that she was a merchantman, and made no preparations to attack her, though assured by his officers that she was an enemy.

(1)   James, *Naval History of Great Britain*, Volume II page 365; Troude, *Batailles Navales de la France*, Tome III page 171.

The French were on the starboard tack, lying to. The *Sibylle* bore steadily down, until, as she approached, the *Forte* crossed her bows and fired a few random shot at her, to which the British ship made no answer. Then, at 12.45 a.m., the *Sibylle* put her helm up, the *Forte* being abaft her

THE ROYAL NAVY

beam, and passed under the enemy's stern, pouring in a most destructive broadside at the very shortest range. She followed this up by closing the *Forte* broadside to broadside, whilst the guns of the French were fired by mistake at one of their prizes. The *Forte* had had to supply crews for seven captures and for this reason was unable to man her forecastle and quarterdeck guns. In consequence, her fire was not very effective.

Early in the action Captain Cook (1) was wounded, and Captain Beaulieu was killed an hour after the battle began. At 2.30 the *Forte* had only four guns which could be used. She therefore stopped her fire and endeavoured to make sail and escape. Discovering her intentions, the *Sibylle*, after twice hailing her to strike, resumed her fire and very quickly brought down the *Forte*'s masts. On this the French ship struck and was taken possession of. The *Sibylle* was much cut up in her masts and rigging. The *Forte* was in a horrible state with her starboard side almost beaten in, and three hundred shot in her hull.

(1)   This gallant officer, a captain of 1794, died of his wounds at Calcutta on May 25th, following. (compilation), *Naval Chronicle*, Volume II page 643. James and others spell his name "Cooke" but the (compilation), *Navy List of the Royal Navy* spelling is here followed. W.L.C.

Name of Ship	Tons	Guns (1)	Broadside (pounds)	Men	Killed	Wounded	Total
Sibylle	1091	48	503	371	5	17	22
Forte	1401	52	610	370?	65	80?	145

2-1/2 hours.

(1)   The *Sibylle* carried twenty-eight 18-pounders, six 9-pounders, and fourteen 32-pounder carronades. The *Forte*'s armament is variously given:

Author	Weight of Shot (pounds)			
	French 24	English 24	8	Carronades 36
Troude	28	2	14	8
James	28		10	4

James has been followed in the text.

In the *Sibylle* were 131 officers and men of the Scotch Brigade, who fought with great credit. It should he noted that in the general opinion of naval men at that time the *Sibylle* was no match for the *Forte*. The latter's weight of broadside, from long guns only, was 448 pounds, as against the *Sibylle*'s 279 pounds The bad shooting of the *Forte* is partly explained by the fact that her gun-quoins had been planed down three days previously. The *Forte* was purchased for the Navy and rated a 44.

On April 9th, the British *San Fiorenzo*, 36, Captain Sir Harry Burrard Neale, and *Amelia*, 38, Captain the Honourable Charles Herbert, were cruising off Belle Isle, where lay three French frigates, the *Cornelie*, 40, *Semillante*, 36, and *Vengeance*, 40, when a squall carried away the *Amelia*'s main top-mast and her two other topgallant masts. (1) On this the three French ships stood out, and, supported by a gunboat, attacked the frigates. A scrambling distant action of three hours followed, after which the French retired, to the great surprise of the British. The *San Fiorenzo* and *Amelia* were much cut up in their rigging. They had to face not only the French ships but also a battery on Hoedic Island. The retreat of the French was explained by the fact that they imagined they were dealing with two cut-down ships of the line.

(1)   James, *Naval History of Great Britain*, Volume II page 376.

On May 8th, the British polacca *Fortune*, 10, Lieutenant Lewis Davis, cruising on the Syrian coast, (1) was attacked by the French brig *Salamine*, 18. After a three hours' desperate engagement the *Fortune* struck, as three French frigates of Rear-Admiral Perree's squadron were seen to be coming up. The *Fortune* had the help of a gunboat, the *Dame de Grace*, which was sunk. Her loss was five.

(1)   James, *Naval History of Great Britain*, Volume II page 379.

On June 9th, the boats of the *Success*, 32, Captain Shuldham Peard, cut out an armed Spanish polacca, laden with merchandise, from the harbour of La Selva. The British loss was four killed and eight wounded out of forty-two.

On August 11th, the British sloops, *Pylades*, 16, Commander Adam Mackenzie, and *Espiegle*, 16, Captain James Boorder with the cutter *Courier*, 10, Lieutenant Thomas Searle, attacked the ex-British brig *Crash*, 12, which was lying between Schiermonnikoog and the Dutch

THE ROYAL NAVY

mainland. (1) The *Courier* led, followed by the other two, and after a fifty minutes action the Dutch flag was hauled down. The British loss was three killed or wounded. On the 12th, the *Crash* and the boats of the other vessels attacked the Dutch schooner *Vengeance*, 6, which was lying under the guns of a battery on Schiermonnikoog. Under a heavy fire the battery was taken and its guns spiked or brought off. The schooner was burnt by her crew. There was no loss on the British side.

(1)   James, *Naval History of Great Britain*, Volume II page 382.

On August 20th, the British *Clyde*, 38, Captain Charles Cunningham, was cruising off Rochefort, when she sighted the French ships *Vestale*, 32, Captain M.M.P. Gaspard, and *Sagesse*, 20. (1) The two separated, and the *Vestale* was followed by the *Clyde*. At 1.30 p.m. the latter was within range, and the action began, the *Clyde* and *Vestale* engaging broadside to broadside. The *Clyde* changed from larboard to starboard of the French ship, passing astern and raking her, and repeated this manoeuvre several times. The *Vestale*'s crew was weak, as thirty or forty men had died in the West Indies of yellow fever; and of those on board many were ill. She had no chance of success against so superior an antagonist. At about 3.20 she struck her flag.

(1)   James, *Naval History of Great Britain*, Volume II page 384; Troude, *Batailles Navales de la France*, Tome III page 177.

Name of Ship	Tons	Guns	Broadside (pounds)	Men	Killed	Wounded	Total
Clyde	1000?	46	425	281	2	3	5
Vestale	946	36? (1)	273 (1)	230	10	22	32

110 minutes.

(1)   James (*Naval History of Great Britain*) calls the *Vestale* a 36-gun frigate and gives her a total of thirty-eight carriage-guns. From Troude (*Batailles Navales de la France*) and from the number of her complement as detailed in James, she appears to have been a 32 of thirty-six carriage guns.

The *Vestale* was not purchased for the Navy.

On August 25th

, off the coast of Guiana, the British *Tamar*, 38, Captain Thomas Western, chased the French corvette *Republicaine*, 28, Captain P.M. Lebozee. (1) The latter during the night escaped into shoal water, whence under cover of darkness she ran for the open sea. At daylight she was seen and pursued. At 5.30 p.m. the *Tamar* came up with her; and, after ten minutes of fighting, the *Republicaine* struck.

(1)   James, *Naval History of Great Britain*, Volume II page 387; Troude, *Batailles Navales de la France*, Tome III page 179.

Name of Ship	Tons	Guns	Broadside (pounds)	Men	Killed	Wounded	Total
Tamar	999	46	425	281	0	2	2
Republicaine		36	266	175	9	12	21

10 minutes.

The *Republicaine*'s eight 36-pounder carronades, counted above, were so badly mounted as to be almost unserviceable.

On September 12th, the British sloops *Arrow*, 28, Commander Nathaniel Portlock, and *Wolverine*, 12, Commander William Bolton, attacked off Harlingen the Dutch brig *Gier*, 14, and ship, *Draak*, 18. (1) The *Wolverine* secured the surrender of the first without loss on either side, but the *Arrow* had a harder task, as she had to work up to the *Draak* under fire, against tide and wind. When close to her enemy she opened, and in fifteen minutes the *Draak* hauled down her colours. The *Wolverine* was then fast coming up.

(1)   James, *Naval History of Great Britain*, Volume II page 388.

Name of Ship	Tons	Guns	Broadside (pounds)	Men	Killed	Wounded	Total
Arrow		28	448	20	1	9	10
Draak	?	24?	358?	180	?	?	?

15 minutes.

THE ROYAL NAVY

The *Draak* was destroyed, and the *Gier* purchased for the Navy.

On September 20th, the British vessels *Camel*, armed storeship, Commander John Lee, and *Rattlesnake*, 16, Commander Samuel Gooch, were lying at anchor in Algoa Bay, South Africa, (1) with masts and yards down, and their commanders and about forty five men serving on shore, when the French *Preneuse*, 36, Captain l'Hermitte, entered the bay and anchored near them without attacking them, though each British vessel fired a shot at her. At 8.30 p.m., since it appeared from the *Preneuse*'s manoeuvres that she intended to board the *Rattlesnake*, (2) that vessel opened fire and was supported by the *Camel* (3) The *Preneuse* at about nine returned the fire, directing her guns mainly upon the *Camel*. The latter ship was hulled below the water-line, and all her crew had to be withdrawn from the guns to the pumps. The *Preneuse*, supposing that the *Camel* was silenced, next turned her fire on the *Rattlesnake*; but at 3.30 a.m., to the surprise of all, she slipped and retreated. The French explanation of this is that the *Preneuse*'s crew was very weak, and that she dreaded attack from a supposed British brig really a prize schooner. The British loss was three killed and thirteen wounded in this action, against very superior force.

(1)   James, *Naval History of Great Britain*, Volume II page 390.
(2)   Temporarily commanded by Lieutenant William Fothergill. W.L.C.
(3)   Temporarily commanded by Lieutenant Charles Shaw. W.L.C.

On October 9th, the *Jupiter*, 50, Captain William Granger, having arrived in Algoa Bay, sailed in quest of the *Preneuse*, and on the 10th, in a heavy gale, sighted her, and chased her. (1) The *Jupiter* could not open her lower deck ports owing to the sea. A running fight continued during the 10th and 11th till 2 p.m. of the latter day, when the *Jupiter* closed. The sea was still so high that the British ship could not use her 24-pounders. The *Preneuse*, though seriously damaged, was handled with great skill. She twice raked her heavier enemy, and at about 5 p.m. so disabled her foe in masts and rigging as to be able to escape. No explanation of the *Jupiter*'s failure can be given. As Troude points out, even if her lower-deck guns were useless, she had her twelve 36-pounder carronades with her 6-pounders, which gave her a broadside of 228 pounds.

(1)   James, *Naval History of Great Britain*, Volume II page 392; Troude, *Batailles Navales de la France*, Tome III page 180; Log of *Jupiter*.

On October 11th, the *Excellent*, 74, Captain the Honourable Robert Stopford, captured off Lorient the French corvette *Arethuse*, 18, Captain Halgan, after an eight hours chase. (1)

(1)   Troude, *Batailles Navales de la France*, Tome III page 183; (compilation), *Gazette de France*, 1799, page 1066.

On October 11th, the British *Revolutionnaire*, 38, Captain Thomas Twysden, captured an exceptionally large and fast French privateer, the *Bordelaise*, 24, on the Irish coast. (1) The *Bordelaise* offered no resistance.

(1)   James, *Naval History of Great Britain*, Volume II page 399; Log of *Revolutionnaire*.

On the 12th, the British *Trincomale*, 16, Commander John Rowe, whilst engaging a French privateer, the *Iphigenie*, 18, in the Strait of Bab-el-Mandeb, blew up, all her crew except two perishing. (1)

(1)   Rowe had been a commander for less than three months. The explosion also sank the *Iphigenie*, about 115 men perishing in her. The British loss was about 98. W.L.C.

On October 15th, the British frigate, *Naiad*, 38, Captain William Pierrepont, cruising in the bay, sighted the two Spanish frigates, *Santa Brigida*, 34, and *Thetis*, 34 with treasure from Mexico on board to the value of £600,000. (1) She at once gave chase, and early next morning saw another ship, a friend, the *Ethalion*, 38, Captain James Young (2nd), which also joined in the chase. A third British frigate, the *Alcmene*, 32, Captain Henry Digby, and a fourth, the *Triton*, 32, Captain John Gore (2nd), arrived on the scene after day broke. The two Spaniards then separated and took different courses. The *Ethalion* pursued the *Thetis*, passing the *Santa Brigida* and firing into her. At 11.30, the *Ethalion* brought the *Thetis* to action, and, after a running fight of an hour, captured her.

THE ROYAL NAVY

Name of Ship	Tons	Guns	Broadside (pounds)	Men	Killed	Wounded	Total
Ethalion	992	46	425	281	0	0	0
Thetis	950?	34?	180	370?	1	9	10

10 minutes.

Meantime, the *Santa Brigida* doubled Cape Finisterre, closely pursued by the *Triton*. The latter was so unfortunate as to strike a reef, but was quickly got off, and at 7 a.m. brought the Spaniard to action. At the same time the *Alcmene*, steering so as to cut off the *Santa Brigida* from the shore, engaged her on the other side. Thus assailed, the *Santa Brigida*, after a vigorous resistance, hauled down her flag. All the three frigates and the *Naiad* were amongst the rocks, whence they succeeded in extricating themselves on a breeze springing up opportunely from the shore.

The Spanish frigates and their captors arrived at Plymouth on the 21st and 22nd. The treasure was in due course removed to London and divided amongst the captors in the following proportion: captains, £40,730 18s each; lieutenants, £5091 7s 3d; warrant-officers, £2468 10s 9-1/2d; midshipmen, £791 17s 0-1/4d; seamen and marines, £182 4s 9-1/2d. The Spanish frigates were not purchased for the Navy.

On October 20th, off Cape Ortegal, the British *Cerberus*, (1) 32, Captain James Macnamara (2nd), discovered a large Spanish convoy of eighty sail, under charge of the *Ceres*, 40, *Diana, Esmeralda, Mercedes*, and an unknown ship, all of 34 guns, besides two brigs. The *Cerberus* at once approached them, closed a frigate, and with extra ordinary audacity, attacked her. The Spaniard was unprepared. She probably never expected a single enemy to venture within the reach of so large a squadron; and at 8.30 her guns are said to have been silenced. The other four Spanish frigates then approached and assailed the intruder, the *Cerberus* being at times engaged on both sides; and at 9.30 Captain Macnamara decided to retire. He succeeded in getting clear of his assailants, and then, at 11 p.m., captured a brig from the convoy and burnt her. The *Cerberus*'s loss was only four wounded. That of the Spaniards is unknown.

On the night of October 24th, the boats of the *Surprise*, 28, Captain Edward Hamilton, cut out the ex-British frigate *Hermione*, 32, from the harbour of Puerto Cabello in Venezuela. (1) The enterprise was a desperate one, as batteries mounting about two hundred guns commanded the harbour. Six boats were employed under the lead of Captain Hamilton himself. They were discovered by two Spanish gun-vessels, and fired on long before they reached the *Hermione*; and, when they got alongside her, they found her crew at quarters. None the less they boarded her, and a desperate fight upon her deck ensued. Captain Hamilton was felled by a clubbed musket, and several of the British were wounded. They drove the Spaniards, however, from the deck, cut the cable, and loosed the foresail and topsails. In spite of a heavy fire from the batteries they carried out their prize with the loss of only 12 wounded. The Spaniards, on the other hand, lost no fewer than 119 killed and 97 wounded out of a crew of 365. This is perhaps the most gallant of the many gallant cutting-out actions of this war, and Captain Hamilton was deservedly knighted for his conduct. The *Hermione* was restored to the Navy under the name first of *Retaliation* and then of *Retribution*.

(1)   James, *Naval History of Great Britain*, Volume II page 405.

ADMIRAL SIR EDWARD HAMILTON, BARONET

(from the engraving by Ridley, after the painting by Thompson)

On November 6th, the British *Speedy,* 14, Commander Jahleel Brenton, whilst waiting for her convoy off Gibraltar, was attacked by twelve Spanish gunboats which endeavoured unsuccessfully to capture two vessels in her charge. (1) She drove them off after a sharp action with the loss of only two killed and one wounded. She was, however, very much cut up in hull. The batteries of Gibraltar gave her no support; the explanation being, as Brenton discovered, that the Governor of Gibraltar had agreed with the Governor of Algeciras, that if the gunboats would not fire on the town of Gibraltar, the batteries would not fire on the gunboats.

(1)   James, *Naval History of Great Britain*, Volume II page 395; Brenton, *Naval History of Great Britain from the Year 1783 to 1822*, Volume I page 487.

On November 15th, the British *Crescent*, 36, Captain William Granville Lobb, and *Calypso*, 16, Commander Joseph Baker with a convoy, fell in with the Spanish *Asia*, 64, *Amfitrite*, 40, and *Galgo*, 16, under Commodore Don F. Montes, bound from San Domingo to Havana. (1) The *Calypso* reconnoitred the Spaniards and stood between them and the British convoy, as also did the *Crescent*. Meantime the convoy had scattered and the *Galgo* was observed to be closing it. On this the *Crescent* made sail from the *Asia* and *Amfitrite*, and in face of them captured and carried off the *Galgo*. The whole convoy reached Jamaica with the loss of only one ship. There must have been the most astonishing incapacity on the part of the Spaniards.

(1)   James, *Naval History of Great Britain*, Volume II page 413.

On November 24th, the British *Solebay*, 32, Captain Stephen Poyntz, discovered off San Domingo four French ships, the flute, *Egyptien*, 18, store-ship, *Eole*, 16, *Levrier*, 12, and *Vengeur*, 8. (1) They bore away for Cape Tiburon, and were followed by Poyntz, until the four were becalmed and separated, when the *Solebay* attacked them in turn and captured them all. Between them, they mounted fifty-eight guns, and were manned by 431 men. The *Eole* (1) was purchased for the Navy and renamed *Nimrod*.

(1)   James, *Naval History of Great Britain*, Volume II page 415. Not in Troude, *Batailles Navales de la France*, so, probably, these vessels were privateers, or hired by privateer companies from the French Navy, or else armed ships with stores on board. (The *Vengeur* was the ex-British schooner *Charlotte*, which had been captured off Cape Francois, under Lieutenant John Thicknesse, earlier in the year. W.L.C.)

(2)   Called *Eolan* in Steel, *Steel's Original and Correct List of the Royal Navy*, and *Goelan* (*Goeland*) in Marshall, *Royal Navy Biography*, Part III Volume I page 753. W.L.C.

On December 11th, the French *Preneuse*, 36, Captain l'Hermitte, was chased off Mauritius by the British *Tremendous*, 74, and *Adamant*, 50, and driven ashore. (1) She was boarded by the British boats and burnt.

THE ROYAL NAVY

(1)   Troude, *Batailles Navales de la France*, Tome III page 184.

On December 17th, the British *Glenmore*, 36, Captain George Duff, and *Aimable*, 32, Captain Henry Raper with a large convoy, fell in with the French *Sirene*, 36, Captain J.M. Renaud, *Bergere*, 18, Captain Bourdichon, and the *Calcutta*, East Indiaman, which the French had just captured, off Madeira. (1) The *Glenmore* mistook the *Calcutta* for a cut-down ship of the line and stood in chase of her and captured her. Meantime the *Aimable* pursued the two French warships, and at 1.30 p.m. was out of sight of her consort. She attacked the *Bergere*, hoping that the *Glenmore* would come up to her aid; but, when this did not happen and the *Sirene* wore and stood towards her, she had to draw off. She remained watching the French ships till nightfall when she rejoined the convoy.

(1)   James, *Naval History of Great Britain*, Volume II page 416; Troude, *Batailles Navales de la France*, Tome III page 186.

In December, a Danish frigate in charge of a convoy resisted an attempted search of her convoy by British vessels and was compelled to accompany the British ships to Gibraltar, but was there eventually released. (1)

(1)   Chevalier, *Histoire de la Marine Francaise dans la Guerre de 1778*, Tome III page 28.

On February 5th, 1800, the British sloops *Fairy*, 16, Commander Joshua Sydney Horton, and *Harpy*, 18, Commander Henry Bazely, off Saint Malo discovered the French frigate *Pallas*, 38, Captain Jacques Epron. (1) The British vessels stood out to sea and were followed by the *Pallas*, which closed and engaged them. An action of over an hour followed, in which the *Harpy* several times raked her opponent. Then the *Pallas* retired, leaving the *Harpy* and *Fairy* too much damaged to follow her.

(1)   James, *Naval History of Great Britain*, Volume III page 3; Troude, *Batailles Navales de la France*, Tome III page 202.

Name of Ship	Tons	Guns	Broadside (pounds)	Men	Killed	Wounded	Total

Pallas	1028	46	498	362	12?	?	12?
Fairy and *Harpy*	(1)	40?	334?	240	5	11	16

1-1/4 hours.

(1)   The *Harpy* was 367 tons.

Repairing their damage, the *Fairy* and *Harpy* made sail in chase of the *Pallas*, when they sighted, coming up ahead, the British *Loire*, 38, Captain James Newman Newman, *Danae*, 20, Captain Lord Proby, and *Railleur*, 16, Commander William Turquand. These joined in the chase, and the *Railleur*, at about 7.45 p.m., compelled the *Pallas* to tack off-shore, when she passed the *Loire* and exchanged fire. At 11 p.m. the *Loire* closed her off the Sept Isles, and began a sharp action with her and a battery on shore. The *Railleur, Harpy*, and *Fairy* all joined in, and the five ships fought running on the starboard tack till 1.30, when the *Harpy* got under the *Pallas*'s stern and gave her several raking broadsides. On this she struck after a brilliant resistance to an overwhelming force.

The *Loire* had on board one hundred "volunteers" from prison-ships who showed great cowardice. The British loss in this action was nine killed and thirty-six wounded; the French loss is unknown. The *Pallas*, a remarkably fine frigate, was purchased for the Navy and renamed *Pique*.

On March 20th, the British *Petrel*, 16, Commander Francis William Austen, off the Riviera, engaged the French *Cerf*, 14, *Lejoille*, 6, and *Ligurienne*, 14, in charge of a convoy. (1) As the British *Mermaid*, 32, was seen to be coming up, though at a great distance, the French vessels made all sail to escape. The *Ligurienne* was overtaken by the *Petrel*, and after a smart fight, in which the French had the support of a coast battery mounting four heavy guns, struck.

(1)   James, *Naval History of Great Britain*, Volume III page 10; Troude, *Batailles Navales de la France*, Tome III page 203.

Name of Ship	Tons	Guns	Broadside (pounds)	Men	Killed	Wounded	Total
Petrel		20?	96?	89?	0	0	0
Ligurienne		16	85	104	2	2	4

1-1/2 hours.

THE ROYAL NAVY

On April 5th, the British ships *Leviathan*, 74, Captain James Carpenter, carrying Rear-Admiral John Thomas Duckworth's flag, *Swiftsure*, 74, Captain Benjamin Hallowell, and *Emerald*, 36, Captain Thomas Moutray Waller, off Cadiz discovered a Spanish convoy. (1) Early on the 6th they captured one of its ships, and later in the day a second. Then, seeing six sail in the north-east, the *Leviathan* and *Emerald* stood towards them, and early on the 7th found that two of them were frigates. At dawn the two British ships bore down upon them and being taken by the Spaniards for vessels of the convoy, were able to get very close. The enemies were hailed to strike, and, thus discovering their mistake, attempted to escape, but were foiled by the *Emerald*, which disabled their sails and rigging. They then struck, and proved to be the *Carmen*, 32, and *Florentina*, 34. They had lost between them twenty-two killed and twenty-six wounded. The British ships apparently suffered no loss. A third Spanish frigate effected her escape.

(1)   James, *Naval History of Great Britain*, Volume III page 13.

On June 3rd, the French corvette *Albanaise*, 12, was captured by the British *Phoenix*, 36, and *Port Mahon*, in the Mediterranean. (1)

(1)   Troude, *Batailles Navales de la France*, Tome III page 210.

On the night of June 10th, the boats of Sir John Borlase Warren's frigate squadron, cruising off the Penmarcks, captured three small French vessels and eight merchantmen in the harbour of Saint Croix with a loss of four men. (1) On the night of the 23rd-24th, a party landed from the boats of the same squadron and stormed and destroyed three small batteries and forts at the mouth of the Quimper River. On the night of July 1st-2nd, the boats boarded and destroyed the French armed ship *Therese*, 20, lying inside Noirmoutier Island, three other armed vessels, and fifteen merchantmen. On returning, the boats grounded upon a sandbank, and ninety-two officers and men were captured by the French. The remaining one hundred fought their way clear.

(1)   James, *Naval History of Great Britain*, Volume III page 15.

On July 7th, the sloop *Dart*, 30, (1) Commander Patrick Campbell with two gun-brigs, (2) four fireships, (3) and the cutters and boats from the *Andromeda*, 32, and *Nemesis*, 28, ran into Dunquerque Road to capture or destroy four French frigates lying there, the *Poursuivante*, 44,

Carmagnole, 40, *Desiree*, 38, and *Incorruptible*, 38. (4) The *Dart* answered a hail in French, and arrived abreast of the inmost frigate but one without a shot being fired. The French vessel then opened on her, and she replied with her 32-pounder carronades, passing on and running on board the innermost enemy. Her men dashed on to the deck of the Frenchman, and in a moment the *Desiree* was carried. She was successfully taken out by her captors and was purchased for the Navy. Meantime the fireships ran up to the other three French frigates, but, though well handled, could not destroy them, and they escaped. The smaller British craft cannonaded the French gunboats. The total British loss in this dashing enterprise was only six killed or wounded.

(1)   32-pounder carronades. W.L.C.

(2)   *Biter*, Lieutenant William Norman, and *Boxer*, Lieutenant Thomas Gilbert. W.L.C.

(3)   *Wasp*, Commander John Edwards (2nd); *Falcon*, Commander Henry Samuel Butt; *Comet*, Commander Thomas Leef; and *Rosario*, Commander James Carthew. W.L.C.

(4)   James, *Naval History of Great Britain*, Volume III page 17; Troude, *Batailles Navales de la France*, Tome III page 191.

On the night of July 26th, three boats from Sir Edward Pellew's squadron, under the command of Lieutenant Jeremiah Coghlan (acting) of the cutter *Viper*, most gallantly cut out the French gun brig *Cerbere*, 7, from Port Louis. (1) The French crew was found at quarters, but, though two of his boats failed to arrive in time, Coghlan boarded. He was driven back and wounded in the thigh, but, returning to the attack, forced his way in and carried her. She was towed out successfully; and Lord Saint Vincent, then in command of the Channel Fleet, was so pleased with Coghlan's conduct that he presented him with a sword and confirmed him as lieutenant, in spite of his not having served his time. (2)

(1)   James, *Naval History of Great Britain*, Volume III page 20; (compilation), *Navy League Journal*, Volume 1 page 195; Osler, *The Life of Admiral Viscount Exmouth*, page 131.

(2)   Coghlan, who was born in 1775, was made a commander in 1804, and a captain in 1810. He died in the latter rank on March 4, 1844. He had been given a C.B. in 1815. W.L.C.

On August 4th, the British *Belliqueux,* 64, Captain Rowley Bulteel with six East Indiamen under her charge, sighted the French frigates

THE ROYAL NAVY

Concorde, 40, Captain J.F. Landolphe, *Franchise*, 36, Captain P. Jurien de la Graviere, and *Medee*, 36, Captain J.D. Coudin, with a prize schooner off the coast of Brazil. (1) Taking the Indiamen for ships of the line, the French scattered. The British pursued, the *Belliqueux* capturing the *Concorde* after a few shots which hurt no one, and the East Indiamen chasing the *Medee* and the *Franchise*. The *Medee* was overtaken by, and after a very short resistance struck to, the Indiamen *Bombay Castle*, John Hamilton, master, and *Exeter*, Henry Meriton, master. The *Franchise* alone escaped.

(1)   James, *Naval History of Great Britain*, Volume III page 23; Troude, *Batailles Navales de la France*, Tome III page 193; Graviere, *Souvenirs d'un Amiral*, Tome II page 23. The names of the French ships were changed purposely in the last-named work. Captain Jurien protested to his senior officer that the supposed ships of the line were only merchantmen, but to no purpose. The *Franchise*, after escaping, cruised for three weeks on the South American coast without seeing a sail. "Was," asks the captain, "the damage which we had caused to commerce worth the loss of two frigates with 700 men? I am far from believing it. ... I assert that commerce-destruction has only a secondary importance in the general outline of war."

On August 20th, the British *Seine*, 38, Captain David Milne, after a six hours chase, came up with the French *Vengeance*, 36, Captain Pitot, off the coast of Puerto Rico. (1) At 4 p.m. the French ship opened fire with her stern-chasers. The *Seine* was not able to use her broadside till 11.30, when she opened fire, taking up a position on the *Vengeance*'s quarter. The fire of the French directed at the *Seine*'s masts caused her to drop behind; but the *Vengeance*, before she escaped from her enemy, lost her foremast and main topmast.

(1)   James, *Naval History of Great Britain*, Volume III page 23; Troude, *Batailles Navales de la France*, Tome III page 215.

Early on the 21st the *Seine* came up again, only to be once more disabled, and once more to refit. At about 9 a.m. she closed the *Vengeance* for the third time and fought the French ship till 10.30, when the latter with foremast, main topmast, and mizenmast gone, and fearfully shattered in hull, struck her flag. She was quite unmanageable. The *Seine* had her mainmast tottering but was not greatly injured.

THE ROYAL NAVY

Name of Ship	Tons	Guns (1)	Broadside (pounds)	Men	Killed	Wounded	Total
Seine	1146	48	498	281	13	29	42
Vengeance	1180	50	434	326	35?	70?	105?

8 to 9 hours.

(1)   Each ship seems to have fought one extra gun at an empty port on the engaged broadside. Troude gives the *Vengeance* forty carriage-guns and a broadside of 311 pounds.

The *Vengeance* was purchased for the Navy but saw no service.

On September 3rd, eight boats from the *Minotaur*, 74, and *Niger*, flute, under Commander James Hillyar, of the latter, rowed in to cut out from Barcelona the Spanish corvettes *Esmeralda*, 22, and *Paz*, 22. (1) The British boats on their way in boarded a Swedish merchantman bound into the port, but quitted as soon as she was within range. The boats, as soon as the Spaniards opened fire, dashed at the *Esmeralda*, and carried her, following up their success by rushing the *Paz*. Both ships were carried off in the face of Spanish gunboats and batteries with a British loss of only three killed and six wounded.

(1)   (compilation), *Annual Register*, 1801 page 87; James, *Naval History of Great Britain*, Volume III page 27; Brenton, *Naval History of Great Britain from the Year 1783 to 1822*, Volume I page 515.

On October 9th, the East Indiaman *Kent*, 26, Robert Rivington, master, after a long and obstinate resistance, was captured in the Bay of Bengal by the French privateer *Confiance*, 26, Robert Surcouf. (1) The *Kent* was not supplied with sufficient muskets to resist the French boarders, who behaved very badly as, indeed, privateers men of both nations only too often did. Rivington fell in the action.

(1)   Norman, *The Corsairs of France*, page 353. Robert Surcouf, one of the greatest of the French corsairs, was born at Saint Malo in 1773, and first went to sea, in a merchantman, in 1789. He was engaged in the slave trade, even after the traffic had been formally abolished by the Republic in 1794, and was in

consequence arrested, but, escaping, became a privateer. In the East Indies he was extraordinarily successful. He was at length appointed an unattached *enseigne* in the navy, but did not serve as such; and, after 1802, contented himself with fitting out privateers, until 1806, when he returned to the East Indies, and gained further successes. After the peace he lived as a shipowner and shipbuilder till his death in 1827. Laughton, *Studies in Naval History*. W.L.C.

On October 22nd, the French corvette *Venus,* 28, was captured in the Atlantic by the British ships *Indefatigable*, 44, and *Fishguard*, 38. (1)

(1)   Troude, *Batailles Navales de la France*, Tome III page 220.

In the evening of October 27th, the boats, under Lieutenant Francis Beaufort, of the British frigate *Phaeton*, 38, Captain James Nicoll Morris, cut out from under the guns of the fortress of Fuengirola, near Malaga, the Spanish polacca *San Josef*, 14. (1) The Spaniards made a desperate resistance, but could not stand against the valour of the British seamen, whose loss was only one killed and four wounded. The *San Josef* lost nineteen wounded. She was purchased for the Navy and renamed the *Calpe*.

(1)   James, *Naval History of Great Britain*, Volume III page 33.

An action which is important as illustrating the value of non-recoil mountings, was that of November 13th, between the British schooner *Milbrook*, of sixteen 18-pounder carronades, mounted on non-recoil principles, (1) and a large French privateer, the *Bellone*, off Oporto. The *Milbrook*, Lieutenant Matthew Smith (2nd), fired eleven broadsides to the enemy's three. The *Bellone* was of far superior force, (2) and succeeded in escaping.

(1)   James, *Naval History of Great Britain*, Volume III page 35.
(2)   Mounting twenty-four long 8-pounders, and six or eight 36-pounder carronades. W.L.C.

On November 17th, a British squadron, under Captain Sir Richard John Strachan, discovered the French corvette *Reolaise*, 20, running along the Morbihan coast, and attempting to gain the shelter of a battery. (1) She was cut off from it by the *Nile*, cutter, Lieutenant George Argles, and ran aground in Port Navalo, striking her colours. The boats of the squadron

THE ROYAL NAVY

approached to cut her out, but she rehoisted her colours, got off the ground, and fired on them. This only postponed her fate, as the boats returned, and, under a heavy fire, boarded and destroyed her with the loss of one killed and seven wounded.

(1)   James, *Naval History of Great Britain*, Volume III page 36; Troude, *Batailles Navales de la France*, Tome III page 220.

On the night of January 3rd, 1801, five boats from the *Melpomene*, 38, Captain Sir Charles Hamilton, crossed the bar of the River Senegal, and without being discovered, approached the French brig *Senegal*, 18, Captain Renou, at anchor in the river. (1) They were close to her when she fired and sank two of the boats. The others pushed alongside her, boarded her, and carried her after a short struggle. The British boats then proceeded to attack a schooner, which had run under the shelter of a battery, but were repulsed. In taking the *Senegal* out she grounded on the bar, and no efforts could get her off. She was, therefore, abandoned, and the boats rowed back to the ship. The loss was heavy, as out of a total of ninety-six officers and men engaged, eleven were killed (2) and eighteen wounded. The *Senegal* was totally lost in the quick sands on which she had struck.

(1)   James, *Naval History of Great Britain*, Volume III page 118; Troude, *Batailles Navales de la France*, Tome III page 245.
(2)   Including Lieutenant William Palmer, Lieutenant of Marines William Vyvian, and Midshipman Robert Main. W.L.C.

On January 17th, the small British schooner *Garland*, (1) and some boats, the whole under Lieutenants Kenneth M'Kenzie and Francis Peachey, approached the French schooner *Eclair*, at anchor under the batteries of Trois Rivieres in the Island of Guadeloupe, under the Swedish flag, boarded her, and carried her off with the loss of five men.

(1)   Troude, *Batailles Navales de la France*, Tome III page 246; James, *Naval History of Great Britain*, Volume III page 120.

On January 20th, the British *Mercury*, 26, Captain Thomas Rogers, in the Mediterranean, fell in with and captured the French *Sanspareille*, 20, Lieutenant G. Renaud, then on her way to Egypt with stores and ammunition for the French Army. (1) Some days previously, in the Gulf of Lions, the same British ship had captured fifteen sail of a French convoy.

(1)   James, *Naval History of Great Britain*, Volume III page 119; Troude, *Batailles Navales de la France*, Tome III page 247.

On January 23rd, the late Spanish *Nuestra Senora de los Dolores*, 1, acting as tender to the British *Abergavenny*, 54, captured in the most gallant way a Spanish preventive schooner, the *Santa Maria*, 6, on the South American coast. (1) The tender chased the Spaniard ashore, followed her and grounded, when a number of British seamen, led by Lieutenant Michael Fitton (acting), swam off to her, sword in mouth, and carried her. She was then destroyed.

(1)   James, *Naval History of Great Britain*, Volume III page 123.

On January 26th, the British *Oiseau*, 36, Captain Samuel Hood Linzee, off Cape Ortegal, sighted the French *Dedaigneuse*, 36, Captain Lacroix, on her way from Cayenne to Rochefort. (1) The French ship was in very bad order. Amongst other defects, the bolts of her cut-water had worked loose and given the bowsprit too much play. Other British frigates, the *Sirius*, 36, and *Amethyst*, 36, came into sight, and the *Dedaigneuse* turned and headed for Ferrol. A long chase followed, but late in the night of the 27th-28th the *Sirius* and *Oiseau* began a running fight. Off Ferrol harbour the French vessel was becalmed, whilst the British pursuers were carried down upon her by a breeze from the sea. After four broadsides the *Dedaigneuse*'s captain was wounded. The French ship struck, seeing another British frigate, the *Immortalite*, approaching. The British suffered no loss, and very little damage. The French loss is unknown. (2) The *Dedaigneuse* was purchased for the Navy.

(1)   James, *Naval History of Great Britain*, Volume III page 123; Troude, *Batailles Navales de la France*, Tome III page 248.
(2)   "Several killed and seventeen wounded," says the *Gazette de France* letter with the usual vagueness.

On January 29th the British corvette *Bordelaise*, 24, Captain Thomas Manby, off Barbados, found three French vessels standing after her. (1) These were the *Curieux*, 18, Captain G. Radelet, *Mutine,* 16, Captain Reybaud, and *Esperance*, 6, Captain Hamon. The British ship shortened sail and waited. The *Curieux* came up, and was at once attacked, whereupon her two consorts beat a prompt retreat. All but two of the *Bordelaise*'s guns were 32-pounder carronades, and those made short work of her audacious assailant. For thirty minutes the two fought at the

THE ROYAL NAVY

89

closest quarters, when the *Curieux* struck, after suffering terrible loss. Her captain paid for his gallantry with the loss of his life. The *Curieux* foundered almost immediately after the action, two British seamen going down in her.

(1)   James, *Naval History of Great Britain*, Volume III page 124.

Name of Ship	Tons	Guns	Broadside (pounds)	Men	Killed	Wounded	Total
Bourdelaise	625	24	361	195	1	7	8
Curieux		18	78	168			(1)

30 minutes.

(1)   About 50 men.

On February 18th, in the southern Atlantic, the British *Penguin*, 18, Captain Robert Mansel, (1) fought a sharp action with three unknown French ships, one looking like a corvette, and the other two apparently merchantmen. (2) The *Penguin* gave chase and compelled one of them to strike. On this she was assailed by the corvette and was so damaged in masts and rigging that she could not pursue her antagonists, who then sheered off. Her foremast went overboard, but her loss was only one man wounded.

(1)   Mansel had been posted on February 14th, but had not received his commission. W.L.C.
(2)   James, *Naval History of Great Britain*, Volume III page 125; Troude, *Batailles Navales de la France*, Tome III page 249; Log of *Penguin*.

On February 19th the British *Phoebe*, 36, Captain Robert Barlow, to the east of Gibraltar, discovered the French frigate *Africaine*, 40, Captain Saunier, steering up the Mediterranean. (1) The *Africaine* was heavily laden, having, besides her crew, four hundred troops for Egypt, six field-guns, and a quantity of arms and ammunition on board. She had parted from the similarly freighted *Regeneree*, 36, some days previously. The *Phoebe* quickly overhauled her enemy, and brought her to close action, steering a parallel course. The French ship had her decks encumbered and was at a great disadvantage. Her only chance lay in boarding the

Phoebe, but this Captain Barlow was adroit enough to prevent. The effect of the *Phoebe*'s well-directed fire upon the crowded decks of the *Africaine* was deadly in the extreme. After two hours' furious fighting, Captain Saunier and Commander J.J. Magendie, the two French senior officers, were wounded, the ship was on fire in several places, and had five feet of water in her hold, and most of her guns were dismounted. She struck her flag.

(1) James, *Naval History of Great Britain*, Volume III page 127; Troude, *Batailles Navales de la France*, Tome III page 250; Bonaparte, *Correspondance de Napoleon Ier*, 5514.

Name of Ship	Tons	Guns	Broadside (pounds)	Men	Killed	Wounded	Total
Phoebe	926	44	407	239	1	12	13
Africaine	1059	44	334	715 (1)	200	144	344

2 hours.

(1) Including 400 troops et cetera.

This action shows clearly the disastrous result of encumbering a warship with soldiers and cargo. The French troops, as a point of honour, insisted on remaining on deck during the action, though their presence was useless, and even harmful; and this contributed to the terrific loss. It was only with extreme difficulty that the *Phoebe* carried her prize into Port Mahon. The *Africaine* was purchased for the Navy, and her name changed to *Amelia*. It appears that the bad shooting of the French who only put three shot into the *Phoebe*'s hull was due to Captain Saunier having planed down the quoins before the day of battle, and to his having actually removed them when the *Phoebe* was in chase of him. Thus the French gunners were compelled to fire high and to endeavour to dismast their enemy. This came to the knowledge of the First Consul, who warned his officers that they were to fire, "not to dismast the enemy, but to do him as much harm as possible."

On March 22nd, the boats of the *Andromache*, 32, and *Cleopatra*, 32, captured a Spanish gunboat on the Cuban coast, but only with heavy loss nine killed and twelve wounded. (1)

THE ROYAL NAVY

(1)   James, *Naval History of Great Britain*, Volume III page 130.

On the night of April 2nd-3rd, the boats of the *Trent*, 36, off the islands of Brehat, captured a French lugger and her prize as these were making for Paimpol. The British loss was two killed and one wounded.

Early in April, the *Speedy*, 14, Commander Lord Cochrane, cruising off the Spanish Mediterranean coast, was decoyed close under the guns of a heavy Spanish xebec disguised as a merchantman. (1) To escape was impossible; to fight, taken unprepared, against such odds, hopeless. Cochrane was sailing under Danish colours. His ship was painted to resemble a Dane; and he placed an officer, who could speak Danish, in Danish uniform at the gangway, and caused him to reply in Danish to the Spaniard's hail. Dissatisfied, the Spaniard sent a boat, which was told that the supposed Dane was from one of the Barbary ports, where the plague was then raging. On this the Spaniards were only too anxious to be off.

(1)   James, *Naval History of Great Britain*, Volume III page 132; Cochrane, *The Autobiography of a Seaman*, page 43.

On May 6th, the *Speedy* met a large Spanish frigate, the *Gamo*. Sailing under American colours till he was close to his enemy, Cochrane, in spite of two broadsides from the Spaniard, which did him no damage, ran alongside, and fired his guns treble-shotted into the foe. The Spaniards attempted to board, but, as soon as Cochrane heard the order given, he sheered off, continuing his fire. A second and a third attempt on the part of the Spaniards were repulsed. Then, running under her big adversary once more, the *Speedy* emptied her whole crew upon the Spaniard's deck, and the *Gamo* was carried, though not without a struggle.

Name of Ship	Tons	Guns	Broadside (pounds)	Men	Killed	Wounded	Total
Speedy	158	14	28	51	3	8	11
Gamo	600	32	190	319	15	41	56

45 minutes.

This is one of the most extraordinary actions of the war, and exhibits in a brilliant light Lord Cochrane's audacity, judgment, and fertility of resource. He carried his big prize safe into harbour, but only with great difficulty.

On May 25th, the boats of the *Mercury*, 28, Captain Thomas Rogers, attempted to cut out the ex-British bomb *Bulldog* from the harbour of Ancona. (1) The British seamen, according to Troude, disarmed suspicion by answering the challenge in French, boarded the *Bulldog*, and carried her without resistance being offered. They then cut the cables which secured her to the mole and had worked her nearly to the entrance of the harbour when they were attacked by a number of French boats, and forced to abandon their prize. Their loss was two killed and four wounded.

(1)   James, *Naval History of Great Britain*, Volume III page 135; Troude, *Batailles Navales de la France*, Tome III page 254.

On June 9th, the *Kangaroo*, 18, Commander George Christopher Pulling, and *Speedy*, 14, Commander Lord Cochrane, attacked a Spanish convoy off Oropesa, under the shelter of a Spanish battery, sank a 20-gun xebec and three gunboats, and captured three merchant brigs. (1) On July 3rd, Rear-Admiral Linois's squadron, of three French sail of the line and one frigate, captured the little *Speedy*, 14, in the Strait of Gibraltar. (2)

(1)   James, *Naval History of Great Britain*, Volume III page 135.
(2)   James, *Naval History of Great Britain*, Volume III page 97.

On the night of July 20th-21st, the boats of the British frigates *Beaulieu*, 40, Captain Stephen Poyntz, and *Doris*, Captain Charles Brisbane, 36, made an attempt to cut out the French corvette *Chevrette,* 20, which was lying in Camaret Bay, but failed to arrive before day had dawned. (1) They retired, but they had been seen, and the *Chevrette* prepared for another attempt by embarking a party of soldiers, which brought her crew up to 339, and by loading her guns to the muzzle with grape. On the following night, the boats of the above frigates with those of the *Uranie*, 38, Captain George Henry Gage, as well, embarked 280 men, and rowed in. Six boats, however, proceeded to chase a French look-out boat, and did not return. The other boats, (2) with 180 men, grew impatient, and dashed at the *Chevrette*. They were received with a heavy fire of great guns and small arms, both from her and from the shore, but pressed on; and the British seamen forced their way on board. A party of topmen, appointed for that purpose, fought their way up her rigging and spread her topsails, and presently the *Chevrette* stood out of the bay. Meantime,

THE ROYAL NAVY

the party on deck carried the forecastle and quarter-deck, and drove the Frenchmen down the hatches. As soon as that had been done the other six boats rejoined. The *Chevrette* was carried off, though fired upon by the French batteries. In the affair the British loss was twelve killed or missing and fifty-seven wounded, whilst the French lost ninety-two killed and sixty-two wounded. The gallantry of the British officers and seamen was above all praise. The *Beaulieu*'s quartermaster, Henry Wallis, who had been ordered to take the *Chevrette*'s helm, fought his way to his post, and continued at it, though badly wounded.

(1)   James, *Naval History of Great Britain*, Volume III page 137; Troude, *Batailles Navales de la France*, Tome III page 255; (compilation), *Naval Chronicle*, Volume VII page 216.

(2)   Under Lieutenants Keith Maxwell, James Pasley, Martin Neville, and Walter Burke; Lieutenant of Marines James Sinclair; and Midshipmen Robert Warren, Sinclair and Warren were killed, and Burke was mortally wounded. W.L.C.

On July 21st, the British hired brig *Pasley*, 16, Lieutenant William Wooldridge, fought a sharp action with a Spanish xebec of twenty-two guns. The xebec escaped. The *Pasley*'s loss was one killed and two wounded. (1)

(1)   James, *Naval History of Great Britain*, Volume III page 149.

On July 31st, the British brig *Sylph*, 18, Commander Charles Dashwood, off Santander, was engaged by a large ship of unknown nationality probably a French or Spanish privateer and after eighty minutes' close fighting had to retire. (1) She was not pursued by the strange ship. On August 1st, the *Sylph* saw her enemy at some distance with her foreyard on the deck, and gave chase, but, by reason of the heavy sea and her own injuries, could not close. The *Sylph*'s loss was one killed and nine wounded.

(1)   James, *Naval History of Great Britain*, Volume III page 145; Marshall, *Royal Navy Biography*, Part I Volume II page 454.

Having repaired her damage, the *Sylph*, cruising off the coast of Spain on September 28th, again encountered an unknown ship, and fought her for over two hours, when the enemy retired. The *Sylph* only had one man wounded. According to Dashwood, the stranger was the French *Artemise*, 40. We may be permitted to feel the gravest doubt as to this. It

94 William Laird Clowes

is impossible to believe that a large and powerful French frigate would have failed to inflict far heavier loss on a small brig if, indeed, she had not captured her. The matter remains a mystery.

On August 18th, (1) the British *Sibylle*, 38, Captain Charles Adam, discovered the French *Chiffonne*, 36, Captain P. Guieysse in Mahe Roads with her foremast out. The *Sibylle* prepared for battle, steered in through a narrow intricate passage, and anchored two hundred yards off the Frenchman with springs on her cables. An action of seventeen minutes followed during which the *Sibylle* had to take the raking fire of a French battery on the island. Then the *Chiffonne* cut her cable, struck her flag, and drifted on a reef. The *Sibylle* sent a boat to take possession, and another to capture the battery, upon which she turned her guns. The battery then surrendered.

(1)   James (*Naval History of Great Britain*, Volume III page 131) gives the date as April 19th. Troude (*Batailles Navales de la France*, Tome III page 259) gives the date as August 20th. Log of *Sibylle*.

Name of Ship	Tons	Guns	Broadside (pounds)	Men	Killed	Wounded	Total
Sibylle	1091	48	503	217 (1)	2	1	3
Chiffonne	845	40	370	190	23	30	53

17 minutes.

(1)   Nominal.

The *Chiffonne* was taken by surprise, and many of her men were on shore. She was got off and was afterwards purchased for the Navy.

On September 2nd, the British *Victor*, 18, Commander George Ralph Collier, off the Seychelles, engaged for ninety minutes the French *Fleche*, 18, Captain J.B. Bonamy. (1) The *Victor* had the heavier metal and soon drove her enemy to flight, but, having received serious injury in her masts and rigging, could not pursue closely. The *Victor* followed at a distance till the 5th when the *Fleche* had disappeared. That afternoon, however, she saw her entering Mahe. The channel was sounded at night and next day the *Victor* stood in and anchored with springs, taking a

THE ROYAL NAVY

95

raking fire during her approach. A fight of two and a half hours followed, when the *Fleche*, in a sinking condition, cut her cables, drove on shore, and was set on fire by her crew. A British party boarded her, but she fell over and sank.

(1)   James, *Naval History of Great Britain*, Volume III page 143; Troude, *Batailles Navales de la France*, Tome III page 262.

Name of Ship	Tons	Guns	Broadside (pounds)	Men	Killed	Wounded	Total
Victor		18	262	120	0	2	2
Fleche		18	78	145	4	?	?

4 hours.

The *Fleche* was eventually raised by the French.

On September 16th, the ex-British bomb *Bulldog* was recaptured off the south coast of Italy by the British frigates *Mercury*, 26, and *Santa Dorotea*, (1) 36.

(1)   Troude, *Batailles Navales de la France*, Tome III page 263.

For the minor actions of the revolutionary war we have the aid of the invaluable *Naval Chronicle*, and of the painstaking James, who appears to have carefully collated *Gazette* letters, logs, courts martial, and what French authorities were accessible in his day. (1) The ship's logs were still kept in a most unsatisfactory way, especially in small craft. For instance, the British frigate *Oiseau* sights the French *Dedaigneuse*, and the log is dumb. But towards the close of the century there is a very distinct improvement, and, as printed forms come into use, more care is exercised.

(1)   The authorities for this war are, besides James and Troude: Brenton, *Naval History* (2 volumes 1837); Chevalier, *Marine Francaise sous la Premiere Republique*, and *Sous le Consulat et l'Empire*; the *Naval Chronicle*, which gives *Gazette* letters, lives of eminent officers and much interesting matter; Schomberg's *Naval Chronology*; courts-martial, logs, List Books, Captains' Letters and Admirals' Dispatches; the various biographies of

great seamen — Nelson (Nicolas), Saumarez (Ross), Pellew (Osler), Dundonald, Saint Vincent (Tucker), Keith (Allardyce), Durham (Murray); Marshall's *Naval Biography*; Ralfe, *Naval Biography*; *Dictionary of National Biography*, the naval biographies in which, by Professor Laughton, are full of research. The compiler takes this opportunity of acknowledging the value of the excellent *Index to James's Naval History*, published by the Navy Records Society, which will be found most useful.

There is a great similarity about all the minor actions between ships. One vessel sights another, gives chase, maintains a running action, closes, rakes, or attempts to rake, gets the enemy's fire under, and brings down his flag. The same characteristics which prevented the French Navy from achieving anything great in the American War are exemplified in the frigate actions of this war, where French ships are concerned. There is the same timidity, the same straining after some ulterior object, the same dislike to damaging the French ship in action, the same firing at the British masts and rigging. To this the loss of at least one action can be directly traced; (1) to this also are probably due in part the very slight losses of men inflicted on British ships in several hotly fought actions. British crews invariably fired at the hulls of their opponents, and strove to kill the men rather than to disable the ship. Chance, as in all battles, plays a considerable part. Israel Pellew shoots away the *Cleopatre*'s wheel, and greatly contributes to one of the most brilliant victories of the war. (2) The bursting of a gun leads not indirectly to the *Ambuscade*'s defeat by an inferior ship. (3)

(1)   *Forte* and *Sibylle*.
(2)   Also Ross, *Memoires and Correspondence of Admiral Lord de Saumarez*, Volume I page 101. The *Reunion*'s wheel was shot away in her action with the *Crescent*. The British gunners seem to have regularly aimed at the wheel, rudder, and steering-gear.
(3)   The court-martial attributed the loss of the *Ambuscade* "to a rapid succession of the most unfortunate accidents."

In this war French ships usually carried large but undisciplined crews and unskilled officers. In these circumstances they were wise to follow Jean Bon Saint Andre's famous advice (1) to "disdain evolutions" and "attempt to board." Thus they could best employ their masses of men. If the shooting of the French crews was wretched and how bad it was these actions show the spirit and fiery courage of the French sailors — seamen

THE ROYAL NAVY

we cannot call them — were above all reproach. They endured enormous losses in innumerable instances before they struck.

(1)   Chevalier, *Histoire de la Marine Francaise dans la Guerre de 1778*, Tome II page 49.

It is interesting to develop further the examination of the influence of weight of metal upon the result of actions. In the American War we have seen that there were very few instances indeed in which the weaker broadside won. That is not the case in the Revolutionary War. Taking important and decisive single ship actions, the results can be tabulated thus:

Navy	Superior Broadside Wins Against	Inferior Broadside Wins Against
British Ships	1	1
French Ships	21	7
Spanish Ships	4	2
Dutch Ships	2	

But in the French Navy the circumstances were quite abnormal, owing to indiscipline, want of seamanship, bad gunnery, and possibly from a hint contained in one of Napoleon's letters — bad powder. (1) The heavier broadside, even in these exceptional circumstances, usually wins the day; and nothing is more noticeable than the steady increase in the force of frigates, so as to ensure having the heavier broadside. The 28-gun ship practically disappears; the 32, the standard cruiser of the American War, gives way to the 36, 38, 40, or to the cut-down ship of the line. The evolution and development which our own day has seen in the size of ships, progress steadily, if slowly. We find, by the close of the war, such frigates as the *Forte* superior by fifty per cent, in weight of metal to the old 50-gun vessel of the line.

(1)   Bonaparte, *Correspondance de Napoleon Ier*, 5476.

In British frigates the carronade was given a very important place. It became larger in calibre, and to a great extent replaced the small guns — 6 and 9-pounders — which had been carried on the forecastle and quarter-deck. In the smaller classes it frequently constituted the entire armament except only for a pair of bow chasers. Owing to its lightness, ease of handling, and rapidity of fire, it was most efficient in action at short ranges, when pitted against long guns, as the instances of the

Glatton, Pelican, Wolverine, and *Milbrook* prove. In the last case, the British ship with non-recoil carronades fired eleven broadsides to her enemy's three. In fact, the carronade was a quick-firer of large calibre but very short range. The wonder is that enemies attacked by British ships so armed did not select a longer range, for the carronade was of little value outside four hundred yards. Probably the strong objection to this weapon, which we find expressed by many experienced and able officers, was that it limited our tactics and constrained close action. In French ships of and above the size of frigates, the 36-pounder carronade is regularly carried during this war: in small French craft, however, there are often no carronades. In Spanish vessels 24-pounder carronades are carried. (1)

(1)   Cochrane, *The Autobiography of a Seaman*, page 51. The *Gamo* had two 24-pounder carronades.

The two conspicuous instances where British ships were taken after a well-contested action, are those of the *Leander* and *Ambuscade*. The first was overpowered by a ship of more than twice her strength, on which she had inflicted enormous loss; the second was beaten under peculiar circumstances by a ship of inferior force. She had an indifferent Captain and a weak crew: she was surprised and she was boarded.

Examining the seven important instances in which a French vessel hauled down her flag to an inferior opponent, we find that in three cases there were other British ships at hand. Even where these do not fire a shot, the moral effect must be great. To fight without a chance of success, when the sacrifice of life is productive of no result, demands almost superhuman courage. The other four instances are those of the *Pique, Tamise, Vestale*, and *Forte*. The *Pique* was raked, and when we know that in the case of the *Reunion* a single raking shot killed or wounded twenty-one men out of a crew of 320, (1) we see what that might mean. She was entangled and held in an awkward position for some minutes under this raking fire. The defeat of the *Tamise* was probably due to the French trick of firing at the masts of the enemy; and, in any case, she was superior to the British ship which captured her by only ten per cent in weight of broadside. The advantage of the *Vestale* in weight of metal was still smaller, and she was attacked by an exceptionally smart captain, Bowen, the hero of Tenerife. She inflicted heavy loss upon the victor. Lastly, the *Forte* was, if French authorities can be believed, badly manned and most indifferently commanded. She

THE ROYAL NAVY 99

was superior by twenty per cent to the *Sibylle*, which captured her, but she fired high.

(1)   Ross, *Memoires and Correspondence of Admiral Lord de Saumarez*, Volume I page 111.

The Spanish instances need not be examined. As a fighting force the Spanish Navy was worthless, and it may be doubted whether the hearts of the Spanish officers were in the war. The same may be said of the Dutch in minor actions. The numerous engagements with privateers which are for the most part omitted in these pages are not very instructive. From want of discipline a privateer, unless of quite exceptional size, was not formidable to a man-of-war.

There are several remarkable instances wherein powerful French ships were captured after a brisk engagement, in which the British loss was trivial to a degree. The *Crescent, Unicorn, Revolutionnaire,* and *Indefatigable* each captured an enemy without having a man killed or even seriously wounded. The losses they inflicted were respectively 81, 51, 20, and 42. The first case illustrates the admirable skill in manoeuvring and seamanship of the best of our naval officers. (1) The *Crescent*'s opponent was virtually equal in force and was superior in size.

(1)   Ross, *Memoires and Correspondence of Admiral Lord de Saumarez*, Volume I page 112.

Other instances in which the British losses were insignificant and the French losses very heavy are those of the *Proserpine* (9 killed and wounded to 75 killed and wounded in the enemy), *Seahorse* (18 to 80), *Lively* (2 to 41), *Santa Margarita* (5 to 51), *Sibylle* (22 to 145), and *Phoebe* (13 to 344). In this last case the enemy was crowded with troops, and the result was a simple massacre. But to this result contributed the French practice of firing to dismast. A British officer on board the *Crescent* noted that "the enemy (the *Reunion*) fired so high that scarcely any shot struck the hull of the *Crescent*." (1) In the *Africaine*, which the *Phoebe* handled so severely, the French captain had actually removed the quoins of his guns, to compel his men to shoot high.

(1)   Ross, *Memoires and Correspondence of Admiral Lord de Saumarez*, Volume I page 102.

The skill of the British officers and men is clearly shown by the celerity with which they refitted their ships when damaged in masts and rigging. The famous examples of the *Vanguard* in 1798 and Saumarez's ships after their action with Linois belong to the major operations. In the minor actions the instance of the *Seine* is very striking. After some hours' firing she is so damaged by the French *Vengeance* in her masts that she drops behind. She refits and comes up again, and again is more or less disabled. A second time she refits; a third time she closes and then takes her enemy.

There are several actions in which British merchantmen repulsed the attack of powerful French frigates or privateers; one or two in which they captured French ships through mistake on the part of the latter. Such successes were, however, obtained by few but East Indiamen. They were formidable-looking ships, having at a distance the appearance of frigates or small vessels of the line; and they were usually well commanded, had disciplined crews, and invariably carried a light armament of such guns as 9-pounder carronades and 12-pounder long guns. An East Indiaman, the *Pigot*, repulsed two French privateers, together mounting sixty guns; and five East Indiamen captured these privateers some days later. Five East Indiamen were mistaken by Sercey's squadron for ships of the line and left unmolested. The French *Medee* surrendered to two East Indiamen which she mistook for vessels of the line. In general, the merchant ship was too badly manned, too much encumbered, too feebly armed, and too weakly built to have any chance against the privateer, much less against the warship.

Very many of the minor actions took place in the Bay, the Bay of Biscay, which was very thoroughly scoured by British cruisers. Taking the year 1796 we find that five 44s, ten 38s, five 36s, five 32s, and eight sloops or brigs were cruising in the Channel and in the Bay. (1) Besides these, eleven small vessels were employed on convoy duty. In the North Sea, off Brest with the Channel Fleet, and on the British coast, were yet more frigates and small craft, whilst the List Book gives the strength of 44s, frigates, and small craft on foreign station in January 1797, thus: 44s, seven; frigates, sixty-four; sloops, et cetera, forty-four. Of these, most were engaged in convoy duty, commerce protection, and watching the enemy's ports. The total so employed was even larger in 1798-1801 than in 1796, seeing that the Navy steadily expanded.

(1)   Schomberg, *Naval Chronology*, Volume II page 4, 532, 533.

SMALLER VESSELS ON FOREIGN STATION, JANUARY 1797

Class	East Indies	Jamaica	Leeward Islands	Mediterranean	Nova Scotia
44s	3	2	1		1
Frigates	14	10	14	19	7
Small	5	10	14	10	5

APPENDIX TO CHAPTERS XXXV AND XXXVI

A. LIST OF H.M. SHIPS TAKEN, DESTROYED, BURNT, FOUNDERED OB WRECKED DURING THE WAR OF THE FRENCH REVOLUTION, 1793-1801, AND OF LOSSES TO THE END OF 1802.

Year 1793			
Date	**Name of Ship**	**Guns**	**Commander Remarks**
May 27	*Hyaena*	24	Captain William Hargood
			Taken by *Concorde* 40 in West Indies
Jun 1	*Advice,* cutter	4	Lieutenant Edward Tyrrel
			Wrecked on Key Bokell, Honduras
Oct 4	*Thames*	32	Captain James Cotes
			Taken by three French frigates going to Gibraltar. Retaken June 7, 1796
Nov 20	*Scipion*	74	
			Accidentally burnt off Leghorn
Dec 16	*Pigmy,* cutter	14	Abraham Pulliblank (1)
			Wrecked on the Motherbank
Dec 18	*Vigilante,* cutter	4	
			Taken by the French at Toulon
Dec 18	*Alerte* (not in commission)	14	
			Taken by the French at Toulon
Dec 18	*Conflagration,* fireship	14	Commander John Loring
			Burnt on evacuation of Toulon
Dec 18	*Vulcan,* fireship	14	Commander Charles Hare
			Expended at Toulon
Dec 18	*Union,* gunboat		
			Blown up at Toulon

THE ROYAL NAVY

Dec		*Vipere*, cutter	4	
				Wrecked in Hyeres Bay

Year 1794

Date		Name of Ship	Guns	Commander Remarks
Jan	7	*Moselle*	24	Commander Richard Henry Alexander Bennett
				Taken on entering Toulon by mistake
Jan	30	*Amphitrite*	18	Captain Anthony Hunt
				Wrecked in the Mediterranean
Feb		*Spitfire*, cutter	6	Commander T.W. Rich (1)
				Capsized off San Domingo with all hands
Mar	8	*Convert*, ex *Inconstant*	32	Captain John Lawford
				Wrecked on Grand Cayman
Apr	11	*Proselyte*, floating battery	24	Commander Walter Serocold
				Sunk by batteries at Bastia
Apr		*Ardent*	64	Captain Robert Manners Sutton
				Accidentally blown up off Corsica with all hands
May	8	*Placentia*		Lieutenant Alexander Shippard
				Lost at Newfoundland
May	10	*Castor*	32	Captain Thomas Troubridge
				Taken by Admiral Nielly's squadron off Cape Clear
May		*Alert*	16	Commander Charles Smith
				Taken by *Unite* 40 off Ireland
Jun	28	*Rose*	28	Captain Matthew Henry Scott
				Wrecked on Rocky Point, Jamaica
Jun		*Speedy*	14	Commander George Eyre
				Taken by French frigates off Nice

Jun		*Ranger,* cutter	14	Lieutenant Isaac Cotgrave
				Taken by a French squadron off Brest
Jul	14	*Hound*	16	Commander Richard Piercy
				Taken by *Seine* and *Galatee* coming from West Indies
Aug	24	*Impetueux* (not in commission)	74	
				Accidentally burnt at Portsmouth
Aug		*Scout*	16	Commander Charles Robinson
				Taken by two French frigates off Cape Bona
Nov	6	*Alexander*	74	Rear-Admiral Richard Rodney Bligh
				Taken by a French squadron off Sicily
Nov	26	*Pylades*	16	Commander Thomas Twysden
				Wrecked on Isle of Nest, Shetlands
Nov	26	*Actif,* brig	10	Commander John Harvey (2nd)
				Foundered off Bermuda
Nov		*Espion*	16	Commander William Hugh Kittoe
				Taken by three French frigates
Dec	22	*Daphne*	20	Captain William Edward Cracraft
				Taken by two French men-of-war. Retaken December 28, 1797

Year 1795

Date		Name of Ship	Guns	Commander / Remarks
Mar	7	*Berwick*	74	Captain Adam Littlejohn
				Taken by the French fleet in the Mediterranean

THE ROYAL NAVY

Date		Name of Ship	Guns	Commander / Remarks
Mar	14	*Illustrious*	74	Thomas Lenox Frederick
				Wrecked near Avenza
May	1	*Royne*	98	Captain George Grey
				Accidentally burnt at Spithead
May		*Mosquito,* floating battery	5	Lieutenant William McCarthy (1)
				Lost on coast of France with all hands
Jun		*Flying Fish,* schooner	6	Lieutenant George Seaton
				Taken in West Indies by two French privateers
Aug	2	*Diomede*	44	Captain Matthew Smith
				Wrecked near Trincomale
Oct	7	*Censeur*	74	Captain John Gore
				Taken by a French squadron off Cape Saint Vincent
Nov	12	*Fleche*	14	Lieutenant Charles Came
				Wrecked in San Fiorenzo Bay
Dec	9	*Nemesis*	28	Captain Samuel Hood Linzee
				Taken by two French men-of-war at Smyrna. Retaken March 9, 1796
Dec	11	*Shark,* Dutch hoy	4	Lieutenant Watson
				Carried by her crew into La Hougue
Dec	29	*Amethyst*	38	Captain Thomas Affleck
				Lost at Alderney

Year 1796

Date		Name of Ship	Guns	Commander / Remarks
		Scourge	16	Commander William Stap
				Foundered off the Dutch coast
Feb	11	*Leda*	36	Captain John Woodley (1)
				Capsized in a squall

Feb	12	*Saint Pierre*		
				Wrecked off Point Negro
Apr	4	*Spider,* hired lugger		Lieutenant James Oswald
				Collided with *Ramillies*
Apr	11	*Ca Ira*	80	Captain Charles Dudley Pater
				Accidentally burnt in San Fiorenzo Bay
May	13	*Salisbury*	50	Captain William Mitchell
				Wrecked near San Domingo
Jun	10	*Arab*	16	Commander Stephen Seymour (1)
				Wrecked near Point Penmarck
Jul	15	*Trompeuse*	16	Commander Joshua Rowley Watson
				Wrecked near Kingsale
Jul		*Active*	32	Captain Edward Leveson Gower
				Wrecked in the Saint Lawrence
Jul		*Sirene*	16	Commander Daniel Guerin (1)
				Wrecked in the Bay of Honduras
Aug	27	*Undaunted,* ex *Arethuse*	38	Captain Robert Winthrop
				Wrecked on Morant Keys
Aug		*Bermuda*	14	Commander Thomas Maxtone (1)
				Foundered in Gulf of Florida
Sep	22	*Amphion*	32	Captain Israel Pellew
				Accidentally burnt in Hamoaze
Oct	2	*Experiment,* brig	10	Lieutenant George Hayes
				Taken by the Spaniards in the Mediterranean
Oct	3	*Narcissus*	20	Captain Percy Fraser
				Wrecked off New Providence

THE ROYAL NAVY

Oct	10	*Malabar*	54	Captain Thomas Parr
				Foundered coming from West Indies
Oct	20	*Poulette*	26	Captain [?] Edwards
				Burnt at Ajaccio as unserviceable
Oct	20	*Bellette*	24	Commander John Temple
				Burnt at Ajaccio as unserviceable
Nov	3	*Helena*	14	Commander Jermyn John Symonds (1)
				Foundered on Dutch coast with all hands
Nov		*Berbice*, brig	8	Lieutenant John Tresahar
				Wrecked at Dominica
Nov		*Vanneau*, brig	8	Lieutenant John Gourly
				Wrecked at Porto Ferrajo
Dec	7	*Reunion*	36	Captain Henry William Bayntun
				Wrecked in the Swin
Dec	14	*Vestale*	36	
				Retaken after capture on December 13
Dec	19	*Courageux*	74	Captain Benjamin Hallowell
				Wrecked below Ape's Hill
Dec	21	*Bombay Castle*	74	Captain Thomas Sotheby
				Wrecked in the Tagus
Dec	24	*Cormorant*	18	Lieutenant Thomas Gott (1)
				Accidentally blown up at Port au Prince
Dec	27	*Hussar*	28	Captain James Colnett
				Wrecked near Isle Bas
Dec	31	*Curlew*	18	Commander Francis Ventris Field (1)
				Foundered in the North Sea

Year 1797			
Date	**Name of Ship**	**Guns**	**Commander** **Remarks**
Jan 2	*Vipere*		Captain Henry Harding Parker (1)
			Foundered off the Shannon
Jan	*Hermes*		Captain William Mulso (1)
			Foundered at sea
Jan 14	*Amazon*	36	Captain Robert Carthew Reynolds
			Wrecked near Isle Bas
Feb 24	*Bloom*, tender	14	Lieutenant Andrew Congalton
			Taken by the French off Holyhead
Feb 24	*Brighton*, tender	14	
			Taken by the French off Holyhead
Apr 27	*Albion*, floating battery	60	Captain Henry Savage
			Wrecked in the Swin
Apr	*Tartar*	28	Captain Honourable Charles Elphinstone
			Wrecked off San Domingo
May 17	*Providence*, discovery ship	16	Captain William Robert Broughton
			Wrecked in the Pacific
May	*Lacedemonian*	12	Commander Matthew Wrench
			Taken by the French in the West Indies
May	*Port Royal*, schooner	10	Lieutenant Elias Man
			Taken in the West Indies
Jun 15	*Fortune*	16	Commander Valentine Collard
			Wrecked near Oporto
Jul 24	*Fox*, cutter		Lieutenant John Gibson (1)
			Destroyed before Santa Cruz

THE ROYAL NAVY

Jul	31	*Artois*	38	Captain Sir Edmund Nagle
				Wrecked on the French coast
Jul	31	*Mignonne*	32	Captain Honourable Philip Wodehouse
				Burnt as unserviceable at Porto Ferrajo
Sep	22	*Hermione*	32	Captain Hugh Pigot (2nd) (1)
				Carried by mutinous crew into La Guaira
Nov	16	*Tribune*	32	Captain Scory Barker (1)
				Wrecked off Halifax
Nov	16	*Hope,* hired lugger	10	
				Run down in the Channel
Dec	27	*Hunter*	18	Commander Tudor Tucker
				Wrecked on Bog Island, Virginia
Dec		*Growler*	12	Lieutenant John Hollingsworth (1)
				Taken off Dungeness by two French rowboats
Dec		*Swift*	18	Commander Thomas Hayward (1)
				Foundered in the China Seas
Dec		*Pandour*	14	Lieutenant Samuel Mason (1)
				Foundered in the North Sea
Dec		*Resolution*	14	Lieutenant William Huggett (1)
				Foundered at sea
Dec		*Marie Antoinette,* schooner	10	Captain John M'Inerheny (1)
				Carried by mutinous crew into a French West Indies port

Year 1798

Date		Name of Ship	Guns	Commander / Remarks
Jan	3	*George*	4	Captain Michael Mackey (1)
				Taken by two Spanish privateers
Feb	3	*Raven*	18	Commander John William Taylor Dixon
				Wrecked at the mouth of the Elbe
Apr	4	*Pallas*	32	Captain Honourable Henry Curzon
				Wrecked on Mount Batten Point
Apr	12	*Lively*	32	Captain James Nicoll Morris
				Wrecked near Rota Point, Cadiz
May	23	*De Braak*	16	Commander James Drew (1)
				Capsized in the Delaware
Jun	23	*Rover*	16	Commander George Irwin
				Wrecked in the Gulf of Saint Lawrence
Jun	29	*Pique*	36	Captain David Milne
				Wrecked on the French coast
Jul	18	*Aigle*	38	Captain Charles Tyler
				Wrecked off Cape Farina
Jul	24	*Resistance*	44	Captain Edward Pakenham (1)
				Accidentally blown up in the Strait of Banca
Jul	26	*Garland*	28	Captain James Athol Wood
				Wrecked off Madagascar
Jul		*Princess Royal,* cutter	8	
				Taken by a French privateer
Aug	15	*Etrusco,* armed transport	24	Commander George Reynolds
				Foundered coming from the West Indies
Aug	18	*Leander*	50	Captain Thomas Boulden

THE ROYAL NAVY

				Thompson
				Taken by the *Genereux* 74. Retaken March 3, 1799
Aug	26	*Crash*	12	Lieutenant Bulkley Mackworth Praed
				Taken on the coast of Holland. Retaken August 11, 1799
Oct	13	*Jason*	38	Captain Charles Stirling
				Wrecked near Brest
Nov	12	*Petrel*	16	Commander Charles Long
				Taken by three Spanish frigates. Retaken November 13, 1798
Nov	26	*Medusa*, armed transport	50	Commander Alexander Becher
				Wrecked on the coast of Portugal
Nov		*Margaret,* tender		Lieutenant John Pollexfen (1)
				Lost off the Irish coast
Dec	3	*Kingfisher*	18	Lieutenant Frederick Lewis Maitland (2nd)
				Wrecked on Lisbon Bar
Dec	10	*Colossus*	74	Captain George Murray (3rd)
				Wrecked off Sicily
Dec	14	*Ambuscade*	32	Captain Henry Jenkins
				Taken by *Bayonnaise* 28
Dec		*Hamadryad*	36	Captain Thomas Elphinstone
				Wrecked off the Portuguese coast
Dec		*Neptune*, lugger	6	[?] Gormer
				Run down off Beachy Head
Dec		*Caroline,* tender		Lieutenant Whittle (1)
				Lost in the East Indies

Year 1799

Date		Name of Ship	Guns	Commander / Remarks
Jan	7	*Apollo*	38	Captain Peter Halkett
				Wrecked on coast of Holland; crew saved
Jan	12	*Weazel*	14	Commander Honourable Henry Grey (1)
				Wrecked in Barnstaple Bay; nearly all lost
Feb	1	*Proserpine*	28	Captain James Wallis
				Wrecked in the Elbe; nearly all saved
Feb	2	*Nautilus*	16	Commander Henry Gunter
				Wrecked off Flamborough Head; crew saved
Feb		*Charlotte,* schooner	8	Lieutenant John Thicknesse
				Taken by the French off Cape Francois. Retaken November 22
Feb		*Mosquito,* schooner	6	Lieutenant Thomas White
				Taken by Spanish frigates off Cuba
Feb		*Grampus,* store ship	26	Captain George Hart
				Wrecked on Barking Shelf; crew saved
Mar	18	*Torride*	2	
				Taken by the French in Egypt. Retaken same day
Apr	22	*Brave,* hired lugger	12	Lieutenant Gardiner Henry Guion
				Run down in the Channel; crew saved
May	8	*Fortune*	10	Lieutenant Lewis Davis
				Taken by French frigates; coast of Syria

THE ROYAL NAVY

May	8	*Dame de Grace,* gunboat		
				Taken by French frigates; coast of Syria
May	23	*Deux Amis*	14	Lieutenant Henry Smith Wilson
				Wrecked on the Isle of Wight; crew saved
Jun	6	*William Pitt,* lugger	14	Lieutenant Haswell
				Taken by Spanish gunboats, Mediterranean
Jul	7	*Penelope,* hired cutter	18	Lieutenant Daniel Hamline
				Taken by *N.S. del Carmen,* Mediterranean
Aug	28	*Contest*	14	Lieutenant John Ides Short
				Wrecked on the coast of Holland; crew saved
Sep	28	*Blanche,* store ship	18	Commander John Ayscough
				Wrecked in the Texel; crew saved
Sep	28	*Fox*	14	Lieutenant William Wooldridge (?)
				Wrecked in the Gulf of Mexico; crew saved
Oct	9	*Lutine*	36	Captain Lancelot Skynner (1)
				Wrecked off Vlieland; nearly all lost
Oct	12	*Trincomale*	16	Commander John Rowe (1)
				Blown up in action; crew lost
Oct	14	*Nassau,* store ship	36	Captain George Tripp
				Wrecked on coast of Holland; nearly all saved
Oct	19	*Impregnable*	98	Captain Jonathan Faulknor (2nd)
				Wrecked near Langstone; crew saved

Oct	25	*Amaranthe*	14	Commander John Blake
				Wrecked on coast of Florida; 22 lost
Nov	5	*Orestes*	18	Commander William Haggitt (1)
				Foundered in the East Indies; crew lost
Nov	16	*Espion,* ex *Atalante,* store ship	16	Commander Jonas Rose
				Wrecked on the Goodwin; crew saved
Dec	5	*Sceptre*	64	Captain Valentine Edwards (1)
				Wrecked in Table Bay; 291 lost
Dec	25	*Ethalion*	38	Captain John Clarke Searle
				Wrecked off Penmarck; crew saved

Year 1800

Date		Name of Ship	Guns	Commander Remarks
Jan	5	*Mastiff*	12	Lieutenant James Watson
				Wrecked near Yarmouth; nearly all saved
Jan	21	*Weymouth,* armed transport	26	Commander Ambrose Crofton
				Wrecked on Lisbon Bar; crew saved
Jan	26	*Brazen*	18	Commander James Hanson (1)
				Wrecked near Brighton; all but one lost
Mar	10	*Repulse*	64	Captain James Alms (2nd)
				Wrecked off Ushant; nearly all saved
Mar	17	*Queen Charlotte*	100	Vice-Admiral Lord Keith, Captain Andrew Todd (1)
				Accidentally burnt off Leghorn; nearly all lost
Mar	17	*Danae,* ex	20	Captain Lord Proby

THE ROYAL NAVY

		Vaillante		
				Carried by mutinous crew into Brest
May	17	*Trompeuse*	18	Commander J. Parker Robinson (1)
				Supposed foundered in Channel; crew lost
May	17	*Railleur*	14	Commander John Raynor (1)
				Supposed foundered in Channel; crew lost
May	17	*Lady Jane,* hired cutter	8	Lieutenant W. Bryer (1)
				Supposed foundered in Channel; crew lost
May	20	*Cormorant*	20	Captain Honourable Courtenay Boyle
				Wrecked on-coast of Egypt; crew saved
Jul	7	*Comet,* fireship		Commander Thomas Leef
				Expended in Dunquerque Road
Jul	7	*Falcon,* fireship		Commander Samuel Butt
				Expended in Dunquerque Road
Jul	7	*Rosario,* fireship		Commander James Carthew
				Expended in Dunquerque Road
Jul	7	*Wasp,* fireship		Commander John Edwards (2nd)
				Expended in Dunquerque Road
Aug	10	*Dromedary,* store ship	24	Commander Bridges Watkinson Taylor
				Wrecked near Trinidad; crew saved
Sep	6	*Stag*	32	Captain Robert Winthrop
				Wrecked in Vigo Bay; crew saved

Sep	26	*Hound*	18	Commander William James Turquand (1)
				Wrecked near Shetland; crew lost
Sep		*Diligence*	18	Commander Charles Bayne Hodgson Ross
				Wrecked near Havana; crew saved
Oct	9	*Chance,* ex *Galgo*	18	Commander George Samuel Stovin (1)
				Foundered in West Indies; nearly all lost
Oct	13	*Rose,* hired cutter	10	Lieutenant Smith
				Taken by the Dutch in the Ems
Oct		*Martin*	16	Commander Honourable Matthew Saint Clair (1)
				Supposed foundered in North Sea; crew lost
Nov	4	*Marlborough*	74	Captain Thomas Sotheby
				Wrecked near Belle Isle; crew saved
Nov	9	*Havik*	16	Commander Philip Bartholomew
				Wrecked off Jersey; crew saved
Nov	23	*Albanaise*	14	Lieutenant Francis Newcombe
				Carried by mutinous crew into Malaga
Nov		*Active,* cutter	12	Lieutenant J. Hamilton
				Taken by the French and Dutch in the Ems. Retaken May 16, 1801
Dec	2	*Sir Thomas Pasley,* brig	16	Lieutenant C.J. Nevin
				Taken by two Spanish gunboats, Mediterranean

THE ROYAL NAVY

Dec		Urchin, gun vessel		Lieutenant Thomas Pearson Croasdaile
				Foundered in Tetuan Bay

Year 1801

Date		Name of Ship	Guns	Commander Remarks
Jan	1	Requin	10	Lieutenant Samuel Powell
				Wrecked near Quiberon; crew saved
Jan	9	Constitution, hired cutter	12	Lieutenant William Humphrey Faulknor
				Taken by two French cutters. Retaken same night
Jan	29	Incendiary, fireship	14	Commander William Dalling Dunn
				Taken by the squadron of M. Ganteaume
Feb	2	Legere	18	Commander Cornelius Quinton
				Wrecked near Cartagena, South America; crew saved
Feb	10	Sprightly, cutter	12	Lieutenant Robert Jump
				Taken by the squadron of M. Ganteaume
Feb	13	Success	32	Captain Shuldham Peard
				Taken by the squadron of M. Ganteaume
Feb	14	Telegraph, hired brig	16	Lieutenant Caesar Corsellis (1)
				Supposed foundered off Cape Ortegal
Feb	27	Bulldog, bomb	18	Commander Barrington Dacres
				Taken by the French at Ancona. Retaken September 16, 1801
Feb		Charming Molly, cutter		D. Sheriff, Master
				Foundered coming from Saint Marcon
Feb		Lurcher, hired	12	Lieutenant R. Forbes

		cutter		
				Taken by a French privateer
Mar	16	*Invincible*	74	Rear-Admiral Thomas Totty, Captain John Rennie (1)
				Wrecked on Hasborough Sand; nearly all lost
Mar	23	*Blazer*	12	Lieutenant John Tiller
				Taken by the Swedes at Warberg; restored
Mar	24	*Fulminante*	10	Lieutenant Robert Corbett
				Wrecked on coast of Egypt
Mar	25	*Scout*	18	Commander Henry Duncan (2nd)
				Lost on the Shingles, Isle of Wight; crew saved
Mar		*Nancy,* hired cutter	6	Lieutenant J. Yames
				Taken by a French privateer
Jun	9	*Meleager*	32	Captain Honourable Thomas Bladen Capell
				Wrecked on the Triangles, Gulf of Mexico; crew saved
Jun	24	*Swiftsure*	74	Captain Benjamin Hallowell
				Taken by the squadron of M. Ganteaume
Jun		*Forte*	44	Captain Lucius Ferdinand Hardyman
				Wrecked at Jeddah; crew saved
Jun		*Speedy*	14	Commander Lord Cochrane
				Taken by the squadron of M. Linois
Jul	5	*Hannibal*	74	Captain Solomon Ferris
				Taken by the squadron of M. Linois
Jul	7	*Augustus,* gun vessel	1	Lieutenant James Scott
				Wrecked in Plymouth Sound; crew saved
Jul	21	*Jason*	36	Captain Honourable John

THE ROYAL NAVY

Date		Name of Ship	Guns	Commander / Remarks
				Murray
				Wrecked near Saint Malo; crew saved
Jul		*Iphigenia*	32	Commander Hassard Stackpoole
				Accidentally burnt at Alexandria; crew saved
Aug	11	*Lowestoft*	32	Captain Robert Plampin
				Wrecked off Inagua, West Indies; crew saved
Sep	4	*Proselyte*	32	Captain George Fowke
				Wrecked off Saint Martin, West Indies; crew saved
Oct	25	*Bonetta*	18	Captain Thomas New
				Wrecked on the Jardines, Cuba; crew saved
Nov		*Utile*	16	Commander Edward Jekyll Canes (1)
				Capsized in the Mediterranean; crew lost
Nov		*Cockchafer,* hired lugger	8	V. Philpot
				Foundered off Guernsey; crew saved
Nov		*Friendship,* gun vessel	2	
				Foundered off Guernsey; crew saved
Nov		*Babet*	20	Captain Jemmett Mainwaring (1)
				Supposed foundered in the West Indies; crew lost
Year 1802				
Date		**Name of Ship**	**Guns**	**Commander** **Remarks**
Mar	2	*Sensible*		Commander Robert Sause
				Wrecked off Ceylon; crew saved

Mar	29	*Assistance*	50	Captain Richard Lee
				Wrecked near Dunquerque; crew saved
Mar		*Scout*	18	Captain Henry Duncan (2nd) (1)
				Foundered off Newfoundland; crew lost
Mar		*Fly*	14	Commander Thomas Duvall (1)
				Foundered off Newfoundland; crew lost

(1)   Commander lost life on the occasion.

THE ROYAL NAVY

FRENCH LOSSES, 1793-1801

LIST OF ENEMY'S MEN-OF-WAR TAKEN, DESTROYED, OR BURNT, AND, SO FAR AS CAN BE ASCERTAINED, WRECKED OR FOUNDERED DURING THE WAR OF THE FRENCH REVOLUTION, 1793-1801

B. FRENCH.
French National Ships

Year 1793

Date		Name of Ship	Guns	Fate
Feb	15	*Leopard*	74	Foundered in Cagliari Bay
Feb		*Vengeur* (supposed)	74	Wrecked near Ajaccio
Apr	16	*Goeland*	14	Taken by *Penelope*, Captain B.S. Rowley, West Indies
May	21	(unknown)	36	Destroyed by the Spaniards at Saint Pietro
May	28	*Prompte* (1)	20	Taken by *Phaeton*, Captain Sir A.S. Douglas, Bay of Biscay
Jun	3	*Curieux,* brig	14	Taken by *Inconstant*, Captain A. Montgomery, West Indies
Jun	6	*Vanneau*	6	Taken by *Colossus*, Captain C.M. Pole, Bay of Biscay
Jun	9	*Eclair* (1)	22	Taken by *Leda*, Captain G. Campbell, Mediterranean
Jun	18	*Cleopatre* (1) (as *Oiseau*)	36	Taken by *Nymphe*, Captain E. Pellew, off Start (2)
Jul	25	*Lutine*	12	Taken by *Pluto*, Commander J.N. Morris, Newfoundland

Aug	29	*Commerce de Marseille* (1)	120	Taken at Toulon by Lord Hood
		Pompee (1)	74	
		Puissant (1)	74	
		Scipion (1)	74	
		Arethuse (1) (as *Undaunted*)	40	
		Topaze (1)	36	
		Perle (1) (as *Amethyst*)	40	
		Aurore (1)	36	
		Lutine (1) (as 32)	36	
		Poulette (1)	26	
		Belette (1)	28	
		Proselyte (1)	36	
		Moselle (1)	20	
		Mulet	18	
		Sincere	18	
		Tarleton	14	
		Alceste	36	Taken at Toulon by Lord Hood, given to Sardinians
		Embroye (?)	20	Taken at Toulon by Lord Hood, given to Neapolitans
		Petite Aurore	18	Taken at Toulon by Lord Hood, given to Spaniards
Sep		*Convention Nationale*	10	Taken by Commodore John Ford, San Domingo
Oct	11	*Imperieuse* (1)	38	Taken by Vice-Admiral John Gell off Genoa
Oct	17	*Modeste* (1)	36	Taken by *Bedford*, Captain R. Man (3rd), et cetera, off Genoa
Oct	20	*Reunion* (1)	36	Taken by *Crescent*, Captain J. Saumarez, off Cherbourg (2)
Nov	25	*Inconstante* (1) (as *Convert*)	36	Taken by *Penelope* and *Iphigenia* off San Domingo

THE ROYAL NAVY

Nov	27	*Blonde*	28	Taken by *Latona* and *Phaeton* off Ushant
Nov	30	*Espiegle* (1)	36	Taken by *Nymphe* and *Circe* off Ushant
Dec	18	*Triomphant*	80	Destroyed at the evacuation of Toulon
		Destin	74	
		Centaure	74	
		Duguay Trouin	74	
		Heros	74	
		Liberte, ex *Dictateur*	74	
		Suffisant	74	
		Themistocle	74	
		Tricolor, ex *Lys*	74	
		Victorieuse	36	
		Montreal	32	
		Iris	32	
		Auguste	24	
		Caroline	24	
Dec	30	*Sans Culotte*	22	Taken by *Blanche*, Captain C. Parker (2nd), West Indies
		Revolutionnaire	20	
		Vengeur	12	

Year 1794

Date		Name of Ship	Guns	Fate
Jan	12	*Trompeuse* (1)	18	Taken by *Sphinx*, Captain R. Lucas, off Cape Clear
Jan	23	*Vipere* (1)	16	Taken by *Flora*, Captain Sir J.B. Warren, Channel
Feb	19	*Minerve* (1) (as *San Fiorenzo*)	38	Taken at San Fiorenzo
Feb	19	*Fortunee*	36	Destroyed at San Fiorenzo
Mar	16	*Actif* (1)	16	Taken by *Iphigenia*, Captain P. Sinclair, West Indies
		Espiegle (1)	12	
Mar	17	*Bienvenue* (1) (as *Undaunted*)	28	Taken by Vice-Admiral Sir J. Jervis, at Martinique (2)
		Avenger	16	
Mar	28	*Liberte*	14	Taken by *Alligator*, Captain T. Surridge,

				Jamaica
Apr	23	*Pomone* (1)	44	Taken by Commodore
		Babet (1)	20	Sir J.B. Warren, off Isle Bas
Apr	23	*Engageante* (1)	36	Taken by *Concorde*, Captain Sir R.J. Strachan. Channel
Apr	23	*Guadeloupe*	16	Taken by Vice-Admiral Sir J. Jervis, Guadeloupe
May	5	*Duguay Trouin*	28	Taken by *Orpheus*, Captain H. Newcome, East Indies
May	5	*Atalante* (1) (as *Espion*)	36	Taken by *Swiftsure*, Captain C. Boyles, near Cork
May	5	*Inconnue*	16	Taken and burnt by Lord Howe
May	21	*Fleche* (1)	14	Taken at Bastia by Lord Hood
May	23	*Moselle* (1)	18	Taken by *Aimable*, Captain Sir H. Burrard, off Hyeres
May	23	*Courier,* cutter	10	Taken and scuttled by Lord Howe, Channel
May	25	*Republicaine*	20	Taken and burnt by Lord Howe, Channel
May	29	*Castor* (1)	32	Retaken by *Carysfort*, Captain F. Laforey, off Land's End (2)
Jun	1	*Juste* (1)	80	Taken by Lord Howe, off Ushant (2) (3)
		Sans Pareil (1)	80	
		Amerique (1) (as *Impetueux*)	74	
		Achille	74	
		Northumberland	74	
		Impetueux	74	
		Vengeur	74	Sunk by Lord Howe, off Ushant (2) (3)
Jun	17	*Sibylle* (1)	40	Taken by *Romney*, Captain Hon. W. Paget, at Miconi (2)

THE ROYAL NAVY

Jun	18	*Narcisse*, cutter	14	Taken by *Aurora*, Captain W. Essington, off Shetland
Aug	10	*Melpomene* (1)	40	Taken by Lord Hood at Calvi
		Mignonne (1)	28	
		Auguste, brig	4	
		Providence, brig	4	
		Ca Ira, gunboat	3	
Aug	23	*Volontaire*	36	Driven ashore and destroyed near Penmarck
Aug	23	*Alerte*	12	Driven ashore and destroyed off Pointe du Raz
Aug		*Sirene* (1)	16	Taken by *Intrepid* and *Chichester* near San Domingo
Aug		*Reprisal*	16	Taken by Vice-Admiral Sir John Jervis, West Indies
Sep	7	*Quartidi*	14	Taken by Commodore Sir E. Pellew off Sicily
Oct	21	*Revolutionnaire* (1)	44	Taken by Commodore Sir E. Pellew off Brest
Oct	30	*Jacobin* (1) (as *Matilda*)	24	Taken by *Ganges* and *Montagu*, West Indies
Oct		*Revenge* (1) (as *Hobart*)	18	Taken by *Resistance*, Captain E. Pakenham, South Sunda
Nov	30	*Carmagnole*, schooner	10	Taken by *Zebra*, West Indies
Dec	2	a sloop		Taken by *Beaulieu*, Captain E. Riou, West Indies
Dec	27	*Republicain*	110	Wrecked near Brest
Dec	30	a schooner		Taken by *Blanche*, Captain R. Faulknor (3rd), West Indies

William Laird Clowes

Year 1795			
Date	**Name of Ship**	**Guns**	**Fate**
Jan 5	*Duquesne*	36	Taken by *Bellona*, Captain G. Wilson, West Indies
Jan 6	*Pique* (1)	36	Taken by *Blanche*, Captain R. Faulknor (3rd), West Indies (2)
Jan 8	*Esperance*	22	Taken by *Argonaut*, Captain A.J. Ball, America
Jan	*Neptune*	74	Wrecked in Audierne Bay
Jan	*Scipion*	80	Foundered in a gale
	Neuf Thermidor	80	
	Superbe	74	
Jan	*Duras*	20	Taken by *Bellona* and *Alarm*, West Indies
Feb 10	*Iphigenie*	36	Taken by the Spaniards, Mediterranean
Feb 20	*Requin* (1)	12	Taken by *Thalia*, Captain R. Grindall, Channel
Feb 26	*Curieuse*, schooner	12	Taken by *Pomone*, Captain Sir J.B. Warren, off Groix
Mar 2	*Espion* (1) (as *Spy*)	18	Taken by *Lively*, Captain G. Burlton, off Brest
Mar 13	*Tourterelle* (1)	28	Taken by *Lively*, Captain G. Burlton, off Ushant (2)
Mar 14	*Ca Ira* (1)	80	Taken by Vice-Admiral W. Hotham off Genoa (2)
	Censeur (1)	74	
Mar	*Temeraire*, cutter	20	Taken by *Dido*, Captain G.H. Towry, Mediterranean
Mar 27	*Republicaine*	22	Taken by Rear-Admiral J. Colpoys, Channel
Mar	*Speedy* (1)	14	Taken by *Inconstant*, Captain T.F. Fremantle, Mediterranean
Mar 29	*Jean Bart* (1) (as	18	Taken by *Astraea*,

THE ROYAL NAVY

		Arab)		Captain Lord H. Paulet, Channel (2)
Apr	10	*Gloire* (1)	36	Taken by *Cerberus* and *Santa Margarita*, Channel
Apr	11	*Gentille* (1)	36	Taken by *Hannibal*, Captain J. Markham, Channel
Apr	15	*Jean Bart* (1) (as *Laurel*)	26	Taken by Commodore Sir J.B. Warren off Rochefort
Apr	16	*Expedition*	16	Taken by Commodore Sir J.B. Warren off Belle Isle
Apr	23	*Galatee*	36	Wrecked near Penmarck
May	9	*Eclair,* gun vessel (1)	3	Taken by Captain Sir R.J. Strachan, coast of France
		Crache Feu, gun vessel (1)	3	
May	17	*Prevoyante, en flute* (1)	24	Taken by *Thetis* and *Hussar*, Chesapeake (2)
		Raison, en flute (1)	18	
May	28	*Courier National*	18	Taken by *Thorn*, Commander R.W. Otway, West Indies
May	29	*Prompte* (1)	28	Captured
May	30	*Liberte*	20	Sunk by *Alarm*, Captain David Milne, off Puerto Rico
Jun	23	*Tigre* (1)	74	Taken by Lord Bridport off Lorient (2)
		Alexandre (1)	74	
		Formidable (1) (as *Belleisle*)	74	
Jun	24	*Minerve* (1)	40	Taken by *Lowestoft* and *Dido*, Mediterranean (2)
Jun		*Perdrix* (1)	24	Taken by *Vanguard*, Captain Simon Miller, off Antigua
Jul	3	*Vesuve,* gun vessel (1)	4	Taken by *Melampus* and *Hebe* off Saint Malo
Jul	13	*Alcide*	74	Struck to Admiral Hotham, but accidentally

			blew up, Mediterranean
Jul		*Echoue*	28	Run ashore and destroyed on Rhe by *Phaeton*, Captain Hon. R. Stopford
Aug	16	*Resolue*	10	Taken by Commodore H. Nelson, Alassio Bay
		Republique, gunboat	6	
		Constitution, galley	5	
		Vigilante, galley	5	
Aug	31	*Suffisante* (1)	14	Taken by A. Duncan off the Texel
		Victorieuse (1)	14	
Sep	2	*Assemblee Nationale*	22	Driven ashore by *Diamond*, Captain Sir W.S Smith, off Treguier
Sep	2	*Rude,* gun vessel	12	Burnt by *Pomone*, Captain Sir J.B. Warren, coast of France
Sep	3	*Vigilante,* cutter	6	Taken by *Childers*, Commander R. Dacres, off Saint Brieux
Sep	22	*Sans Culotte*	18	Burnt by *Aimable*, Captain C.S. Davers, West Indies
Oct	10	*Superbe*	22	Taken by *Vanguard*, Captain Simon Miller, West Indies
Oct	10	*Brutus*	10	Taken by *Mermaid* and *Zebra*, West Indies
Oct	14	*Republicain* (1)	18	Taken by *Mermaid* and *Zebra*, West Indies
Oct	15	*Eveille*	18	Taken by Commodore Sir J.B. Warren off Rochefort
Nov		*Droits du Peuple*	36	Wrecked off Trondhjem
Dec	1	*Pandore* (1) (as *Pandour*)	14	Taken by *Caroline*, Captain W. Luke, North Sea

THE ROYAL NAVY

Year 1796			
Date	**Name of Ship**	**Guns**	**Fate**
Mar 9	*Nemesis* (1)	28	Taken by *Egmond*,
	Sardine (1)	22	Captain John Sutton and consorts off Tunis
Mar 10	*Bonne Citoyenne* (1)	20	Taken by *Phaeton*, Captain Honourable R. Stopford, Cape Finisterre
Mar 10	*Aspic*, cutter		Taken by the *Quebec* in Saint George's Channel
Mar 18	*Etourdie*	16	Burnt by *Diamond*, Captain Sir W.S. Smith, and *Liberty, Aristocrat*, off Cape Frehel (2)
Mar	*Favorite*	22	Taken by *Alfred*, Captain T. Drury, off Cape Finisterre
Mar	*Marsouin*	26	Taken by *Beaulieu*, Captain Lancelot Skynner, West Indies
Mar 20	*Etoile,* armed store ship	28	Taken by Commodore Sir J.B. Warren, coast of France
Mar	*Alerte*	14	Taken by *Cormorant*, Commander Joseph Bingham, West Indies
Mar	*Mutine,* brig		Taken by frigates in the Bay
Apr 13	*Unite* (1)	36	Taken by *Revolutionnaire* and consorts, coast of France
Apr 15	*Robuste* (1) (as *Scourge*)	22	Taken by Commodore Sir J.B. Warren off the Saintes
Apr 20	*Unite* (1) (as *Surprise*)	28	Taken by *Inconstant*, Captain T.F. Fremantle, Mediterranean
Apr 21	*Percante* (1) (as *Jamaica*)	26	Taken by *Intrepid*, Captain Charles Carpenter, West Indies
Apr 22	*Virginie* (1)	40	Taken by squadron of Sir

			E. Pellew, *Indefatigable*, off the Lizard (2)
Apr		*Aurore*	10	Taken by *Cleopatra*, Captain C. Rowley, America
Apr	27	*Ecureuil*, lugger	18	Burnt by boats of *Niger*, Captain E.J. Foote, off Penmarck
May	2	*Abeille*, cutter	14	Taken by *Dryad*, Commander J.K. Pulling (acting), off Lizard (1)
May	4	*Volcan*	12	Taken by *Spencer*, Commander A.F. Evans, off Bermuda
May	7	*Cygne*, cutter	14	Taken by *Doris*, Captain Hon. C. Jones, off Scilly
May	8	*Athenienne* (1)	14	Taken by *Albacore*, Commander R. Winthrop, off Barbados
May	31	*Genie*, ketch	3	Taken by Commodore H. Nelson at Oneglia
		Gunboat Number 12	1	
Jun	8	*Tribune*	36	Taken by *Unicorn*, Captain T. Williams (4th), Ireland (2)
Jun	8	*Tamise*, ex *Thames* (1) (as *Thames*)	32	Retaken by *Santa Margarita*, Captain T.B. Martin, Ireland (2)
Jun	10	*Utile*	24	Taken by *Southampton*, Captain J. Macnamara (2nd) off Hyeres (2)
Jun	11	*Trois Couleurs*, brig	10	Taken by Commodore Sir E. Pellew, off Ushant
		Blonde, brig	16	
Jun	13	*Proserpine* (1) (as *Amelia*)	40	Taken by *Dryad*, Captain Lord Amelius Beauclerk, off Cape Clear (2)
Jun	22	*Legere* (1)	22	Taken by *Apollo* and *Doris* off Scilly
Jul	12	*Renommee* (1)	36	Taken by *Alfred*, Captain T. Drury, off San Domingo
Aug	19	*Alerte*	16	Taken by *Carysfort*,

THE ROYAL NAVY

				Captain T. Alexander, East Indies
Aug	22	*Andromaque*	36	Destroyed by Commodore Sir J.B. Warren near Arcachon
Aug	28	*Elisabeth*	36	Taken by Vice-Admiral G. Murray (2nd), North America
Oct	18	*Eliza*	10	Taken by *Fury*, Commander H. Evans, West Indies
Nov	1	*Cerf Volant*	18	Taken by *Magicienne*, Captain W.H. Ricketts, off San Domingo
Nov	13	*Etonnant*	18	Destroyed by *Minerva* and *Melampus* off Barfleur
Nov	13	*Etna* (1) (as *Cormorant*)	18	Taken by *Melampus* and *Childers*, coast of France
Nov	27	*Decius*	28	Taken by *Lapwing*, Captain R. Barton, West Indies, destroyed Nov 28th (2)
Nov	27	*Vaillant,* brig	4	Destroyed by *Lapwing*, Captain R. Barton, West Indies (2)
Dec	3	*Africaine*	18	Taken by *Quebec*, Captain J. Cooke, off San Domingo
Dec	10	*General Leveau*	16	Taken by *Mermaid* and *Resource* off San Domingo
Dec	13	*Vestale*	36	Taken by *Terpsichore*, Captain R. Bowen
Dec	16	*Seduisant*	74	Wrecked near Brest
Dec	30	*Scevola*	44	Foundered off Ireland
Dec	30	*Impatiente*	44	Wrecked near Mizen Head
Dec	31	*Amaranthe* (1)	14	Taken by *Diamond*, Captain Sir R.J. Strachan, off Alderney

Dec		*Justine*, store ship, *en flute*	44	Lost off Irish coast

Year 1797

Date		Name of Ship	Guns	Fate
Jan	5	*Tortue* (1) (later *Ariane*)	40	Taken by *Polyphemus*, Captain G. Lumsdaine, off Ireland
Jan	7	*Ville de Lorient, en flute*	36	Taken by *Doris, Unicorn,* and *Druid* off Ireland
Jan	8	*Suffren,* store ship	44	Sunk by *Majestic, Daedalus,* and *Incendiary* off Ushant
Jan	10	*Atalante* (1)	16	Taken by *Phoebe*, Captain R. Barlow, off Scilly
Jan	12	*Allegre,* store ship		Taken by *Spitfire*, Commander Michael Seymour, off Ushant
Jan	13	*Droits de l'Homme*	74	Wrecked in action with *Indefatigable* and *Amazon* off Penmarck (2)
Jan		*Surveillante*	36	Scuttled in Bantry Bay
Feb	13	a schooner	2	Taken by *Matilda*, Captain H. Mitford, off Barbados
Mar	9	*Resistance* (1) (as *Fishguard*)	40	Taken by *San Fiorenzo* and *Nymphe* off Brest (2)
		Constance (1)	22	
Mar		*Modeste*	20	Taken by *Fox*, Captain Pulteney Malcolm, off Vizagapatam
Apr	17	*Hermione*	36	Destroyed by *Thunderer* and *Valiant*, off San Domingo
May	13	*Jalouse* (1)	18	Taken by *Vestal*, Captain C. White, North Sea
May	29	*Mutine* (1)	14	Cut out by boats of *Minerve* and *Lively*, Lieutenant T.M. Hardy, Santa Cruz (2)
Jun	12	*Harriette*	6	Taken by *Aigle*, Captain

THE ROYAL NAVY

				C. Tyler, off Lisbon
Jul	17	*Calliope*	36	Destroyed by Commodore Sir J.B. Warren off coast of France
Jul	17	*Freedom, en flute*	8	Taken and burnt by Commodore Sir J.B. Warren off coast of France
Aug	11	a ship corvette	22	Taken and bilged by Commodore Sir J.B. Warren off coast of France
Aug	11	a brig, gun vessel	12	Taken and sunk by Commodore Sir J.B. Warren off coast of France
Aug	20	*Gaite* (1)	20	Taken by *Arethusa*, Captain T. Wolley, Atlantic
Aug	23	*Egalite, chasse-maree*	8	Taken by Commodore Sir J.B. Warren, coast of France
Aug	27	*Petit Diable,* cutter	18	Taken and bilged by Commodore Sir J.B. Warren, coast of France
Sep	10	*Espoir* (1)	16	Taken by *Thalia*, Captain Lord H. Paulet, Mediterranean
Oct	9	*Decouverte*	18	Taken by *Unite*, Captain C., Channel
Oct	14	*Ranger* (1)	14	Taken by *Indefatigable*, Captain Sir E. Pellew, off Tenerife, retaken
Nov	6	*Venturier,* ex *Ranger* (1)	14	Retaken by *Galatea*, Captain G. Byng
Nov	12	*Eperviere*	16	Taken by *Cerberus*, Captain John Drew, off Ireland
Nov		*Meduse*	40	Foundered on passage from America

Dec	22	*Nereide* (1)	36	Taken by *Phoebe*, Captain R. Barlow, off Scilly (2)
Dec	28	*Daphne* (1) (as 20)	30	Retaken by *Anson*, Captain P.C. Durham, Bay of Biscay
Dec		*Republique Triomphante*	14	Taken by *Severn* and *Pelican*, West Indies

Year 1798

Date		Name of Ship	Guns	Fate
Jan	5	*Cheri*	26	Taken by *Pomone*, Captain R.C. Reynolds, Bay of Biscay, and foundered
Jan	16	*Desiree*	6	Taken by pinnace, Lieutenant Samuel Pym, of *Babet*, West Indies
Feb	16	*Scipion*	20	Taken by *Alfred*, Captain T. Totty, Guadeloupe
Feb	26	*Souris, chasse-maree*	16	Taken by *Badger*, Lieutenant C.P. Price, and consorts, Saint Marcon
Apr	5	*Sainte Famille, chasse-maree*		Taken by *Impetueux* and *Sylph*
Apr	19	*Arrogante,* gun vessel (1)	6	Taken by *Jason*, Captain C. Stirling, off Brest
Apr	21	*Hercule* (1)	74	Taken by *Mars*, Captain A. Hood, off Bec du Raz (2)
May	1	*Quatorze Juillet*	74	Accidentally burnt at Lorient
May	7	*Flibustier*		Taken during attack on Saint Marcon by *Badger* and *Sandfly* (2)
May	13	*Mondovi* (1)	16	Cut out by boats (Lieutenant W. Russell) of *Flora*, at Cerigo
May	31	*Confiante*	36	Run ashore and destroyed by *Hydra*, Captain Sir F. Laforey, near Le Havre

THE ROYAL NAVY

Jun	22	*Corcyre*	16	Taken by *Flora*, Captain R.G. Middleton, off Sicily
Jun	22	*Egalite*	20	Destroyed by *Aurora*, Captain H. Digby, Bay of Biscay
Jun	27	*Sensible*	36	Taken by *Seahorse*, Captain E.J. Foote, Mediterranean
Jun	30	*Seine* (1)	40	Taken by *Jason*, Captain C. Stirling, and *Pique*, Captain David Milne
Aug	1	*Orient*	120	Burnt in action with Rear-Admiral Sir H. Nelson
Aug	1	*Franklin* (1) (as *Canopus*)	80	Taken in Aboukir Bay by Rear-Admiral Sir H. Nelson (2) (3)
		Tonnant (1)	80	
Aug	1	*Timoleon*	74	Destroyed by her crew after action with Rear-Admiral Sir H. Nelson (2) (3)
		Guerrier	74	Taken and burnt in Aboukir Bay by Rear-Admiral Sir H. Nelson (2)
		Heureaux	74	
		Mercure	74	
		Spartiate (1)	74	Taken in Aboukir Bay by Rear-Admiral Sir H. Nelson (2)
		Conquerant (1)	74	
		Aquilon (1) (as *Aboukir*)	74	
		Souverain Peuple (1) (as *Guerrier*)	74	
		Artemise	36	Burst after action with Rear-Admiral Sir H. Nelson (2)
		Serieuse	36	Sunk in action with Rear-Admiral Sir H. Nelson (2)
Aug	3	*Aventuriere*	14	Cut out by boats (Lieutenant T.G. Shortland) of *Melpomene*

				and *Childers*, Corigiou
Aug	7	*Vaillante* (1) (as *Danae*)	20	Taken by *Indefatigable*, Captain Sir E. Pellew, Bay of Biscay
Aug	7	*Liguria* (Genoese)	26	Taken by *Espoir*, Commander Loftus Otway Bland, Mediterranean (2)
Aug	11	*Fortune* (1) (as 10)	18	Taken by *Swiftsure*, Captain B. Hallowell, coast of Egypt; retaken May 8th, 1799
Aug	12	*Neptune*	20	Taken by *Hazard*, Commander W. Butterfield, coast of Ireland
Aug	22	*Legere* (1), gun vessel	6	Taken by *Alcmene*, Captain G. Hope, off Alexandria
Aug	24	*Decade* (1)	36	Taken by *Magnanime* and *Naiad*, off Finisterre
Aug	25	*Torride* (1), ketch	7	Taken by boats (Lieutenant W. Debusk) of *Goliath*, off Aboukir; retaken March 18, 1799
Sep	1	*Reunion*	6	Taken by *Oiseau*, Captain C. Brisbane, East Indies
Sep	2	*Anemone,* gun vessel	4	Destroyed off Damietta by *Seahorse* and *Emerald*
Oct	12	*Hoche* (1) (as *Donegal*)	74	Taken by Commodore Sir J.B. Warren, coast of Ireland
		Embuscade (1) (as *Ambuscade*)	36	
		Coquille	36	
		Bellone (1) (as *Proserpine*)	36	
Oct	13	*Resolue* (1)	36	Taken by *Melampus*, Captain Graham Moore, coast of Ireland
Oct	18	*Loire* (1)	40	Taken by *Anson*, Captain

THE ROYAL NAVY

Date		Name of Ship	Guns	Fate
				P.C. Durham and *Kangaroo*, Commander E. Brace, Ireland
Oct	20	*Immortalite*	40	Taken by *Fishguard*, Captain T.B. Martin, off Brest (2)
Oct	29	*Fulminante,* cutter	8	Taken by *Espoir*, Captain Loftus Otway Bland, Mediterranean
Nov	17	*Fouine,* lugger	8	Taken by *Sylph*, Commander John Chambers White, off Brest
Nov	20	*Hirondelle*	20	Taken by *Phaeton*, *Ambuscade*, and *Stag* in the Channel
Dec	28	*Wilding,* armed transport	14	Taken by *Spitfire*, Commander Michael Seymour, Bay of Biscay

		Year 1799		
Date		**Name of Ship**	**Guns**	**Fate**
Feb	9	*Prudente*	36	Taken by *Daedalus*, Captain H. Lidgbird Ball, Cape of Good Hope
Feb	28	*Forte* (1)	44	Taken by *Sibylle*, Captain E. Cook, Bengal (2)
Mar	1	*Marianne*	4	Taken by Commodore Sir W.S. Smith, coast of Syria
Mar	3	*Leander* (1)	50	Taken by Russians and Turks at Corfu; restored to Britain
Mar	3	*Brune*	28	Taken by Russians and Turks at Corfu
Mar	18	*Hirondelle*	16	Taken by *Telegraph*, Lieutenant. J.A. Worth, off Isle Bas (2)
Mar	18	*Negresse* (1)	6	Taken by Commodore Sir W.S. Smith, coast of Syria
		Foudre	8	
		Dangereuse (1)	6	
		Marie Rose	4	

		Dame de Grace (1)	4	
		Deux Freres	4	
		Torride	2	
Mar		*Courier*	16	Taken by *Zealous*, Captain Samuel Hood, Mediterranean
Apr	4	*Sans Quartier*	14	Taken by *Danae*, Captain Lord Proby, coast of France
Apr	27	*Rebecca, chasse-maree*	16	Taken by *Black Joke*, Lieutenant J. Nicolson, off Ushant
Apr		a corvette	16	Taken by *Lion*, Captain Manley Dixon, Mediterranean
Jun	18	*Junon* (1) (as *Princess Carlotte*)	38	Taken by squadron under Captain John Markham, Mediterranean
		Alceste (1)	36	
		Courageuse (1)	38	
		Salamine (1) (as 16)	16	
		Alerte (1) (as *Minorca*)	14	
Aug	20	*Vestale*	36	Taken by *Clyde*, Captain C. Cunningham, mouth of Garonne
Aug	20	*Hussard* (1) (as *Surinam*)	18	Taken by Vice-Admiral Lord Hugh Seymour, Surinam
Aug	26	*Republicaine*	28	Taken by *Tamar*, Captain Thomas Western, off Surinam
Sep	13	*Saint Jacques*	6	Taken by *Triton*, Captain John Gore (2), off Lorient
Oct	10	*Arethuse* (1) (as *Raven*)	18	Taken by *Excellent*, Captain Hon, R. Stopford, off Lorient
Oct	12	*Iphigenie*	24	Blown up in action with *Trincomale*, Commander John Rowe, Red Sea
Nov	10	*Charente*	35	Wrecked off Lorient

THE ROYAL NAVY

Nov	22	*Egyptienne, en flute,*	20	Taken by *Solebay*, Captain Stephen Poyntz, off San Domingo
		Eole (1) (as *Nimrod*)	16	
		Levrier	12	
		Vengeur (ex British *Charlotte*)	8	
Dec	11	*Preneuse*	36	Destroyed by boats (Lieutenant Edward Grey) of *Tremendous* and *Adamant*, off Port Louis

Year 1800

Date		Name of Ship	Guns	Fate
Jan	7	*Brule Gueule*	20	Wrecked off Brest
Feb	6	*Pallas (*1) (as *Pique*)	38	Taken by *Loire, Danae*, and consorts *Fairy* and *Harpy*, coast of France (2)
Feb	9	a polacre (Genoese)	14	Driven ashore and destroyed by *Pearl*, Captain S.J. Ballard, Mediterranean
Feb	10	*Vedette*	14	Taken by *Triton*, Captain John Gore, coast of France
Feb	18	*Genereux* (1)	74	Taken by Rear-Admiral Lord Nelson, Mediterranean
		Ville de Marseille, store ship		
Feb	19	*Gun Vessel Number 57*	1	Taken by *Aristocrat*, Lieutenant Corbet James d'Auvergne, Cape Frehel

Mar	21	*Ligurienne*	16	Taken by *Petrel*, Commander F.W. Austen, near Marseille (2)
Mar	30	*Guillaume Tell* (1) (as *Malta*)	80	Taken by *Lion, Foudroyant*, and *Penelope*, Mediterranean (2)
Apr	13	*Diligente*	6	Taken by cutter (Master Buckley) of *Calypso*, West Indies
Apr	13	*Neptune,* schooner	4	Taken by *Mayflower*, privateer, J. le Blair, coast of France
May	5	*Dragon*	14	Taken by *Cambrian* and *Fishguard*, Channel
May	20	*Prima,* galley	2	Taken by boats under Commander Philip Beaver, Genoa
May	31	*Legere,* lugger	3	Taken by *Netley*, Lieutenant F. Godolphin Bond, Mediterranean
Jun	1	*Cruelle* (1)	16	Taken by *Mermaid*, Captain R. Dudley Oliver, off Toulon
Jun	6	*Insolente*	18	Burnt by boats (Lieutenant John Pilfold) of *Impetueux*, Bay of Biscay
Jun	11	*Nochette,* gunboat	2	Taken by boats of squadron of Sir J.B. Warren, off Penmarck
		a *chasse-maree*	10	
		a *chasse-maree*	6	
Jun		*Diligente*	12	Taken by *Crescent*, Captain W. Granville Lobb, West Indies
Jun	7	*Revanche*	4	Taken by *Phoenix*, Captain Laurence W. Halsted, Mediterranean

THE ROYAL NAVY

141

Jul	2	*Therese*	20	Taken and burnt by boats (Lieutenant H. Burke) of *Renown*, *Fishguard*, and *Defence*, Bourgneuf Bay
		a lugger	12	
		a gunboat	6	
		a gunboat	6	
		a cutter	6	
Jul	8	*Desiree*	38	Taken by *Dart*, Commander Patrick Campbell, Dunquerque Road (2)
Jul	29	*Cerbere*	7	Cut out by boat (Lieutenant Jeremiah Coghlan, acting, of *Viper)* of *Impetueux*, Port Louis (2)
Jul		*Boudeuse*		Destroyed to provide fuel, Valetta
Aug	5	*Concorde*	40	Taken by *Belliqueux*, Captain Rowley Bulteel, and consorts, off Rio
Aug	5	*Medee*	36	Taken by Indiamen *Bombay Castle* and *Exeter*, off Rio
Aug	21	*Diane* (1) (as *Niobe*)	40	Taken by *Northumberland, Genereux*, and *Success*, off Malta
Aug	25	*Vengeance*	40	Taken by *Seine*, Captain David Milne, in Mona Passage (2)
Sep	1	*Capricieuse*	6	Taken by *Termagant*, Commander W. Skipsey, off Corsica
Sep	4	*Athenien* (1) (Maltese)	64	Taken at the surrender of Valetta
		Diego (Maltese)	64	
		Cartagenoise	36	
Oct	8	*Quid pro Quo*	8	Taken by *Gipsy*, Lieutenant Coryndon Boger, off Guadeloupe
Oct	22	*Venus* (1) (as *Amaranthe*)	28	Taken by *Indefatigable* and *Fishguard* off

Date		Name of Ship	Guns	Fate
				Portugal
Nov	17	*Reolaise*	20	Driven ashore by *Nile,* Lieutenant G. Argles, and burnt by boats (Lieutenant W. Hennah) of squadron

Year 1801

Date		Name of Ship	Guns	Fate
Jan	3	*Senegal*	18	Cut out and destroyed by boats (Lieutenant T. Dick) of *Melpomene,* Senegal
Jan	18	*Aurore* (1)	16	Taken by *Thames,* Captain William Lukin, Channel
Jan	18	*Eclair* (1) (as 12)	<u>4</u>	Cut out by *Garland,* tender, Lieutenant Kenneth Mackenzie, Guadeloupe
Jan	20	*Sans Pareille*	20	Taken by *Mercury,* Captain Thomas Rogers, off Sardinia
Jan	28	*Dedaigneuse* (1)	36	Taken by *Oiseau, Sirius,* and *Amethyst,* off Portugal
Jan	29	*Curieuse*	18	Taken by *Bordelaise,* Captain Thomas Manby, off Barbados; foundered
Jan		*Bombarde, gun vessel*	1	Taken by *Boadicea,* Captain R. Goodwin Keats off Brest
Feb	16	*Furieuse,* xebec	6	Taken by *Minorca,* Commander George Miller, Mediterranean
Feb	19	*Africaine* (1)	40	Taken by *Phoebe,* Captain Robert Barlow, Mediterranean (2)
Feb	20	*Arc,* cutter		Taken by boats of *Excellent,* Quiberon Bay
Apr	9	*General Brune*	14	Taken by *Amethyst,* Captain John Cooke,

THE ROYAL NAVY

				Channel
Apr		*Laurette*	26	Taken by *Arrogant*, Captain E. Oliver Osborn, East Indies
May	27	*Corvesse* (?) despatch vessel	1	Taken by *Corso*, Commander William Ricketts, Mediterranean
May	28	*Egypte*	16	Taken by *Heureaux*, Captain Loftus Otway Bland, off Barbados
Jun	23	*Tigre* (suspected pirate)	8	Taken by boats of *Mercury* and *Corso*, Gulf of Venice
Jul	12	*Saint Antoine*	74	Taken by Rear-Admiral Sir James Saumarez off Gibraltar (2)
Jul	22	*Chevrette*	20	Cut out by boats (Lieutenant Keith Maxwell of *Beaulieu)*, *Doris, Uranie*, and *Robust*, near Brest (2)
Jul	25	a corvette	10	Taken by *Determine*, Captain John Clarke Searle, off Alexandria
Aug	3	*Carrere* (1)	38	Taken by *Pomone*, Captain E.L. Gower, off Elba
Aug	10	*Eveille,* lugger	2	Taken by cutter (Midshipman Francis Smith of *Atalante*) Quiberon Bay
Aug	19	*Chiffonne* (1)	36	Taken by *Sibylle*, Captain Charles Adam, off Seychelles
Aug	21	four howitzer boats (1 gun each)	4	Taken or destroyed by boats (Lieutenant James John Charles Agassiz) of Captain Jonas Rose's squadron, near Etaples
Sep	2	*Succes* (1) (as *Success*)	22	Retaken by *Pomone, Phoenix*, and *Minerve* off Vado

Sep	2	*Bravoure*	36	Driven ashore
Sep	2	*Causse*	64	Taken at capitulation of Alexandria; delivered to Turkey
		Justice	40	
		unknown Venetian	32	
		Egyptienne (1)	44	Taken at capitulation of Alexandria; retained
		Regeneree (1)	36	
		unknown Venetian	32	
Sep	7	*Fleche*	18	Sank after capture by *Victor*, Commander George Ralph Collier, East Indies
Sep	16	*Bulldog* (1)	18	Retaken by *Champion*, Captain Lord William Stuart, near Gallipoli

(1)   Added to the Royal Navy.
(2)   Medals granted in 1849 in pursuance of *Gazette* notice of June 1st, 1847.
(3)   Flag officers' and captains' gold medals.

C. DUTCH
Ships of the Batavian Republic

Year 1795				
Date		**Name of Ship**	**Guns**	**Fate**
Aug	18	*Willemstad* (1) (as *Princess*)	26	Taken by Vice-Admiral Sir G.K. Elphinstone, Simon's Bay
		Ster, armed brig	14	
Aug	20	*Brak* (1) (as *De Braak*)	14	Detained by *Fortune*, Commander Francis Wooldridge, Falmouth
Aug	22	*Alliantie* (1) (as *Alliance, 20*)	36	Taken by *Stag, Reunion, Isis*, and *Vestal*, off Norway
Aug	28	*Komeet* (1) (as *Penguin*)	18	Taken by *Unicorn*, Captain Thomas Williams (4th), Irish station
Oct	22	*Overijssel* (1)	64	Taken by *Polyphemus*, Captain George Lumsdaine, Queenstown

THE ROYAL NAVY

Oct		*Maria Louise*	14	Taken by *Rattlesnake*, Commander Edward Ramage, Cape of Good Hope

Year 1796

Date		Name of Ship	Guns	Fate
Jan		*Harlingen* (1) (as *Amboyna*)	10	Taken by Rear-Admiral Peter Rainier, East Indies
Mar		*Zefir* (1) (as *Eurus*)	36	Detained by *Andromeda, Ranger*, and *Kite*, Firth of Forth
Mar	4	*Zeeland* (1) as *Zealand*	64	Taken by Vice-Admiral Richard Onslow at Plymouth
		Brakel (1)	54	
		Tholen (1) (as *Thulen*)	40	
		Meermin (1) (as *Miermin*)	16	
		Pijl (1)	16	
Apr	22	*Vlugheid*	12	Taken by Admiral Duncan, coast of Norway
Apr	23	*Thetis*	24	Taken by Commander Thomas Parr at Demerara
		Zeemeeuw	12	
May	12	*Argo* (1) (as *Janus*)	6	Taken by *Phoenix*, Captain Lawrence W. Halsted, et cetera, North Sea
May	12	*Echo*	12	Driven ashore by *Pegasus*, Captain Ross Donnelly, Vriesland
		Gier	12	
May	12	*Mercurius* (1) (as *Hermes*)	12	Taken by *Sylph*, Commander John Chambers White, off the Texel
Jun	8	*Jason* (1) (as *Proselyte*)	36	Brought into Greenock by mutinous crew
Jul	6	*Bataaf*	12	Taken by *Roebuck*, Commander Alexander S. Burrowes, off Barbados
Aug	17	*Dordrecht* (1) (as *Dortrecht*)	64	Surrendered to Vice-Admiral Sir G.K. Elphinstone, Saldanha Bay
		Revolutie (1) (as *Prince Frederick*)	64	

	Maarten Harpertzoon Tromp (1) (as *Van Tromp*)	54	
	Castor (1) (as *Saldanha*)	44	
	Brave (1) (as *Braave*)	40	
	Bellona (1) (as *Vindictive*)	24	
	Sirene (1) (as *Laurel*)	26	
	Havik (1) (as *Havick*)	18	
	Vrouw Maria	16	

Year 1797

Date		Name of Ship	Guns	Fate
Oct	11	*Vrijheid* (1)	74	Taken by Admiral Adam Duncan in the battle off Camperdown (2) (3)
		Jupiter (1) (as *Camperdown*)	72	
		Haarlem (1)	68	
		Admiraal Tjerk Hiddes de Vries (1) (as *Admiral Devries*)	68	
		Gelijkheid (1)	68	
		Wassenaar	64	
		Hercules (1) (later *Delft*)	64	
		Alkmaar (1)	56	
		Delft	54	Taken by Admiral Duncan off Camperdown (2) (3), sunk
		Monnikendam	44	Taken by Admiral Duncan off Camperdown (2) (3), lost
		Embuscade	32	Taken by Admiral Duncan off Camperdown (2) (3), retaken

THE ROYAL NAVY

Oct		Yonge Frans (?)	10	Taken by *Resistance*, Captain Edward Pakenham, East Indies
		Yonge Lansier (?)	10	
		Wakker (?)	10	
		Limbi	8	
		Ternate	4	
		Resource (?)	6	
		Juno	4	

Year 1798

Date		Name of Ship	Guns	Fate
Oct	24	Waakzaamheid (1)	24	Taken by *Sirius*, Captain Richard King, North Sea
		Furie (1) (as Wilhelmina)	36	

Year 1799

Date		Name of Ship	Guns	Fate
Apr	26	Helena	8	Taken by *Virginie*, Captain George Astle, East Indies
		Helena	12	
		Brak	12	
May	24	a brig	6	Taken by *Arrogant* and *Orpheus*, East Indies
Aug	11	Crash (1)	12	Retaken by *Pylades*, Commander Adam Mackenzie and consorts off Groningen (2)
Aug	14	a *schuyt* (1) (as Undaunted)	2	Taken by *Pylades*, Commander Adam Mackenzie and consorts off Groningen
Aug	14	Weerwraak, gun vessel	6	Burnt by *Pylades*, Commander Adam Mackenzie and consorts off Groningen (2)
Aug	20	Kemphaan (1) (as Camphaan)	16	Taken by Vice-Admiral Lord Hugh Seymour, Surinam
Aug	28	Verwachting	64	Taken by Vice-Admiral Andrew Mitchell, Nieuwe Diep, Texel
		Broederschap	54	
		Hector (1) (as Pandour)	44	
		Duif	44	

		Expeditie	44	
		Belle Antoinette	44	
		Constitutie	44	
		Unie	44	
		Heldin (1)	28	
		Minerva (1) (as *Braak*)	24	
		Venus (1) (as *Amaranthe*)	24	
		Valk	24	
		Alarm	24	
Aug	30	*Washington* (1) (as *Princess of Orange*)	70	Surrendered to Vice-Admiral Andrew Mitchell, in the Vlieter, Texel
		Gelderland (1)	64	
		Admiraal De Ruijter (1) (as *De Ruyter*)	64	
		Utrecht	64	
		Cerberus (1) (as *Texel*)	64	
		Leijden (1)	64	
		Beschermer (1)	56	
		Batavier (1)	56	
		Amphitrite (1)	44	
		Mars (1) (as *Vlieter)* rasee	44	
		Embuscade (1)	32	
		Galatie (1)	16	
Sep		*Valk*	20	Taken by Vice-Admiral Andrew Mitchell, Zuijder Zee, but lost November 10th, 1799
Sep	12	*Draak*	24	Taken by *Arrow*, Commander Nathaniel Portlock and *Wolverine*, Commander William Bolton, off Vlie (2)
		Gier (1)	14	
Sep	15	*Dolfijn* (1) (as *Dolphin*)	24	Surrendered to *Arrow*, Commander Nathaniel Portlock and *Wolverine*, Commander William Bolton, off Vlie (2)

THE ROYAL NAVY

Oct	9	*Lijnx*	12	Taken by boats of *Circe*,
		Perseus	8	Captain Robert Winthrop, River Ems
Oct		four gunboats, 1 gun each	4	Cut out by boats of *Dart, Hasty, Defender, Cracker*, and *Iris*, coast of Holland
Year 1800				
Date		**Name of Ship**	**Guns**	**Fate**
Aug	23	a brig (1) (as *Admiral Rainier*)	16	Taken by *Daedalus, Centurion, Braave*, and *Sibylle*, East Indies
Oct	28	5 gunboats		Burnt by *Admiral Rainier*, Lieutenant W.H. Dobbie, Carawang River
Oct	30	3 gunboats		Taken by *Admiral Rainier*, Lieutenant W.H. Dobbie, Carawang River

(1) Added to the Royal Navy.
(2) Medals granted in 1849 in pursuance of *Gazette* notice of June 1st, 1847.
(3) Flag officers' and captains' gold medals.

D. SPANISH
Ships of the Royal Spanish Navy

Year 1796				
Date		**Name of Ship**	**Guns**	**Fate**
Sep	16	*Princesa*	16	Detained by *Seahorse*, Captain George Oakes, off Corunna
Oct	13	*Mahonesa* (1)	24	Taken by *Terpsichore*, Captain Richard Bowen, off Cape de Gata (2)
Nov	2	*San Pio*	18	Taken by *Regulus*, Captain William Carthew, Atlantic
Nov	23	*Galgo*	18	Taken by *Alarm*, Captain Edward Fellowes, off Grenada
Dec	2	*Corso* (1)	18	Taken by *Southampton*, Captain James Macnamara, off Monaco
Dec	20	*Santa Sabina*	40	Taken by *Minerve*, Captain

				George Cockburn, Mediterranean; retaken December 21st, 1796 (2)

Year 1797

Date		Name of Ship	Guns	Fate
Feb	14	*Salvador del Mundo* (1)	112	Taken by the fleet of Admiral Sir John Jervis, K.B., off Cape Saint Vincent (2) (3)
		San Josef (1)	112	
		San Nicolas (1)	80	
		San Ysidro (1)	80	
		San Vincente	80	Burnt to prevent capture by Rear-Admiral H. Harvey, Trinidad
		Arrogante	74	
		Gallardo	74	
		Santa Cecilia	34	
		San Damaso (1)	74	Taken by Rear-Admiral H. Harvey, Trinidad
Mar	12	*Los Magellanes*	<u>4</u>	Taken by *Dover*, Lieutenant H. Kent, coast of Portugal
Apr	26	*Ninfa* (1) (as *Hamadryad*)	34	Taken by *Irresistible*, Captain George Martin, Lisbon station
Apr	26	*Santa Elena*	34	Destroyed by *Irresistible*, Captain George Martin, near Cadiz
May	24	*Nuestra Senora del Rosario* (1) (as *Rosario*)	20	Taken by *Romulus* and *Mahonesa*, off Cadiz
Jun	21	*San Francisco*	14	Taken by *Santa Margarita*, Captain George Parker, off Ireland
Nov	14	*Bolador*	16	Taken by *Majestic*, Captain George Blagden Westcott, Lisbon station

Year 1798

Date		Name of Ship	Guns	Fate
May		*San Antonio*, packet	6	Taken by *Endymion*, Captain Sir Thomas Williams (4th), off Ireland
May	8	*Receviso*	6	Taken by *Aurora*, Captain H.

THE ROYAL NAVY

Date		Name of Ship	Guns	Fate
				Digby, Lisbon station
Jul	15	*Santa Dorotea* (1)	34	Taken by *Lion*, Captain Manley Dixon, off Cartagena (2)
Sep	16	*Velosa Aragonesa, en flute*	30	Taken by *Aurora*, Captain H. Digby, off the Azores
Nov	13	*Petrel*	16	Retaken by *Argo*, Captain James Bowen, Mediterranean
Nov	15	a brig on the stocks (1) (as *Port Mahon*)		Taken at the capture of Minorca
		14 gunboats		
Nov	28	*San Leon*	16	Taken by *Santa Dorotea, Stromboli, Perseus*, and *Bulldog*, Lisbon station

Year 1799				
Date		**Name of Ship**	**Guns**	**Fate**
Jan	2	*Valiente,* packet	12	Taken by *Cormorant*, Captain Lord Mark Robert Kerr, off Malaga
Feb	6	*Santa Teresa* (1)	34	Taken by *Argo*, Captain James Bowen, off Majorca
Feb	22	*Africa,* xebec	14	Taken by *Espoir*, Commander James Sanders, Mediterranean
Mar	16	*Guadalupe*	34	Driven ashore by *Centaur* and *Cormorant*, Mediterranean
Mar	16	*Urca Cargadora*	12	Burnt by *Prompte*, Captain Thomas Dundas, West Indies
Mar	19	*Vincejo* (1)	18	Taken by *Cormorant*, Captain Lord Mark Robert Kerr, Mediterranean
Mar	24	*Golondrina,* packet	4	Taken by *Mermaid* and *Sylph* off Corunna
May		*Pajaro,* packet	4	Taken by *Alarm*, Captain Robert Rolles, Gulf of Florida
Jun 23		*San Antonio*	14	Taken by *Terpsichore*, Captain William Hall Gage, Mediterranean
Jul		*Feliz*	14	Taken by *Alarm*, Captain Robert Rolles, West Indies
Jul		*Sandoval* (?)	4	Taken by *York* and consorts,

Date		Name of Ship	Guns	Fate
				West indies
Aug	6	*Infanta Amalia* (1) (as *Porpoise*)	12	Taken by *Argo*, Captain James Bowen, off coast of Portugal
Sep		a packet	2	Taken by *Mayflower*, privateer, Mediterranean
		a gunboat	8	
Oct	17	*Thetis*	34	Taken by *Ethalion*, Captain James Young (2nd), and consorts off Ferrol
Oct	18	*Santa Brigida*	34	Taken by *Naiad, Alcmene,* and *Triton* off Cape Finisterre
Oct	25	*Hermione* (1) (as *Retribution*)	34	Cut out of Puerto Cabello by boats of *Surprise*, Captain Edward Hamilton (2) (3)
Nov	15	*Galgo* (1)	16	Taken by *Crescent*, Captain William Granville Lobb, Atlantic

Year 1800

Date		Name of Ship	Guns	Fate
Jan	26	*Nuestra Senora del Carmen*	16	Taken by *Penelope*, Captain Henry Blackwood, Mediterranean
Feb		*Cuervo*	4	Taken by *Alarm*, Captain Robert Rolles, West Indies
Apr	7	*Carmen* (1) (as 36)	34	Taken by Rear-Admiral John Thomas Duckworth off Cadiz
		Florentina (1) (as 36)	34	
Jun	22	*Cortez*	4	Taken by *Flora*, Captain Robert Gambier Middleton, Lisbon station
Jun		*Nuestra Senora del Carmen,* felucca	2	Destroyed by *Bonetta*, Commander H. Vansittart, West Indies
Jun	29	*Gibraltar,* gunboat	10	Taken by *Anson*, Captain Philip Calderwood Durham, off Gibraltar
		Salvador, gunboat	10	
Jun		a gunboat	2	Taken by *Rattler*, Commander John Mathias Spread, West

THE ROYAL NAVY

153

Date		Name of Ship	Guns	Fate
				Indies
Jul	27	*Cantabra*	18	Taken by *Apollo*, Captain Peter Halkett, off Havana
Aug	20	*Veloz*	4	Taken by *Clyde*, Captain Charles Cunningham, Channel
Sep	3	*Concepcion*, alias *Esmeralda*	22	Cut out by boats (Commander James Hillyar) of *Minotaur* and *Niger*, Barcelona
		Paz	22	
Sep	30	*Vivo*	14	Taken by *Fishguard*, Captain Thomas Byam Martin, coast of Spain
Oct	27	*San Josef,* polacca	8	Cut out by boats (Lieutenant Francis Beaufort) of *Phaeton*, near Malaga (2)
Nov	10	*Resolucion*	18	Taken and destroyed by *Apollo*, Captain Peter Halkett, Gulf of Mexico

Year 1801

Date		Name of Ship	Guns	Fate
Jan	6	*Reina Luisa*	2	Taken by *Hind*, Captain Thomas Larcom, off Jamaica
May	6	*Gamo,* xebec	30	Taken by *Speedy*, Commander Lord Cochrane, near Barcelona
May	16	*Alcudia*		Cut out by boats of *Naiad* and *Phaeton*, near Pontevedra
		Raposo		
Jun	8	*Duides,* cutter	8	Taken by *Constance*, Captain Zachary Mudge, off Vigo
Jun	9	a xebec	20	Sunk in action by *Kangaroo* and *Speedy*, under a battery, Oropesa
		2 gunboats		
Jul	5	5 gunboats		Sunk in action by Rear-Admiral Sir James Saumarez, Algeciras
Jul	12	*Real Carlos*	112	Burnt in action with Rear-Admiral Sir James Saumarez, south of Gibraltar (2)
		San Hermenegildo	112	
		Perla	24	Sunk after action with Rear-Admiral Sir James Saumarez, south of Gibraltar (2)
Aug	20	*Neptuno,* pierced for 20		Taken by boats of *Fishguard*, *Diamond*, and *Boadicea*,

William Laird Clowes

	guns		Corunna
	a gunboat	1	
Sep 24	*Limeno*	18	Taken by *Chance*, privateer, coast of Peru

(1)   Added to the Royal Navy.

(2)   Medals granted in 1849 in pursuance of *Gazette* notice of June 1st, 1847.

(3)   Flag officers' and captains' gold medals.

DANISH

Ships of the Danish Royal Navy Lost to Vice-Admiral Lord Nelson at Copenhagen April 2nd, 1801 (1)

Name of Ship	Guns	Fate
Sjoelland	74	Taken and burnt
Dannebrog	62	Blew up after action
Infoedstretten	61	Taken and burnt
Holsteen (2)	60	Taken
Proevesteen	56	Taken and burnt
Jylland	48	Taken and burnt
Valkyrien	48	Taken and burnt
Charlotte Amalie	26	Taken and burnt
Aggershuus	20	Sunk after action
Haien	20	Taken and burnt
Kronborg	20	Taken and burnt
Nyborg	20	Sunk after action
Rendsborg	20	Driven ashore and burnt
Svoerdfisken	20	Taken and burnt
Soehesten	18	Taken and burnt

(1)   Medals granted in 1849 in pursuance of *Gazette* notice of June 1st, 1847.

(2)   Added to the Royal Navy.

THE ROYAL NAVY

CHAPTER XXXVII

VOYAGES AND DISCOVERIES, 1793-1802

Sir Clements Markham, K.C.B, F.R.S.

Broughton to the Pacific – Philip and Hunter to Botany Bay – Matthew Flinders – George Bass — Voyage of Flinders in the Investigator – Wreck of the Porpoise – French bad faith

When Lieutenant William Robert Broughton left the *Chatham* in 1793, and took home dispatches, crossing Mexico from San Blas to Vera Cruz, it was under consideration whether another surveying and exploring expedition should not be sent to the North Pacific. Captain James King had observed that the navigation of the sea between Japan and China offered the largest field for discovery; and his remark had received attention from the Lords of the Admiralty. The result was that Lieutenant Broughton (1) was appointed to the *Providence* with secret orders, on October 3rd, 1793. This vessel was a sloop of war of 400 tons, carrying 16 guns with a complement of 115 men. She had just returned from the service of conveying bread-fruit plants from Tahiti to the West Indies, under the command of Captain William Bligh. Broughton had three Lieutenants under him, Zachary Mudge, George Forbes Freeman Young, and James Giles Vashon; Mr. John Crossley shipped as astronomer, William Chapman was the master, and John Cawley, master's mate. On October 21st, 1794, the *Providence* sailed from Saint Helens, reached Sydney in August, 1795, and arrived in Tahiti in the end of November.

(1)   Broughton was made a commander in January 1795, and a captain on January 28th, 1797. W.L.C.

Memories of Cook were dear to the Tahitians, who gave every assistance to English ships and supplied them amply with fresh provisions After rating the chronometers at Point Venus, Broughton shaped a course for the Sandwich Islands. On December 17th, 1795, he discovered a low island covered with trees, which he named Caroline after the daughter of Sir Philip Stephens, Secretary to the Admiralty. On January 8th, 1796, he anchored in Karakakoa Bay. There the error and rate of chronometers was again ascertained, and uniform kindness and goodwill were displayed by the natives. The murder of Captain Cook, in a moment of blind rage, was deeply deplored, for he had been loved and respected by them. At that time Kamehameha I had made himself sovereign of all the islands but Kauai.

From Hawaii the *Providence* went to Lahaina in Maui, and thence to Waikiki Bay in Oahu, where Kamehameha was preparing for the conquest of Kauai. Captain Broughton left the Sandwich Islands on February 2nd, 1796, arriving at Nootka Sound on the 15th of March; and, after some stay in the Strait of Juan de Fuca, anchored at Monterey in June. He then, with the advice of his officers, decided upon a plan to survey the coast of Asia from the island of Saghalien to the Nankin River with the Kurile and Japan islands, thinking that such survey would complete a knowledge of the North Pacific, and would be very acceptable to geographers.

Returning to the Sandwich Islands, the vessel was steered thence to the westward, and sighted the Japanese island of Yesso on the 12th of September. Broughton anchored in Endermo Bay, in the island of Yesso, examined the whole western coast of Niphon, and passed through the Strait of Sangaar into the Gulf of Tartary. On November 11th, the *Providence* was off the entrance to the Bay of Tokio, and soon afterwards had a glorious view of Fusi-yama, towering above the high land and covered with snow. In December she arrived at Macao, where Commander Broughton purchased a small schooner to assist him in the work of surveying. He took on board fifteen months' provisions and completed a thorough refit. All the men were in good health, and the work was recommenced with the brightest prospects in April 1797.

But within a month the circumstances had entirely altered. Broughton was navigating among the islands to the east of Formosa. In the evening of May 17th white water was reported to Lieutenant Vashon, the officer of the watch, ahead and on both bows. Directly afterwards the ship struck

THE ROYAL NAVY 157

upon a coral reef: the helm having been put up, and the sails being all full. When Captain Broughton came on deck his opinion was that, if the helm had been put a-lee on seeing the danger, the ship would have cleared it. Vashon was tried by court-martial and dismissed his ship. (1)

(1)   He was also dismissed the service, but was reinstated, and reached the rank of Captain on May 28th, 1802. W.L.C.

The wind freshened, the sea began to break with great force, and the leak rapidly increased on the pumps. There was no hope of saving the vessel, which fell over on her broadside; and the people were all got into the boats. They made sail with the schooner, to the south-west, and were very hospitably received on the island of Typing, or Myako-sima, by the inhabitants. Returning to Canton, arrangements were made for passages home, for officers and men, in the East India Company's ships.

Captain Broughton continued the survey in the small schooner with a select body of officers and men. His operations embraced an examination of the Pescadores and Lu-Chu Islands, and of the southern and eastern coasts of Japan; and in August 1797, he was again off the island of Yesso. Passing through the Strait of Sangaar, the little schooner was taken up the east coast of Yesso and Saghalien to latitude 52d north Captain Broughton came to the conclusion that he would be unable to pass through the narrow strait into the sea beyond. On September 16th, therefore, he turned to the south, along the western side of the Gulf of Tartary, a name given by Broughton on the 24th. He examined the coast of Corea, and anchored in the harbour of Chosan, where he was able to learn something of Corea and its inhabitants.

Proceeding southwards in October, Broughton found himself among the cluster of islands off the south coast of Corea, one of which is Port Hamilton; and he surveyed the large island of Quelpart. The only chart he had on board was that by van Kuelen, which was of little use as a guide; and his surveys were laid down without aid from other sources. The little schooner returned from her adventurous voyage, and anchored safely in Macao Roads on November 27th, 1797. Captain Broughton and his officers then took passages to England, arriving in February 1799, after an absence of four years. The narrative of his voyage was published in 1804.

The most important results of Captain Cook's voyages of discovery were the colonisation of Australia and New Zealand, and the establishment of large civilised communities of English race in the southern hemisphere. On January 19th, 1788, nine years after the great navigator's death, Captain Arthur Phillip arrived at Botany Bay in H.M. brig *Supply*, followed by Captain John Hunter in the *Sirius* with six transports and three store ships. (1)

(1)   Phillip flew a broad pennant as commodore of the expedition, and left England in the *Sirius* with Hunter as his captain, Lieutenant Henry Lidgbird Ball commanding the *Supply*; but on November 25th, 1787, Phillip shifted his broad pennant to the *Supply*, and proceeded, leaving Hunter, in the *Sirius*, to follow. The six transports were the *Scarborough, Lady Penrhyn, Friendship, Charlotte, Prince of Wales*, and *Alexander*, having on board convicts guarded by marines. The three store ships were the *Golden Grove, Fishburn*, and *Borrowdale*. W.L.C.

Soon after wards they removed to Port Jackson, a much better harbour three leagues to the northward, where the town of Sydney was founded. Captain Phillip was the first Governor of New South Wales. Early in 1795, Captain Hunter arrived at Sydney with H.M.S. *Reliance* and *Supply*, to relieve Captain Phillip. On board the *Reliance* there was a young midshipman whose ardour for discovery secured for him the illustrious position of the foremost maritime explorer of Australia.

The name of this midshipman was Matthew Flinders. Born in 1774 at Donington, near Boston, in Lincolnshire, where his father was a medical man, young Flinders was filled with a longing to go to sea by having read *Robinson Crusoe*. The boy succeeded in learning navigation, and at length he was allowed to join the Navy in 1790 on board the *Scipio*, 64, Captain Thomas Pasley, at Chatham. He served in the *Providence* with Bligh, in the second voyage to Tahiti, to transport plants of the bread-fruit to the West Indies, and he was in the *Bellerophon* at the battle of the 1st of June 1794.

Arriving at Port Jackson in the *Reliance* in September 1795, Flinders soon found that there was no survey of the coast beyond Captain Cook's general chart. He at once conceived a project to supply the deficiency. In Mr. George Bass, the surgeon of the *Reliance*, he had the good fortune to find a friend whose ardour for discovery was equal to his own. Flinders and Bass determined to complete the examination of the coast of New South Wales, by all such opportunities as the duties of the ship, and the means at their disposal, would admit.

CAPTAIN MATTHEW FLINDERS, R.N.

The plans of the young explorers were discouraged by the authorities. They, however, had resolution and perseverance. All official help and countenance were withheld. But they managed, by their own unaided exertions, to equip a small boat called the *Tom Thumb* (1) and they sailed in her with a crew consisting of themselves and one boy. In their first voyage they explored for a considerable distance the George River, which falls into Botany Bay. Their second enterprise was to examine a large river, which was said to fall into the sea to the south of Botany Bay.

(1)   She was but eight feet long. (compilation), *Naval Chronicle*, Volume XXXII page 181. W.L.C.

Leaving Port Jackson on March 25th, 1795, Flinders and Bass sailed along the coast until, in the first watch of the 29th, a gale of wind sprang up from the south. In a few minutes the waves began to break. The danger to which the little boat was exposed, was increased by the darkness of the night, and the uncertainty of finding any place of shelter. Flinders steered with an oar, and it required the utmost care to prevent the boat from broaching to. A single wrong movement, or a moment's inattention, would have sent them to the bottom. Bass kept the sheet in his hand, drawing in a few inches occasionally when he saw a particularly heavy sea following. The boy was kept constantly at work baling out. After running for a hour in this critical situation, some breakers were distinguished ahead. The boat's head was brought to the wind at a favourable moment, sail and mast were got down, and the oars were got out. Pulling towards the reef during the intervals of the heaviest seas, they found that it terminated in a point and in a few minutes they were in smooth water under its lee. Such were the perils that the ardent explorers gallantly faced in the cause of geographical discovery.

In 1798, Bass undertook a voyage to the southward of Port Jackson in a whale boat with a crew of five convicts. He explored six hundred miles of coastline. In this open boat, exposed during the greater part of the time to very tempestuous weather, Bass persevered until he had discovered the entrance to the strait which now bears his name, separating Australia from Tasmania. This feat has few equals in the annals of maritime enterprise.

The zeal of Flinders (1) and Bass was at length rewarded. The Governor of New South Wales gave them the use of the *Norfolk*, a sloop of twenty-five tons with authority to complete the discovery of Bass's Strait. They had a good crew of eight naval volunteers, and twelve weeks' provisions. Sailing from Port Jackson on the 7th of October 1798, they thoroughly explored the coasts of Tasmania and the adjacent islands, where seals and birds abounded.

(1)   Flinders was made a lieutenant in 1798, a commander on February 16th, 1801, and a captain on May 7th, 1810.

Bass landed on one islet where he had to fight his way with the seals up the hill side; and, when he arrived at the top, he was obliged to make a path with his club amongst the albatrosses. These birds were sitting on their nests and covered the surface of the ground.

Flinders made regular astronomical observations throughout this very important voyage, and he returned to Port Jackson on the 11th of January

THE ROYAL NAVY   161

1799. The main result of the voyage was the complete examination of the strait between Australia and Tasmania. At the special request of young Flinders, it received, from Governor Hunter, the name of Bass's Strait. Flinders made one more exploring voyage to the northward of Port Jackson, before returning to England on board the *Reliance* in 1800.

When the charts based on the discoveries of Flinders and Bass were published, men of science were strongly impressed with the great importance of completing the work, and making a thorough examination of all the coasts of Australia. Sir Joseph Banks, the President of the Royal Society, submitted a plan to the Government; and it was decided that such a voyage should be undertaken. The right man was selected to do the work. Young Flinders was appointed to the command.

In January 1801, Flinders took command of the *Investigator*. (1) a north country-built ship of 334 tons, closely resembling the vessels employed in Captain Cook's voyages. Crowds of volunteers eagerly came forward for the service. The instructions were to examine first the south coast of Australia from King George's Sound to Bass's Strait, then the north-west coast, then the Gulf of Carpentaria and the coast to the westward. The instructions were signed by Lord Saint Vincent, Captain Thomas Troubridge, and Captain John Markham. They were accompanied by extracts from a memoir by Mr. Alexander Dalrymple (2) on the winds and weather. A passport was also granted by the French government, promising protection to a voyage undertaken solely for the advancement of science.

(1)   Ex-*Xenophon.*
(2)   The hydrographer.

There were two lieutenants on board, one being Samuel William Flinders, the commander's brother. The master was John Thistle, and there were eight midshipmen, including the future Sir John Franklin. The astronomer was John Crossley, and the botanist was Robert Brown, so well-known afterwards, in the scientific world, as the "Princeps Botanicorum." On the 18th of July 1801, the expedition sailed from Spithead, and, using Vancouver's chart, the *Investigator* was anchored in King George's Sound on the 9th of December.

The voyage was continued along the south coast of Australia in January 1802, and a careful survey was made from King George's Sound to Port Phillip. The new discoveries included the great Gulfs of Spencer and

Saint Vincent; and the surrounding coasts, which were all laid down with remarkable accuracy. It was near Thistle Island, at the entrance of Spencer Gulf, that Mr. Thistle the master, and a young midshipman named Taylor, were lost by the capsizing of a cutter. Commander Flinders deplored the death of the master, who had served with him in his previous voyage round Tasmania and was a most valuable officer.

The numerous Lincolnshire names, including Donington and Spilsby the birthplaces of Flinders and Franklin, given to points on the coast, show from what county the commander hailed.

On April 27th, the *Investigator* anchored at Port Phillip, which had been discovered and named ten weeks earlier by Lieutenant James Murray, who had come from Port Jackson in the *Lady Nelson*, brig. Flinders, however, made a complete examination of this great sheet of water.

The *Investigator* arrived at Port Jackson on the 9th of May 1802, all on board being in better health and spirits than when they left Spithead; for Flinders promoted the happiness of the men by strict discipline combined with kindly sympathy and consideration; and health was preserved by closely following the system of Captain Cook — cleanliness, wholesome food, and free circulation of air in the messing and sleeping place. An observatory was temporarily established at Port Jackson, where young Franklin was appointed assistant. The brig, *Lady Nelson*, commanded by Lieutenant Murray, was placed under the orders of Commander Flinders at Port Jackson.

In July 1802, the examination of the coast to the northward was commenced, as well as of the Barrier Reef, of which Flinders wrote an interesting description. In October, he proceeded onwards to Torres Strait and the Gulf of Carpentaria; but the ship was in a most unseaworthy condition. It was found that most of the timbers were rotten, and that, even with fine weather, she would not hold together for more than six months. Nevertheless Flinders continued the survey for some time longer, as far along the north coast of Australia as Melville Bay. In June 1803, he returned to Port Jackson.

The *Investigator* was quite unfit for further use. Old, crazy, and leaky when she was bought, she was a vessel such as, in our days, would not be deemed fit for the business of a collier. It was a school of hardship and rough work, yet full of interest for an ardent young sailor. It was in discovering many a reef and island, and many a mile of coast line, that

THE ROYAL NAVY 163

John Franklin's mind became imbued with that sincere love of geographical discovery which marked his career through life. Flinders was the example, and the Australian survey was the nursery which reared one of the greatest of our Arctic navigators, the discoverer of the North-West Passage. Able, brave, and modest, Flinders was exactly the man to awaken similar qualities in his officers.

The *Investigator* was condemned, and a small vessel named the *Porpoise* was hired to take the officers and men to England. On the 10th of August 1803, she sailed from Port Jackson, homeward bound with two other vessels in company, the *Bridgewater* and *Cato*. In the evening of the 17th, all the ships being still in company, and going about eight knots under double-reefed topsails, breakers were seen ahead from the forecastle of the *Porpoise*. The helm was immediately put down, but she missed stays, and in another minute was carried among the breakers. Striking upon a coral reef, she took a fearful heel over on her beam ends, the foremast going over the side at the second or third shock. Soon the hold was full of water, but luckily she went over with the upper deck away from the surf. The *Cato* struck on the reef about two cables' length from the *Porpoise*, fell over towards the surf, and her masts went by the board. The *Bridgewater* escaped, and her dastardly master — his name was Palmer — made sail, leaving his consorts to their fate.

During the night, Commander Flinders and his first lieutenant, Robert Merrick Fowler, employed the people in making a raft and securing water and provisions on it. The *Cato*, having fallen over to windward with her deck exposed to the waves, the decks were torn up and everything was washed away. The only safe place for the unfortunate crew was in the port fore chains, where they were all crowded together. In this situation, some clinging to the chain plates and dead eyes, others holding to one another, they passed the night. With daylight there appeared a dry sandbank about half a mile distant, sufficiently large to receive the shipwrecked people and such provisions as could be saved. The *Porpoise*'s boats were brought as near to the *Cato* as possible, the crew jumping from the fore chains and swimming to them through the surf. All got safe to the boats except three young lads, who were drowned. All next day the people worked hard, landing water and provisions on the sandbank. The ships soon broke up, but two boats were saved.

Commander Flinders took command of the combined ships' companies. He resolved to lay down two decked boats, capable of conveying all the shipwrecked people to Port Jackson, and also to send the cutter for assistance. The latter service would be one of great danger, and Flinders, therefore, resolved to perform it himself. He started on the 25th of August with a crew of fourteen men, and, after a perilous voyage of 750 miles in an open boat, he safely reached Port Jackson on September 8th. The ship *Rolla*, bound to China, was engaged to call at the reef, and take the shipwrecked people on board. This was successfully done; and young Franklin was one of those who went home by Canton.

Flinders was anxious to return to England direct with his charts and notebooks. He was supplied with a smaller schooner of twenty-nine tons, called the *Cumberland*. Passing through Torres Strait the little vessel sprang a leak, and Commander Flinders was obliged to put into Mauritius. There he was perfidiously made a prisoner of war by the French governor, contrary to the established usage of civilised nations, and to the written promise of the French government. The governor, whose name was Decaen, used the quibble that the passport was for the *Investigator*, not the *Cumberland*. (1)

(1)   He also charged Flinders with being an impostor. *Naval Chronicle*, Volume XIV page 332. W.L.C.

Surveyors and explorers, whose work is intended to benefit the whole world, are allowed to pass free in time of war, and this Decaen disgraced his country and himself by detaining Flinders. He was kept a prisoner for nearly seven years. It broke his heart. Released at length in June 1810, he returned to England in the following October. He was three years preparing the narrative of his voyage in two quarto volumes and an atlas, which were published in 1814. His work finished, the great surveyor died on July 19th of the same year. Flinders had extraordinary natural gifts as a surveyor. He was one of the first to investigate the deviation caused by the iron in ships. He it was who first suggested the name of Australia. He was a man of remarkable talent, but modest and unassuming, and though he was a strict disciplinarian, he was beloved by all who served under him.

With the voyage of Flinders ended, the long and glorious labours of naval discoverers, which had been continuous for forty years. From 1764 to 1804, Byron, Wallis, Carteret, Cook, Phipps, Vancouver, Broughton and Flinders had advanced geographical science, and made discoveries, the results of which are incalculable. They created and trained a school of marine surveyors, but they also trained Nelson, Riou, Vashon, and others, the heroes of Trafalgar and many other sea fights, and the saviours of their country. After 1804 there was a pause for some years, though, even during that time of stress, surveying was not entirely neglected. In 1818, Great Britain was once more aroused to a sense of her duties, as the leader of exploration and discovery among the nations of the earth.

INDEX OF CITATIONS IN VOLUME 4B
+
by

David Mignery
2023

This index represents my best effort at correctly identifying the sources cited in William Clowes' history. It should be used with caution. The works attributed to each author are only those which are referenced in this volume. Documents are listed with "anonymous" authors when the author's name is lost to history. "Compilations" are large collections of documents assembled by generally anonymous compilers.

Author	Particulars
Bonaparte	Napoleon Bonaparte, 1769 to 1821, French general, First Consul, Emperor of France as Napoleon I, Napoleon III ordered the publication of the *Correspondance de Napoleon Ier* in 1859.
Brenton	Edward Pelham Brenton, 1774 to 1839, British Royal Navy officer, author of *Naval History of Great Britain from the Year 1783 to 1822*, two volumes, 1837.
Charnock	John Charnock, 1756 to 1807, English, author of *History of Marine Architecture*, 1778.
Chevalier	Louis Edouard Chevalier, 1824 to 1907, unidentifiable French historian, author of *Histoire de la Marine Francaise dans la Guerre de 1778,* Paris 1877 and

THE ROYAL NAVY

Histoire de la Marine Francaise sous la Première République.

Clarke — James Stanier Clarke, 1766 to 1834, English cleric, naval writer, Royal navy chaplain, The Life of Admiral Lord Nelson, K.B co-author with John M'Arthur of *The Life of Admiral Lord Nelson, K.B.*, Fishers's edition.

Cochrane — Thomas Cochrane, 1775 to 1860, British admiral, mercenary, politician, commander-in-chief of the West Indies and North American stations, commander of the Chilean Navy and the Brazilian Imperial Navy, Earl of Dundonald, Marquess of Maranhao, author of *The Autobiography of a Seaman*, 1890 edition.

Graviere — Edmond Jurien de la Graviere, 1812 to 1892, French naval officer, author of *Souvenirs d'un Amiral.*

Guillon — Edouard Louis Maxime Guillon, 1849 to 1929, French historian and journalist, author of *La France et l'Irlande Pendant la Revolution.*

Hennequin — Joseph-Francois-Gabriel Hennequin, 1775 to 1842, French naval officer, biographer, author of *Biographie Maritime.*

James — William James, 1780 to 1827, British lawyer and military historian, author of *Naval History of Great Britain*, London 1886 edition, octavo.

Laughton — Sir John Knox Laughton, 1830 to 1915, British naval historian, Professor of Modern History at King's College London, co-founder of the Navy Records Society, author of *Studies in Naval History,* published by the Royal United Services Institute in 1896.

M'Arthur — John McArthur, 1755 to 1840, British naval officer, co-author with James Clarke of *The Life of Admiral Lord Nelson, K.B.*, Fisher's edition.

Marshall	John Marshall, 1784 to 1837, English biographer, officer in the Royal Navy, author of the *Royal Navy Biography*, 12 volumes 1823 to 1829.
Murray	probably Alexander Murray, 1775 to 1813, Scottish minister, philologist, linguist and biographer, Professor of Hebrew and Semitic languages at Edinburgh University, author of *Memoir of the Naval Life and Service of Admiral Sir Philip C.H.C. Durham*.
Nelson	Horatio Nelson, 1758 to 1805, the famed British admiral, author of *The Dispatches and Letters of Vice Admiral Lord Viscount Nelson*, edited by Nicholas Harris Nicolas.
Nicolas	Nicholas Harris Nicolas, 1799 to 1848, English antiquary, naval officer, barrister, member of the Society of Antiquaries and the American Antiquarian Society, author of the incomplete *History of the Royal Navy*. Editor of *The Dispatches and Letters of Vice Admiral Lord Viscount Nelson*.
Norman	Charles Boswell Norman, 1846 to 1926, British Army captain in the East India Company and writer on military matters, author of *The Corsairs of France*.
Osler	Edward Osler, unidentifiable author of *The Life of Admiral Viscount Exmouth*, 2nd edition.
Ralfe	James Ralfe, active 1820 to 1829, British naval historian, author of *The Naval Biography of Great Britain*.
Ross	John Lockhart Ross, 1777 to 1856, Scottish Royal Navy officer, polar explorer, writer, editor of *Memoires and Correspondence of Admiral Lord de Saumarez*.
Schomberg	Isaac Schomberg, 1753 to 1813, British Royal Navy officer, author of *Naval Chronology, or an Historical Summary of Naval and Maritime Events, From the Time of the Romans to the Treaty of Peace,* 1802 edition.

THE ROYAL NAVY

Steel
David Steel, 1763 to 1803, unidentifiable author of *Steel's Original and Correct List of the Royal Navy*.

Troude
Onisme-Joachim Troude, 1807 to 1886, French naval officer and naval historian, author of *Batailles Navales de la France*.

Tucker
Jedediah Stephens Tucker, unidentifiable author of *Memoirs of Admiral the Right Hon. the Earl of St. Vincent*.

Williams
Gomer Williams, unidentifiable author of the *History of the Liverpool Privateers and Letters of Marque with an Account of the Liverpool Slave Trade*. London, 1897.

(compilation)
Annual Register; a long-established reference work, written and published each year, which records and analyses the year's major events, developments, and trends throughout the world. It was first written in 1758 under the editorship of Edmund Burke, and has been produced continuously since that date.

(compilation)
Gazette de France; founded by Theophraste Renaudot and published its first edition on 30 May 1631. It progressively became the mouthpiece of one royalist faction, the Legitimists. Renamed *La Gazette,* it was finally discontinued in 1915.

(compilation)
Naval Chronicle; a British periodical published monthly between 1799 and 1818, founded by James Stanier Clarke and John McArthur.

(compilation)
Navy League Journal; a publication of the Navy League of Great Britain now merged with the Marine Society and Sea Cadets headquartered in London.

(compilation)
Navy List of the Royal Navy; annual lists of active and reserve officers, and biennial lists of retired officers published by the Royal Navy.

(compilation)
Public Record Office, Minutes of Courts Martial; records currently maintained by the British National Archives.

William Laird Clowes

THE ROYAL NAVY

GENERAL INDEX

A.

Abeille, ship, 39, 126.
Abergavenny, ship, 85.
Aboukir, 132.
Aboukir Bay, 131.
Aboukir, ship, 131.
Achille, ship, 120.
Actif, ship, 100, 119.
Active, ship, 102, 112.
Adam, Charles, 91, 139.
Adamant, ship, 76, 135.
Admiraal de Ruijter, ship, 144.
Admiraal Tjerk Hiddes de Vries,
        ship, 142.
Admiral de Vries, ship, 142.
Admiral Devries, ship, 142.
Admiral Rainier, ship, 145.
Admirals' Dispatches, 92.
Admiralty, 18, 36.
Admiralty, Lords of the, 151.
Admiralty, Secretary to the,
        152.
Advice, ship, 98.
Affleck, Thomas, 101.
Africa, 54, 71.
Africa, ship, 66, 147.

Africaine, ship, 86, 87, 96, 127,
        138.
Agamemnon, ship, 16.
Agassiz, Charles, 139.
Aggershuus, ship, 150.
Aigle, ship, 106, 129.
Aimable, ship, 43, 44, 77, 120,
        124.
Aix, Isle of, 54.
Ajaccio, 103, 117.
Alarm, ship, 32, 122, 123, 144,
        145, 147, 148.
Alassio Bay, 124.
Albacore, ship, 126.
Albanaise, ship, 79, 112.
Albion, ship, 104.
Alceste, ship, 34, 118, 134.
Alcide, ship, 124.
Alcmene, ship, 73, 132, 148.
Alcudia, ship, 17, 149.
Alderney, 101, 128.
Alert, ship, 99.
Alerte, ship, 25, 98, 121, 125,
        127, 134.
Alexander, ship, 100, 154.
Alexander, Thomas, 127.
Alexandre, ship, 123.

Alexandria, 59, 115, 132, 139, 140.
Alfred, ship, 42, 125, 126, 130.
Algeciras, 149.
Algeciras, Governor of, 75.
Algerine, 50.
Algoa Bay, 71, 72.
Alkmaar, ship, 142.
Allardyce, Alexander, 92.
Allegre, ship, 128.
Allemand, Zacharie Jacques Theodore, 16-18.
Alliance, ship, 33, 140.
Alliantie, ship, 33, 140.
Alligator, ship, 120.
Alms, James (2nd), 33, 110.
Amaranthe, ship, 110, 128, 138, 144.
Amazon, ship, 37, 38, 41, 104, 128.
Amboyna, ship, 141.
Ambuscade, ship, 63-65, 93, 95, 107, 132, 133.
Amelia, ship, 41, 68, 69, 87, 126.
America, 81, 122, 126, 130.
American, 19, 88.
American War, 93, 94.
Amerique, ship, 120.
Amethyst, ship, 85, 101, 118, 138, 139.
Amfitrite, ship, 76.
Amphion, ship, 46, 102.
Amphitrite, ship, 99, 144.
Ancona, 89, 113.
Andromache, ship, 50, 87.
Andromaque, ship, 44, 127.
Andromeda, ship, 79, 141.
Anemone, ship, 132.
Anguilla, 47.
Anson, ship, 35, 41, 51, 53, 54, 130, 133, 148.

Antelope, ship, 19.
Antigua, 123.
Antoinette, ship, 105.
Ape's Hill, 103.
Apollo, ship, 41, 61, 108, 126, 149.
Aquilon, ship, 131.
Arab, ship, 102, 123.
Aragonesa, ship, 147.
Arc, ship, 138.
Arcachon, 127.
Arctic Ocean, 159.
Ardent, ship, 99.
Arethusa, ship, 20, 21, 25, 51, 52, 129.
Arethuse, ship, 72, 102, 118, 135.
Argles, George, 83, 138.
Argo, ship, 33, 39, 66, 141, 147, 148.
Argonaut, ship, 29, 122.
Ariane, ship, 128.
Aristocrat, ship, 35, 125, 135.
Arrogant, ship, 45, 139, 143.
Arrogante, ship, 54, 130, 146.
Arrow, ship, 71, 144.
Artemise, ship, 32, 33, 90, 131.
Artois, ship, 25, 26, 35, 51, 105.
Asia, 152.
Asia, ship, 76.
Aspic, ship, 35, 125.
Assemblee Nationale, ship, 34, 124.
Assistance, ship, 116.
Astle, George, 143.
Astraea, ship, 30, 31, 33, 123.
Atalante, ship, 19, 22, 23, 110, 120, 128, 139.
Athenien, ship, 137.
Athenienne, ship, 126.
Atlantic Ocean, 59, 83, 86, 129, 145, 148.

THE ROYAL NAVY

173

Audacious, ship, 23.
Audierne Bay, 25, 51, 122.
Auguste, ship, 119, 121.
Augustus, ship, 114.
Aurora, ship, 121, 131, 147.
Aurore, ship, 118, 126, 138.
Austen, Francis William, 78, 136.
Australia, 153, 154, 156-160.
Australian, 159.
Auvergne, Corbet James d', 135.
Avenger, ship, 119.
Aventurier, ship, 58.
Aventuriere, ship, 132.
Avenza, 101.
Ayaldi, Captain Don T., 47.
Ayscough, John, 109.
Azores Archpelago, 147.

B.

Bab-el-Mandeb, Strait of, 73.
Babet, ship, 20, 21, 115, 120, 130.
Badger, ship, 130.
Baker, Joseph, 76.
Ball, Alexander John, 122.
Ball, Henry Lidgbird, 66, 133, 154.
Ballantyne, George, 20.
Ballard, Samuel James, 54, 135.
Banca, Strait of, 57, 106.
Banks, Joseph, 157.
Bannister, George, 62.
Bantry Bay, 128.
Barbados, Island of, 85, 126, 128, 138, 139, 141.
Barbary, 88.
Barcelona, 82, 149.
Barfleur, 127.
Barker, Scory, 105.

Barking Shelf, 108.
Barlow, Robert, 52, 86, 128, 130, 138.
Barnstaple Bay, 108.
Barrier Reef, 158.
Bartholomew, Philip, 112.
Barton, Robert, 47, 127.
Bas, Isle de, 58, 103, 104, 121, 135.
Bass, George, 154-157.
Basseterre, 44.
Bass's Strait, 156, 157.
Bastia, 99, 121.
Bataaf, ship, 142.
Batavian Republic, 141.
Batavier, ship, 145.
Bayntun, William Henry, 103.
Bayonnaise, ship, 63-65, 108.
Bazely, Henry, 77.
Beachy Head, 108.
Beauclerk, Lord Amelius, 39, 41, 127.
Beaufort, Francis, 83, 150.
Beaulieu, Captain, 67.
Beaulieu, ship, 44, 89, 90, 122, 126, 140.
Beaver, Philip, 137.
Bec du Raz, 131.
Becher, Alexander, 108.
Bedford, ship, 119.
Beens, Captain, 30.
Belette, ship, 119.
Belhomme, Lieutenant P.J.P., 20.
Belle Antoinette, 144.
Belle Isle, 68, 113, 124.
Belleisle, ship, 124.
Bellerophon, ship, 154.
Bellette, ship, 103.
Belliqueux, ship, 80, 137.
Bellona, ship, 122, 142.
Bellone, ship, 83, 132.

Benaud, Jean Marie, 26.
Bencoolen, 20.
Bengal, 133.
Bengal, Bay of, 67, 82.
Bennett, Richard Henry
Alexander, 99.
Berbice, ship, 103.
Beresford, John Poo, 32, 45.
Bergere, ship, 77.
Bergeret, Captain, 37.
Berkeley, Velters Cornwall, 50.
Bermuda Islands, 38, 51, 100,
126.
Bermuda, ship, 102.
Berry, Edward, 60-62.
Berwick, ship, 100.
Beschermer, ship, 144.
Betsy, ship, 41.
Bienvenue, ship, 119.
Bigot, Lieutenant J.G., 55.
Bingham, Joseph, 125.
Biscay, Bay of (the Bay), 10,
17, 27, 35, 52, 59, 97,
117, 126, 130-133, 136.
Biter, ship, 80.
Black Joke, ship, 134.
Blackwood, Henry, 57, 148.
Blair. J. le, 136.
Blake, John, 110.
Blanche, ship, 27-29, 48, 109,
119, 121, 122.
Bland, Loftus Otway, 58, 132,
133, 139.
Blazer, ship, 114.
Bligh, Richard Rodney, 100.
Bligh, William, 151, 154.
Blonde, ship, 41, 119, 126.
Bloom, ship, 104.
Boadicea, ship, 138, 150.
Bog Island, 105.
Boger, Coryndon, 137.
Bolador, ship, 146.

Bolton, William, 71, 144.
Bombarde, ship, 138.
Bombay Castle, ship, 81, 103,
137.
Bompard, Jean Baptiste
Francois, 13, 14.
Bona, 37.
Bona, Cape, 100.
Bonamy, Captain J.B., 91.
Bonaparte, Napoleon, 94, 162.
Bond, Francis Godolphin, 136.
Bonetta, ship, 115, 148.
Bonhomme Richard, ship, 64.
Bonne Citoyen, ship, 35, 125.
Boorder, James, 69.
Bordeaux, 54.
Bordelaise, ship, 72, 85, 138.
Borrowdale, ship, 154.
Boston, Lincolnshire, 154.
Boston, ship, 13-15.
Botany Bay, 153, 155.
Boudeuse, ship, 137.
Boulogne, 65.
Bourde, Captain, 55.
Bourdelaise, ship, 86.
Bourdichon, Captain, 77.
Bourdonnais, Captain la, 35.
Bourgneuf Bay, 137.
Bowen, James, 66, 147, 148.
Bowen, Richard, 47, 48, 95,
127, 145.
Bowyer, Robert, 43.
Boxer, ship, 80.
Boyle, Courtenay, 111.
Boyles, Charles, 22, 120.
Boyne, ship, 31.
Braak, ship, 144.
Braave, ship, 142, 145.
Brace, Edward, 133.
Brak, ship, 140, 143.
Brakel, ship, 141.
Brave, ship, 108, 142.

THE ROYAL NAVY

Bravoure, ship, 140.
Brazen, ship, 110.
Brazil, 80.
Brehat, 88.
Brenton, Edward Pelham, 14,
162.
Brenton, Jahleel, 75.
Brest, 10, 25, 29, 30, 36, 37, 41,
50, 54, 97, 100, 107,
111, 121, 122, 127, 128,
130, 133, 135, 138, 139.
Brest fleet (Escadre de
l'Atlantique), 50.
Breton, 34, 35.
Bridgewater, ship, 159.
Bridport, Lord (Alexander
Hood), 123.
Briggs, Joseph, 64.
Brighton, 110.
Brighton, ship, 104.
Brilliant, ship, 57, 58.
Brisac, George, 10.
Brisbane, Charles, 34, 89, 132.
Bristol, 50.
Britain, 52, 133.
Britannia, ship, 20.
British East India Company, 20,
22, 49, 52, 77, 80-82,
97, 137, 153.
British Royal Navy, 13, 16, 18,
22-24, 26, 29, 31, 33,
37-41, 46, 47, 49-51,
55, 57, 59, 63, 66, 68,
70, 71, 74, 76, 78, 80,
82, 83, 85, 87, 91, 94,
97, 140, 145, 150, 154.
Broederschap, ship, 143.
Broughton, William Robert,
104, 151-153, 160.
Brown, Mr., ship master, 64.
Brown, Robert, 157.
Bruillac, Captain A.A.M., 54.

Brule Greule, ship, 135.
Brune, ship, 34, 133.
Brutus, ship, 23, 35, 42, 124.
Bryer, Lieutenant W., 111.
Buchanan, John, 66.
Buckley, Master, 136.
Bulldog, ship, 89, 92, 113, 140,
147.
Bulteel, Rowley, 80, 137.
Burke, Henry, 137.
Burke, Walter, 90.
Burlton, George, 29, 122.
Burrard, Captain H., 120.
Burrowes, Alexander
Saunderson, 141.
Butt, Henry Samuel, 80, 111.
Butterfield, William, 59, 132.
Byng, George, 129.
Byron, John, 160.

C.

Ca Ira, ship, 102, 121, 122.
Cadiz, 47, 48, 51, 79, 106, 146,
148.
Cagliari Bay, 117.
Calcutta, 68.
Calcutta, ship, 77.
Calliope, ship, 51, 129.
Calpe, ship, 83.
Calvi, 121.
Calypso, ship, 76, 136.
Camaret Bay, 89.
Cambrian, ship, 136.
Came, Charles, 101.
Camel, ship, 71, 72.
Campbell, George, 117.
Campbell, Patrick, 79, 137.
Camperdown, 142.
Camperdown, ship, 142.
Camphaan, ship, 143.
Canada, ship, 54.

Canary Islands, 52.
Candia (Crete), 59.
Canes, Edward Jekyll, 115.
Canon, Captain A., 31, 52.
Canopus, ship, 131.
Cantabra, ship, 149.
Canton, 153, 160.
Capell, Thomas Bladen, 62, 114.
Capricieuse, ship, 137.
Carawang River, 145.
Caribe, River, 63.
Caribs, the, 35.
Carmagnole, ship, 17, 18, 79, 121.
Carmen, ship, 79, 148.
Caroline Island, 152.
Caroline, ship, 107, 119, 124.
Carpentaria, Gulf of , 157, 158.
Carpenter, Charles, 32, 125.
Carpenter, James, 78.
Carpentier, Lieutenant J.M.M., 39.
Carrere, ship, 139.
Cartagena, 47, 48, 56, 147.
Cartagena, Colombia, 113.
Cartagenoise, ship, 137.
Carteret Bay, 31.
Carteret, Philip, 160.
Carthew, James, 80, 111.
Carthew, William, 145.
Carysfort, ship, 23, 120, 127.
Castor, ship, 23, 99, 120, 142.
Cato, ship, 159.
Causse, ship, 140.
Cawley, John, 151.
Cayenne, 54, 59, 62, 85.
Censeur, ship, 101, 122.
Centaur, ship, 147.
Centaure, ship, 119.
Centurion, ship, 22, 26, 27, 145.
Cerbere, ship, 80, 137.

Cerberus, ship, 30, 74, 123, 129, 144.
Ceres, ship, 48, 49, 74.
Cerf Volant, ship, 127.
Cerf, ship, 78.
Cerigo, 55, 130.
Ceylon, 115.
Champain, William, 63.
Champion, ship, 140.
Chance, ship, 112, 150.
Channel Fleet, 80, 97.
Channel Islander, 24.
Channel Islands, 15, 20.
Chapman, William, 151.
Charente, ship, 54, 135.
Charleston, 19.
Charlotte Amalie, ship, 150.
Charlotte, ship, 76, 108, 135, 154.
Charming Molly, ship, 113.
Chatham, 154.
Chatham, ship, 151.
Cherbourg, 15, 21, 118.
Cheri, ship, 130.
Chesapeake Bay, 123.
Chesapeake Peninsula, 29.
Chevrette, ship, 89, 139.
Chichester, ship, 121.
Chiffonne, ship, 91, 139.
Childers, ship, 10, 58, 124, 127, 132.
China, 151, 160.
China Seas, 105.
Chosan, 153.
Church, Stephen George, 45.
Cigogne, ship, 36.
Circe, ship, 15, 19, 119, 145.
Citoyenne Francais, ship, 10.
Clark, William, 45.
Clear, Cape, 41, 99, 119, 126.
Cleopatra, ship, 87, 126.
Cleopatre, ship, 11-13, 93, 117.

THE ROYAL NAVY

Clyde, ship, 69, 70, 134, 149.
Cochrane, Alexander Forester
    Inglis, 32, 88, 89, 114,
    149.
Cockburn, George, 48, 146.
Cockchafer, ship, 115.
Coghlan, Jeremiah, 80, 137.
Cole, Francis, 23, 36.
Collard, Valentine, 104.
Collier, George Ralph, 91, 140.
Colnett, James, 103.
Colossus, ship, 107, 117.
Colpoys, John, 30, 122.
Comet, ship, 80, 111.
Commerce de Marseille, ship,
    118.
Concepcion, ship, 149.
Concorde, ship, 11, 20, 21, 36-
    38, 80, 98, 120, 137.
Confiance, ship, 82.
Confiante, ship, 131.
Conflagration, ship, 98.
Congalton, Andrew, 104.
Conil Bay, 51.
Conquerant, ship, 131.
Conseil, Captain, 27.
Constance, ship, 50, 128, 149.
Constitutie, ship, 144.
Constitution, ship, 113, 124.
Contest, ship, 109.
Convention National, ship, 118.
Convert, ship, 99, 118.
Cook, Edward, 53, 67, 68, 133.
Cook, H.B., engraver, 43.
Cook, James, 152-154, 157,
    158, 160.
Cooke, John, 127, 139.
Cooke, John (2nd), 50.
Copenhagen, 150.
Coquille, ship, 36, 132.
Corbett, Robert, 114.
Corcyre, ship, 54, 131.

Corea, 153.
Corfu, 61, 62, 133.
Corigiou, 132.
Cork, 22, 120.
Cormorant, ship, 103, 111, 125,
    127, 147.
Cornelie, ship, 68.
Correjou, 58.
Corsellis, Caesar, 113.
Corsica, 99, 137.
Corso, ship, 139, 145.
Cortez, ship, 148.
Corunna, 145, 147, 150.
Corvesse, ship, 139.
Cotes, James, 15, 18, 98.
Cotgrave, Isaac, 100.
Coudin, Captain J.D., 80.
Courageuse, ship, 134.
Courageux, ship, 103.
Courcy, Michael de, 62.
Coureuse, ship, 30.
Courier National, ship, 32, 123.
Courier, ship, 26, 27, 69, 120,
    134.
Courtenay, George William
    Augustus, 13, 14.
Crache Feu, ship, 123.
Cracker, ship, 145.
Cracraft, William Edward, 27,
    100.
Crash, ship, 69, 107, 143.
Crescent, ship, 15, 16, 23, 24,
    76, 93, 96, 118, 136,
    148.
Croasdaile, Thomas Pearson,
    113.
Crofton, Ambrose, 110.
Crossley, John, 151, 157.
Cruelle, ship, 136.
Cuba, 87, 108, 115.
Cuervo, ship, 148.
Culverhouse, John, 49.

Cumberland, ship, 160.
Cunningham, Charles, 69, 134, 149.
Curieuse, ship, 122, 138.
Curieux, ship, 85, 86, 117.
Curlew, ship, 103.
Curzon, Henry, 106.
Cybele, ship, 26, 27, 45.
Cygne, ship, 126.

D.

Dacres, Barrington, 113.
Dacres, Richard, 124.
Daedalus, ship, 66, 128, 133, 145.
Dalrymple, Alexander, 157.
Dame de Grace, ship, 69, 109, 134.
Damietta, 132.
Danae, ship, 59, 78, 111, 132, 135.
Dangereuse, ship, 134.
Danish (Dane), 77, 88.
Danish Royal Navy, 150.
Dannebrog, ship, 150.
Daphne, ship, 27, 53, 100, 130.
Dart, ship, 79, 137, 145.
Dashwood, Charles, 90.
Davers, Charles Sydney, 124.
Davis, Lewis, 69, 108.
De Braak, ship, 106, 140.
De Ruyter, ship, 144.
Debusk, William, 132.
Decade, ship, 62, 132.
Decaen, Charles Mathieu Isidore, 160.
Decasse, Captain, 32.
Decius, ship, 47, 127.
Decouverte, ship, 129.
Dedaigneuse, 85, 92, 136.
Defence, ship, 137.

Defender, ship, 145.
Delaware River, 106.
Delft, ship, 142.
Delorme, Captain, 32.
Demerara, 141.
Deniau, Francois A., 15.
Desgarceaux, Commodore, 20.
Desirade, 27.
Desiree, ship, 79, 80, 130, 137.
Destin, ship, 119.
Determine, ship, 139.
Deux Amis, ship, 109.
Deux Freres, ship, 134.
Diamond, ship, 25, 31, 34, 35, 37, 124, 125, 128, 150.
Diana, ship, 25, 74.
Diane, ship, 137.
Dick, Thomas, 138.
Dickson, Edward Stirling, 63.
Dictateur, ship, 119.
Dictionary of National Biography, 92.
Dido, ship, 32, 33, 122, 123.
Diego, ship, 137.
Digby, Henry, 73, 131, 147.
Diligence, ship, 112.
Diligente, ship, 136.
Diomede, ship, 26, 27, 101.
Dixon, John William Taylor, 106.
Dixon, Manley, 56, 134, 147.
Dobbie, William Hugh, 145.
Dolfijn, ship, 144.
Dolphin, ship, 144.
Dominica, 103.
Donegal, ship, 132.
Donington, 154, 158.
Donnelly, Ross, 141.
Dordrecht, ship, 142.
Doris, ship, 41, 89, 126, 128, 139.
Dortrecht, ship, 142.

THE ROYAL NAVY

Doudoux, Captain, 35.
Douglas, Andrew Snape, 117.
Dover, ship, 146.
Downman, Hugh, 54.
Draak, ship, 71, 144.
Dragon, ship, 136.
Drew, James, 106.
Drew, John, 129.
Droits de l'Homme, ship, 128.
Droits du Peuple, ship, 124.
Dromedary, ship, 111.
Druid, ship, 23, 128.
Drury, Thomas, 42, 125, 126.
Dryad, ship, 39, 41, 126.
Duckworth, John Thomas, 78,
148.
Duff, George, 77.
Duguay Trouin, ship, 22, 119,
120.
Duides, ship, 149.
Duif, ship, 143.
Duncan, Adam, 34, 39, 124,
141, 142.
Duncan, Henry (2nd), 114, 116.
Dundas, Thomas, 147.
Dundonald, Lord (Thomas
Cochrane), 92, 163.
Dungeness, 105.
Dunkirk (Dunquerque), 29, 116.
Dunn, William Dalling, 113.
Dunquerque Road, 79, 111, 137.
Duquesne, ship, 122.
Durand Linois, C.A.L., 36.
Duras, ship, 122.
Durham, Philip Calderwood,
148.
Durham, Philip Charles, 19, 35,
53, 54, 92, 130, 133.
Dutch, 33, 39, 62, 63, 69, 71,
94, 95, 101, 112.
Dutch coast, 101, 103.
Duvall, Thomas, 116.

E.

East Indies, 22, 83, 97, 107,
110, 120, 127, 132,
139-141, 143, 145.
Echo, ship, 141.
Echoue, ship, 124.
Éclair, ship, 84, 117, 123, 138.
Ecureuil, ship, 38, 126.
Edwards, Captain (unknown),
103.
Edwards, John, 14.
Edwards, John (2nd), 80, 111.
Edwards, Valentine, 110.
Egalite, ship, 129, 131.
Egero, 33.
Egmond, ship, 125.
Egypt, 84, 86, 108, 111, 114,
132.
Egypte, ship, 139.
Egyptien, ship, 76.
Egyptienne, ship, 135, 140.
Elba, Island of , 139.
Elbe, River, 65, 106, 108.
Elisabeth, ship, 45, 127.
Eliza, ship, 127.
Ellison, Joseph, 23.
Elphinstone, Charles, 104.
Elphinstone, George Keith, 93,
110, 140, 142.
Elphinstone, Thomas, 107.
Embroye, ship, 118.
Embuscade, ship, 13-15, 132,
142, 144.
Emerald, ship, 50, 79, 132.
Ems, River, 112, 145.
Endermo Bay, 152.
Endymion, ship, 146.
Engageante, ship, 20, 21, 120.
England, 10, 62, 153, 154, 157,
159, 160.

English, 13, 18, 68, 152, 153.
English Channel, 12, 29, 39, 97, 105, 108, 111, 119, 120, 122, 123, 129, 133, 136, 138, 139, 149.
Eolan, ship, 76.
Eole, ship, 76, 135.
Eperviere, ship, 129.
Epron, Jacques, 77.
Erqui, 35.
Esmeralda, ship, 74, 82, 149.
Esperance, ship, 29, 85, 122.
Espiegle, ship, 19, 69, 119.
Espion, ship, 23, 25, 29, 100, 110, 120, 122.
Espoir, ship, 58, 59, 66, 129, 132, 133, 147.
Essington, William, 121.
Etaples, 139.
Ethalion, ship, 73, 110, 148.
Etna, ship, 127.
Etoile, ship, 36, 125.
Etonnant, ship, 127.
Etourdie, ship, 35, 125.
Etrusco, ship, 106.
Europe, 10.
Eurus, ship, 141.
Eurydice, ship, 23.
Evans, Andrew Fitzherbert, 38, 126.
Evans, Henry, 127.
Eveille, ship, 124, 139.
Excellent, ship, 72, 135, 138.
Exeter, ship, 81, 137.
Expeditie, ship, 144.
Expedition, ship, 123.
Experiment, ship, 102.
Eyre, George, 99.

F.

Factory Island, 54.

Fairy, ship, 77, 78, 135.
Falcon, ship, 80, 111.
Falmouth, 140.
Farina, Cape, 106.
Faulknor, Jonathan (2nd), 11, 25, 109.
Faulknor, Robert (3rd), 27, 28, 121, 122.
Faulknor, William Humphrey, 113.
Favorite, ship, 125.
Feliz, ship, 147.
Fellowes, Edward, 145.
Ferris, Solomon, 114.
Ferrol, 85, 148.
Field, Francis Ventris, 103.
Finisterre, Cape, 11, 21, 62, 73, 125, 132.
Firth of Forth, 141.
Fisgard, 50.
Fishburn, ship, 154.
Fishguard, 50.
Fishguard, ship, 50, 83, 128, 133, 136-138, 149, 150.
Fitton, Michael, 85.
Flamborough Head, 108.
Fleche, ship, 17, 91, 92, 101, 120, 140.
Flibustier, ship, 130.
Flinders, Matthew, 154-160.
Flora, ship, 20, 21, 25, 54, 55, 119, 130, 131, 148.
Florentina, ship, 79, 148.
Florida, 110.
Florida, Gulf of, 102, 147.
Flushing, 42.
Fly, ship, 116.
Flying Fish, ship, 101.
Foote, Edward James, 38, 55, 126, 131.
Forbes, Lieutenant R., 114.
Ford, John, 118.

THE ROYAL NAVY 181

Formidable, ship, 123.
Formosa, Island of, 152.
Forte, ship, 45, 67, 68, 93, 94, 95, 114, 133.
Fortune, ship, 69, 104, 108, 132, 140.
Fortunee, ship, 16, 119.
Fothergill, William, 72.
Foucaud, Captain, 34.
Fouchet, ship, 17.
Foudre, ship, 134.
Foudroyant, ship, 136.
Fouine, ship, 133.
Fourcaud, Captain, 47.
Fowke, George, 115.
Fowler, Robert Merrick, 159.
Fox, ship, 53, 104, 109, 128.
Fradin, Captain J.B.A., 39.
France, 10, 30, 53, 101, 105, 106, 123-125, 127, 129, 134, 135, 136.
France, First Consul of, 87, 162.
Franchise, ship, 80, 81.
Francois, Cape, 76, 108.
Franklin, John, 157, 158, 160.
Franklin, ship, 131.
Fraser, Percy, 102.
Frederick, Thomas Lenox, 101.
Freedom, ship, 129.
Frehel, Cape, 125, 135.
Fremantle, Thomas Francis, 37, 122, 125.
Frenay, Bay of, 31.
French, 10, 12-32, 34-47, 49-60, 62-73, 76-101, 104-106, 108, 109, 112-114, 117-140, 157, 160.
French Army, 84.
French Navy, 14, 46, 62, 76, 93, 94.
French Republic, 82.

French Republic, Directory of the, 55.
French Royalist, 19.
French Vendeens, 36.
French West Indies, 105.
Friendship, ship, 115, 154.
Fuengirola, 83.
Fulminante, ship, 114, 133.
Furet, ship, 65.
Furie, ship, 62, 63, 143.
Furieuse, ship, 138.
Fury, ship, 127.
Fusi-yama, 152.

G.

Gage, George Henry, 89.
Gage, William Hall, 147.
Gaillard, Captain, 11.
Gaite, ship, 51, 52, 129.
Galatea, ship, 25, 35, 36, 44, 129.
Galatee, ship, 24, 100, 123.
Galatie, ship, 144.
Galgo, ship, 76, 112, 145, 148.
Gallardo, ship, 146.
Gallipoli, 140.
Gamo, ship, 88, 95, 149.
Ganges, ship, 121.
Ganteaume, Honore, 113, 114.
Garland, ship, 84, 106, 138.
Garlies, Lord (George Stewart), 29.
Garonne River, 134.
Gaspard, Captain M.M.P., 69.
Gata, Cape de, 145.
Gay, Captain, 16.
Gazette de France, 92, 165.
Gelderland, ship, 144.
Gelijkheid, ship, 142.
Gell, John, 118.
General Brune, ship, 139.

General Leveau, ship, 127.
Genereux, ship, 59-61, 107, 135, 137.
Genie, ship, 126.
Genoa, 34, 118, 122, 136.
Genoese, 58, 132, 135.
Gentille, ship, 31, 123.
George River, 155.
George, ship, 106.
Gibraltar, 75, 77, 86, 98, 139, 148, 149.
Gibraltar, Governor of, 75.
Gibraltar, ship, 148.
Gibson, John, 104.
Gier, ship, 71, 141, 144.
Gilbert, Thomas, 80.
Gilbraltar, Strait of, 89.
Gipsy, ship, 137.
Gironde River, 44, 54, 63.
Glatton, ship, 42, 94.
Glenmore, ship, 77.
Gloire, ship, 30, 31, 123.
Goelan, ship, 76.
Goeland, ship, 76, 117.
Golden Grove, ship, 154.
Goliath, ship, 132.
Golondrina, ship, 147.
Gooch, Samuel, 71.
Good Hope, Cape of, 133, 141.
Goodwin Sands, 110.
Gore, John, 101, 135.
Gore, John (2nd), 73.
Gormer, (unknown), 107.
Gossett, Abraham, 35.
Gott, Thomas, 103.
Gourly, John, 103.
Gower, Edward Leveson, 102, 139.
Grampus, ship, 108.
Grand Cayman Island, 99.
Granger, William, 72.
Graviere, P. Jurien de la, 80, 81.

Great Britain, 160, 161.
Great Britain, King of, 12, 14, 25.
Greenock, 141.
Grenada, 35, 145.
Grey, Edward, 135.
Grey, George, 31, 101.
Grey, Henry, 108.
Grindall, Richard, 122.
Groix, 122.
Groningen, 143.
Growler, ship, 105.
Guadaloupe, ship, 120.
Guadalupe, ship, 147.
Guadeloupe, 27, 43, 53, 120, 130, 137.
Guadeloupe, Island of, 84.
Guerin, Daniel, 102.
Guernsey, 115.
Guernsey Road, 24.
Guerrier, ship, 131.
Guiana, 70.
Guieysse, Captain P., 91.
Guillaume Tell, ship, 136.
Guine, Enseigne J.F., 51.
Guion, Gardiner Henry, 108.
Gunter, Henry, 108.
Gurupano, 63.

H.

Haarlem, ship, 142.
Haggitt, William, 110.
Haien, ship, 150.
Halgan, Captain, 72.
Halifax, 105.
Halkett, Peter, 108, 149.
Hallowell, Benjamin, 79, 103, 114, 132.
Halsted, Laurence William, 39, 136, 141.
Hamadryad, ship, 51, 107, 146.

THE ROYAL NAVY 183

Hamilton, Charles, 58, 84.
Hamilton, Edward, 74, 75, 148.
Hamilton, John, 81.
Hamilton, Lieutenant J., 112.
Hamline, Daniel, 109.
Hamoaze, 102.
Hamon, Captain, 85.
Hannibal, ship, 31, 114, 123.
Hanson, James, 110.
Hardy, Thomas Masterman, 49, 129.
Hardyman, Lucius Ferdinand, 114.
Hare, Charles, 98.
Hargood, William, 11, 98.
Harlingen, 71.
Harlingen, ship, 141.
Harpy, ship, 77, 78, 135.
Harriette, ship, 129.
Hart, George, 108.
Harvey, Eliab, 25.
Harvey, Henry, 146.
Harvey, John (2nd), 100.
Hasard, ship, 16, 17.
Hasborough Sand, 114.
Hasty, ship, 145.
Haswell, Lieutenant, 109.
Havana, 76, 112, 149.
Havick, 142.
Havik, 112, 142.
Havre, 37.
Hawaii, 152.
Hawaii, Kamehameha I of, 152.
Hayes, George, 102.
Hayward, Thomas, 105.
Hazard, ship, 59, 132.
Hebe, ship, 31, 123.
Hector, ship, 143.
Heldin, 144.
Helena, ship, 103, 143.
Hennah, William, 138.
Henry, Cape, 32, 45.

Herbert, Charles, 68.
Hercule, ship, 130.
Hercules, ship, 142.
Hermes, ship, 104, 141.
Hermione, ship, 74, 105, 128, 148.
Hermitte, Captain l', 71, 76.
Heros, ship, 119.
Heureaux, ship, 131, 139.
Hillyar, James, 82, 149.
Hind, ship, 19, 149.
Hirondelle, ship, 31, 133, 134.
Hobart, ship, 121.
Hoche, ship, 132.
Hoedic Island, 69.
Holland, 107-109, 145.
Hollingsworth, John, 105.
Holsteen, ship, 150.
Holt, (unknown artist), 28.
Holyhead, 104.
Honduras, 98.
Honduras, Bay of, 102.
Hood, Alexander, 130.
Hood, Lord, 118, 120, 121.
Hood, Samuel, 134.
Hood, Samuel (2nd), 19, 20.
Hope, George, 132.
Hope, ship, 105.
Horton, Joshua Sydney, 77.
Hotham, William, 122, 124.
Houghton, ship, 20.
Hound, ship, 24, 100, 112.
Howe, Richard Lord, 23, 120.
Huggett, William, 105.
Hullin, Captain, 52.
Hunt, Anthony, 99.
Hunt, Anthony (2nd), 37.
Hunter, John, 154, 157.
Hunter, ship, 105.
Hussar, ship, 32, 103, 123.
Hussard, ship, 134.
Hyaena, ship, 11, 98.

Hydra, ship, 131.
Hyene, ship, 52.
Hyeres, 120, 126.
Hyeres Bay, 99.
Hyeres Roads, 40.

I.

Illustrious, ship, 101.
Immortalite, ship, 85, 133.
Impatiente, ship, 127.
Imperieuse, ship, 118.
Impetueux, 100, 120, 130, 136, 137.
Impregnable, ship, 19, 109.
Inagua, 115.
Incendiary, ship, 113, 128.
Inconnue, ship, 23, 120.
Inconstant, ship, 37, 99, 117, 122, 125.
Inconstante, ship, 18, 19, 118.
Incorruptible, ship, 42, 79.
Indefatigable, ship, 37, 38, 52, 59, 83, 96, 126, 128, 129, 132, 138.
Index to James's Naval History, 92.
Indian Ocean, 66.
Infanta Amalia, ship, 148.
Infoedstretten, ship, 150.
Insolente, ship, 136.
Intrepid, ship, 121, 125.
Investigator, ship, 157-160.
Invincible, ship, 114.
Iphigenia, ship, 18, 19, 115, 118, 119.
Iphigenie, ship, 73, 122, 135.
Ireland, 49, 72, 99, 107, 126-129, 132, 133, 140, 146.
Iris, ship, 10, 119, 145.
Irresistible, ship, 38, 50, 146.
Irwin, George, 106.

Isis, ship, 33, 140.
Italy, 92.

J.

Jacobin, ship, 121.
Jalouse, ship, 128.
Jamaica, 76, 97, 99, 120, 149.
Jamaica, ship, 125.
James, William, 10, 15, 40, 64, 68, 92, 163.
Janus, ship, 141.
Japan, 151-153.
Jardines Archipelago, 115.
Jason, ship, 52, 54-56, 107, 115, 131, 141.
Java, 49.
Jean Bart, ship, 26, 27, 30, 123.
Jeddah, 114.
Jenkins, Henry, 63-65, 107.
Jersey, Island of, 31, 112.
Jervis, John, 40, 41, 48, 119-121, 146.
Joliff, Captain, 66.
Jones, Charles, 126.
Juan de Fuca Strait, 152.
Jump, Robert, 113.
Juno, ship, 19, 20, 39, 143.
Junon, ship, 134.
Jupiter, ship, 72, 142.
Juste, ship, 120.
Justice, ship, 140.
Justine, ship, 128.
Jylland, ship, 150.

K.

Kamehameha I of Hawaii, 152.
Kangaroo, ship, 89, 133, 149.
Karakakoa Bay, 152.
Kauai, Island of, 152.

THE ROYAL NAVY

Keats, Richard Goodwin, 25, 35, 44, 138.
Keith, Baron and Viscount (George Elphinstone), 93, 110, 140, 142.
Kemphaan, ship, 143.
Kent, Henry, 146.
Kent, ship, 82.
Kerr, Mark Robert, 147.
Key Bokell, 98.
King George's Sound, 157.
King, James, 151.
King, John, 39.
King, Richard, 143.
King, Richard (2nd), 62.
Kingfisher, ship, 107.
Kingsale, 102.
Kite, ship, 141.
Kittoe, Hugh, 100.
Komeet, ship, 140.
Kronborg, ship, 150.
Kuelen, Johannes van, 153.
Kurile Islands, 152.

L.

La Guaira, 105.
La Hougue, 101.
La Rochelle, 56.
La Selva, 69.
Lacedemonian, ship, 104.
Lacroix, Captain, 85.
Lady Jane, ship, 111.
Lady Nelson, ship, 158.
Lady Penrhyn, ship, 154.
Laforey, Francis, 23, 44, 120, 131.
Lahaina, 152.
Landolphe, Captain J.F., 80.
Land's End, 120.
Langstone, 109.
Lapwing, ship, 47, 127.

Larcom, Thomas, 149.
Laroque, Captain J.B.M., 50.
Latona, ship, 119.
Latreyte, Captain, 53.
Laurel, ship, 123, 142.
Laurette, ship, 139.
Lawford, John, 99.
Le Havre, 131.
Leander, ship, 59-62, 95, 107, 133.
Lebozee, Captain P.M., 70.
Leda, ship, 101, 117.
Lee, John, 71.
Lee, Richard, 116.
Leef, Thomas, 80, 111.
Leeward Islands, 97.
Legere, ship, 39, 41, 113, 126, 132, 136.
Leghorn (Livorno), 98, 110.
Leijden, ship, 144.
Lejoille, Captain, 59, 61, 62.
Lejoille, ship, 78.
Lennox, Charles, 49.
Leopard, ship, 117.
Leviathan, ship, 66, 78, 79.
Levrette, ship, 22.
Levrier, ship, 76, 135.
Liberte, ship, 32, 119, 120, 123.
Liberty, ship, 35, 125.
Liguria, ship, 58, 59, 132.
Ligurienne, ship, 78, 136.
Lijnx, ship, 145.
Limbi, ship, 143.
Limeno, ship, 150.
Lincolnshire, 154, 158.
Linois, Charles Alexandre Leon Durand, 22, 36, 89, 96, 114.
Linzee, Samuel Hood, 85, 101.
Lion, ship, 56, 57, 134, 136, 147.
Lions, Gulf of, 84.

Lisbon, 129, 146, 147, 148.
Lisbon Bar, 107, 110.
List Book, 92, 97.
Littlejohn, Adam, 100.
Lively, ship, 25, 29, 30, 96, 106, 122, 128.
Liverpool, 50.
Lizard Peninsula, 37, 126.
Lobb, William Granville, 76, 136, 148.
Loire, ship, 78, 133, 135.
London, 48, 74.
Long, Charles, 107.
Lorient, 30, 56, 72, 123, 130, 135.
Loring, John, 98.
Los Magellanes, ship, 146.
Loss Archipelago, 54.
Lowestoft, ship, 32, 33, 115, 123.
Lucas, Richard, 45, 119.
Lu-Chu Islands, 153.
Luke, William, 124.
Lukin, William, 138.
Lumsdaine, George, 10, 49, 129, 141.
Lurcher, ship, 114.
Lutine, ship, 109, 117, 118.
Lydiard, Charles, 40, 41.
Lys, ship, 119.

M.

Maarten Harpertzoon Tromp, ship, 142.
Macao, 152.
Macao Roads, 153.
Mackenzie, Adam, 69, 143.
Mackenzie, Kenneth, 138.
Mackey, Michael, 106.
Macnamara, James (2nd), 34, 40, 74, 126, 145.

Madagascar, 106.
Madeira, 77.
Magendie, Captain, 29.
Magendie, Commander J.J., 87.
Magicienne, ship, 127.
Magnanime, ship, 62, 132.
Mahe, 91.
Mahe Roads, 91.
Mahonesa, ship, 47, 145, 146.
Main, Dawson, 64.
Main, Robert, 84.
Maine, Gulf of, 45.
Mainwaring, Jemmet, 43, 115.
Maistral, Captain, 16.
Maitland, Frederick Lewis (2nd), 107.
Majestic, ship, 19, 128, 146.
Majorca, 66, 147.
Malabar, ship, 103.
Malaga, 83, 112, 147, 149.
Malays, 57.
Malcolm, Pulteney, 53, 128.
Malta, 19, 55, 137.
Malta, ship, 136.
Maltese, 55, 137.
Man, Robert (3rd), 118.
Manby, Thomas, 85, 138.
Manilla, 53.
Mansel, Robert, 86.
Mansfield, John Moore, 50.
Margaret, ship, 107.
Margarita Island, 63.
Maria Louise, ship, 141.
Marianne, ship, 133.
Marie Antoinette, ship, 105.
Marie Rose, ship, 134.
Marittimo, 55.
Markham, Clements, 151.
Markham, John, 123, 134, 157.
Marlborough, ship, 112.
Mars, ship, 130, 144.
Marseille, 135.

THE ROYAL NAVY

Marsouin, ship, 125.
Martin, George, 146.
Martin, George (2nd), 50.
Martin, ship, 112.
Martin, Thomas Byam, 39, 126,
    133, 149.
Martinique, 119.
Mason, Samuel, 105.
Mastiff, ship, 110.
Matilda, ship, 49, 121, 128.
Maui, Island of, 152.
Mauritius, 26, 35, 55, 66, 76,
    160.
Maxtone, Thomas, 102.
Maxwell, Keith, 90, 139.
Mayflower, ship, 136, 148.
McCarthy, William, 101.
Medee, ship, 10, 46, 47, 80, 81,
    97, 137.
Mediterranean Fleet, 40.
Mediterranean Sea, 32, 50, 58,
    79, 84, 86, 88, 97, 99,
    100, 102, 109, 112, 115,
    117, 122-125, 129, 131-
    136, 138, 139, 146-148.
Medland, T. engraver, 12.
Medusa, ship, 107.
Meduse, ship, 130.
Meermin, ship, 141.
Melampus, ship, 20, 21, 31, 123,
    127, 133.
Meleager, ship, 114.
Melpomene, ship, 16, 58, 84,
    121, 132, 138.
Melville Bay, 158.
Mercedes, ship, 74.
Mercure, ship, 131.
Mercurius, ship, 141.
Mercury, ship, 84, 89, 92, 138,
    139.
Meriton, Henry, 81.

Mermaid, ship, 35, 44, 55, 56,
    78, 124, 127, 136, 147.
Mexico, 73, 151.
Mexico, Gulf of, 109, 114, 149.
Miconi, 121.
Middleton, Robert Gambier, 32,
    54, 131, 148.
Miermin, ship, 141.
Mignonne, ship, 16, 17, 105,
    121.
Milbrook, ship, 83, 94.
Miller, George, 138.
Miller, Simon, 123, 124.
Milne, David, 32, 55, 81, 106,
    123, 131, 137.
M'Inerheny, John, 105.
Minerva, ship, 127, 144.
Minerve, ship, 16, 17, 32, 33,
    48, 49, 119, 123, 128,
    140, 146.
Minorca, 32, 147.
Minorca, ship, 134, 138.
Minotaur, ship, 82, 149.
Mitchell, Andrew, 143, 144.
Mitchell, William, 102.
Mitford, Henry, 128.
Mizen Head, 127.
M'Kenzie (Mackenzie),
    Kenneth, 84, 138.
M'Kinley, George, 35.
Modeste, ship, 118, 128.
Mona Passage, 137.
Monaco, 145.
Mondovi, ship, 55, 130.
Monnikendam, ship, 142.
Montagu, ship, 121.
Montalan, Captain G.S.A., 29.
Monterey, 152.
Montes, Commodore Don F.,
    76.
Montgomery, Augustus, 117.
Montreal, ship, 119.

Moore, Graham, 133.
Morant Keys, 102.
Morbihan, 83.
Morris, James Nicoll, 83, 106, 117.
Mortlock, Lewis, 65.
Moselle, ship, 34, 99.
Mosquito, ship, 101, 108, 118, 120.
Motherbank, the, 98.
Moultson, Jean, 39.
Mount Batten Point, 106.
Mudge, Zachary, 149, 151.
Mulet, ship, 118.
Mullon, Captain, 12, 13.
Mulso, William, 104.
Murray, George (2nd), 127.
Murray, George (3rd), 20, 107.
Murray, James, 158.
Murray, John, 115.
Murray, William Bowman, 64.
Mutine, ship, 35, 61, 62, 85, 125, 128.
Myako-sima (Typing Island), 153.
Mykonos, Island of, 24.

N.

Nagle, Edmund, 25, 26, 35, 105.
Naiad, ship, 54, 62, 73, 132, 148, 149.
Nancy, ship, 114.
Nankin River, 152.
Narcisse, ship, 121.
Narcissus, ship, 102.
Nassau, ship, 109.
Nautilus, ship, 20, 108.
Navy Records Society, 93, 163.
Navy, Commisioner of the, 33.
Neale, Harry Burrard, 50, 68.
Neapolitan, 118.

Negresse, ship, 134.
Negro, Point, 102.
Neirop, Meindert van, 62.
Nelson, Horatio, 16, 48, 59, 60, 62, 92, 124, 126, 131, 135, 150, 160, 164.
Nemesis, ship, 79, 101, 125.
Neptune, ship, 59, 107, 122, 132, 136.
Neptuno, ship, 150.
Nereide, ship, 52, 53, 130.
Nest, Isle of, 100.
Netley, ship, 136.
Neuf Thermidor, ship, 122.
Neuwerk, 65.
Neville, Martin, 90.
Nevin, Lieutenant C.J., 112.
New Jersey, 14.
New Providence, 102.
New South Wales, 154.
New South Wales, Governor of, 154, 156.
New York, 13, 14.
New Zealand, 153.
New, Thomas, 115.
Newcombe, Francis, *.
Newcome, Henry, 22, 120.
Newfoundland, 23, 99, 116, 117.
Newman, James Newman, 55, 78.
Nice, 99.
Nicolson, James, 134.
Nielly, Joseph Marie, 23, 99.
Nieuwe Diep, 143.
Niger, ship, 23, 31, 38, 82, 126, 149.
Nile, Battle of the, 59-61.
Nile, ship, 83, 138.
Nimrod, ship, 76, 135.
Ninfa, ship, 51, 146.
Niobe, ship, 137.

THE ROYAL NAVY

189

Niphon, 152.
Nochette, ship, 136.
Nodin, a French Royalist, 19.
Noirmoutier Island, 79.
Nonsuch, ship, 20.
Nootka Sound, 152.
Norfolk, ship, 156.
Norman, William, 80.
North America, 127.
North Atlantic Ocean, 59.
North Pacific Ocean, 151, 152.
North Sea, 42, 97, 103, 105, 112, 124, 128, 141, 143.
Northumberland, ship, 120, 137.
North-West Passage, 159.
Norway, 33, 140, 141.
Nova Scotia, 97.
Nuestra Senora de los Dolores, ship, 85.
Nuestra Senora del Carmen, ship, 109, 148.
Nuestra Senora del Rosario, ship, 146.
Nyborg, ship, 150.
Nymphe, 11-13, 19-21, 50, 117, 119, 128.

O.

Oahu, Island of, 152.
Oakes, George, 145.
O'Bryen, James, 58.
Oiseau, ship, 13, 29, 85, 92, 117, 138.
Oliver, Robert Dudley Oliver, 136.
Oneglia, 126.
Onslow, Richard, 141.
Oporto, 83, 104.
Orestes, ship, 110.
Orient, ship, 131.
Oropesa, 89, 149.

Orpheus, ship, 22, 120, 143.
Ortegal, Cape, 74, 85, 113.
Osborn, Edward Oliver, 139.
Osborn, Samuel, 26.
Oswald, James, 102.
Otway, Robert Waller, 32, 44, 123.
Overijssel, ship, 141.

P.

Pacific Ocean, 104, 151, 152.
Paget, William, 24, 121.
Paimpol, 88.
Pajaro, ship, 147.
Pakenham, Edward, 57, 106, 121, 143.
Pallas, ship, 77, 78, 106, 135.
Palmer, ship's master, 159.
Palmer, William, 84.
Pandore, ship, 124.
Pandour, ship, 105, 124, 143.
Papillon, ship, 54.
Papin, Captain, 25.
Parker, Christopher (2nd), 119.
Parker, George, 146.
Parker, Henry Harding, 104.
Parr, Thomas, 103, 141.
Pasley, James, 90.
Pasley, ship, 90.
Pasley, Thomas, 154.
Pater, Charles Dudley, 102.
Patriote, ship, 23.
Paulet, Henry, 30, 123, 129.
Paz, ship, 82, 149.
Peachey, Francis, 84.
Peard, Shuldam, 69, 113.
Pearl, ship, 54, 135.
Pegasus, 141.
Pelican, ship, 46, 47, 94, 130.
Pellew, Edward, 12, 13, 20, 25,

36, 37, 52, 59, 80, 92, 117, 121, 126, 129, 132.

Pellew, Israel, 12, 13, 46, 93, 102.

Pembroke, 50.

Penelope, ship, 18, 19, 109, 117, 118, 136, 148.

Penguin, ship, 86, 140.

Penmarck Point (the Penmarcks), 25, 38, 51, 55, 79, 102, 110, 121, 123, 126, 128.

Pensee, ship, 43, 44.

Percante, ship, 38, 125.

Perdrix, ship, 123.

Perla, ship, 149.

Perle, ship, 118.

Perree, Jean-Baptiste, 69.

Perseus, ship, 145, 147.

Peru, 150.

Pescadores Islands, 153.

Petit Diable, ship, 129.

Petite Aurore, ship, 118.

Petrel, ship, 78, 107, 136, 147.

Pevrieu, Etienne, 20, 41.

Phaeton, ship, 35, 54, 83, 117, 119, 124, 125, 133, 149.

Philippine Islands, 53.

Phillip, Arthur, 153, 154.

Philpot, V., 115.

Phipps, Constantine John, 160.

Phoebe, ship, 52, 53, 86, 87, 96, 128, 130, 138.

Phoenix, ship, 39, 79, 136, 140, 141.

Piercy, Richard, 24, 100.

Pierrepont, William, 62, 73.

Pigmy, ship, 98.

Pigot, Hugh (2nd), 105.

Pigot, ship, 20, 97.

Pijl, ship, 141.

Pilfold, John, 136.

Pique, ship, 27-29, 55, 56, 78, 95, 106, 122, 131, 135.

Pitot, Captain, 42, 81.

Placentia, ship, 99.

Plampin, Robert, 115.

Pletsz, Bartholomeus, 62.

Pluto, ship, 117.

Plymouth, 46, 74, 141.

Plymouth Sound, 114.

Pockock, Nicholas, 12.

Pole, Charles Morice, 117.

Pollexfen, John, 107.

Polyphemus, ship, 49, 128, 141.

Pomona, ship, 56.

Pomone, ship, 20-22, 35, 51, 52, 120, 122, 124, 130, 139, 140.

Pompee, ship, 118.

Pontevedra, 149.

Porpoise, ship, 148, 159.

Port au Prince, 103.

Port Hamilton, 153.

Port Jackson, 154-160.

Port Louis, 80, 135, 137.

Port Mahon, 87.

Port Mahon, ship, 79, 147.

Port Navalo, 83.

Port Phillip, 157, 158.

Port Royal, ship, 104.

Porte, Lieutenant la, 59.

Portlock, Nathaniel, 71, 144.

Porto Ferrajo, 103, 105.

Portsmouth, 15, 100.

Portugal, 107, 138, 146, 148.

Portuguese, 50.

Poulette, ship, 103, 118.

Poursuivante, ship, 79.

Powell, Samuel, 113.

Poyntz, Stephen, 76, 89, 135.

Praed, Bulkley Mackworth, 107.

Preneuse, ship, 71, 72, 76, 135.

Preston, d'Arcy, 48.

THE ROYAL NAVY

191

Prevoyante, ship, 32, 123.
Price, Charles Papps, 130.
Prima, ship, 136.
Prince Frederick, ship, 142.
Prince of Wales, ship, 154.
Princeps Botanicorum (Robert
    Brown), 157.
Princesa, ship, 145.
Princess Carlotte, ship, 134.
Princess of Orange, ship, 144.
Princess Royal, ship, 106.
Princess, ship, 140.
Proby, William Allen, Lord, 78,
    111, 134.
Proevesteen, ship, 150.
Prompte, ship, 32, 117, 123,
    147.
Proselyte, ship, 99, 115, 118,
    141.
Proserpina, ship, 56, 66.
Proserpine, ship, 36, 41, 56, 65,
    96, 108, 126, 132.
Providence, ship, 104, 121, 151,
    152, 154.
Prudente, ship, 26, 27, 45, 66,
    133.
Puerto Cabello, 74, 148.
Puerto Rico, 81, 123.
Puissant, ship, 118.
Pulliblank, Abraham, 98.
Pulling, George Christopher, 89.
Pulling, John King, 39, 126.
Pullock Harbour, 53.
Purchet, Captain, 50.
Pylades, ship, 69, 100, 143.
Pym, Samuel, 130.

Q.

Quartidi, ship, 121.
Quatorze Juillet, ship, 130.
Quebec, ship, 35, 125, 127.

Queen Charlotte, ship, 110.
Queenstown, 141.
Quelpart Island, 153.
Quiberon, 113.
Quiberon Bay, 138, 139.
Quid pro Quo, ship, 137.
Quimper River, 79.
Quinton, Cornelius, 113.

R.

Radelet, Captain G., 85.
Raffy, Lieutenant R.G., 58.
Railleur, ship, 78, 111.
Rainier, Peter, 49, 141.
Raison, ship, 32, 45, 123.
Ramage, Edward, 141.
Ramillies, ship, 102.
Ranger, ship, 52, 100, 129, 141.
Raper, Henry, 77.
Raposo, ship, 149.
Rassurante, ship, 42.
Rattler, ship, 149.
Rattlesnake, ship, 71, 72, 141.
Raven, ship, 106, 135.
Raynor, John, 111.
Raz, Pointe du, 35, 36, 121.
Real Carlos, ship, 149.
Rebecca, ship, 134.
Receviso, ship, 147.
Red Sea, 135.
Regeneree, ship, 45, 54, 57, 58,
    86, 140.
Regiment, Alsace, 64.
Regulus, ship, 145.
Reina Luisa, ship, 149.
Reliance, ship, 154, 157.
Renaud, Captain J.N., 77.
Renaud, Lieutenant G., 84.
Rendsborg, ship, 150.
Rennie, John, 114.
Renommee, ship, 42, 126.

Renou, Captain, 84.
Renown, ship, 137.
Reolaise, ship, 52, 83, 138.
Reprisal, ship, 121.
Republicain, ship, 121, 122,
    124.
Republicaine, ship, 23, 35, 42,
    70, 71, 120, 134.
Republique Triomphant, ship,
    130.
Republique, ship, 124.
Repulse, ship, 110.
Requin, ship, 29, 113, 122.
Resistance, ship, 22, 50, 57,
    106, 121, 128, 143.
Resolucion, ship, 149.
Resolue, ship, 20, 21, 124, 133.
Resolution, ship, 105.
Resource, ship, 127, 143.
Retaliation, ship, 74.
Retribution, ship, 74, 148.
Reunion, ship, 15, 16, 33, 93,
    95, 96, 103, 118, 132,
    140.
Revanche, ship, 39, 136.
Revenge, ship, 121.
Revolutie, ship, 142.
Revolutionary War, 94.
Revolutionnaire, ship, 25, 26,
    36, 37, 72, 73, 96, 119,
    121, 125.
Reybaud, Captain, 85.
Reynolds, George, 106.
Reynolds, Robert Carthew, 37,
    104, 130.
Rhe, Isle of, 124.
Rich, Commander T.W., 99.
Richer, Lieutenant J.B.E., 63,
    65.
Ridley, engraver, 75.
Rio de Janeiro, 137.
Riou, Edward, 121, 160.

Riouffe, Captain, 18.
Riviera, the, 78.
Rivington, Robert, 82.
Robinson Crusoe by Defoe,
    154.
Robinson, Charles, 100.
Robinson, J. Parker, 111.
Robust, ship, 50, 139.
Rochefort, 17, 69, 85, 123-125.
Rocky Point, 99.
Roebuck, ship, 141.
Rogers, Thomas, 84, 89, 138.
Rolla, ship, 160.
Rolles, Robert, 147, 148.
Romney, ship, 24, 121.
Romulus, ship, 146.
Rondeau, Captain J.M., 24.
Rosario, ship, 80, 111, 146.
Rose, Jonas, 110, 139.
Rose, ship, 99, 112.
Ross, Charles Bayne Hodgson,
    112.
Rota Point, 106.
Rover, ship, 106.
Rowe, John, 73, 109, 135.
Rowley, Bartholomew Samuel,
    18, 117.
Rowley, Charles, 126.
Royal Society, President of the,
    157.
Royne, ship, 101.
Rude, ship, 124.
Ruse, ship, 65.
Russell, William, 130.
Russian, 62, 133.

S.

Sabina, ship, 48, 49.
Sagesse, ship, 69.
Saghalien Island, 152, 153.
Saint Albans, ship, 22.

THE ROYAL NAVY

Saint Andre, Jean Bon, 93.
Saint Antoine, ship, 139.
Saint Brieux, 124.
Saint Clair, Matthew, 112.
Saint Croix, 79.
Saint George's Channel, 35, 125.
Saint Helens, 151.
Saint Jacques, ship, 135.
Saint Kitts, 47.
Saint Lawrence River, 102.
Saint Lawrence, Gulf of, 106.
Saint Malo, 31, 77, 82, 115, 123.
Saint Marcon, 113, 130.
Saint Martin, 115.
Saint Pierre, ship, 102.
Saint Pietro, 117.
Saint Vincent, Cape, 101, 146.
Saint Vincent, Gulf of, 157.
Saint Vincent, Lord, 80, 92, 157.
Sainte Famille, ship, 130.
Saintes, the, 125.
Salamine, ship, 69, 134.
Saldanha Bay, 142.
Saldanha, ship, 142.
Salisbury, ship, 102.
Salvador del Mundo, ship, 146.
Salvador, ship, 148.
Samboangon, 53.
San Antonio, ship, 146, 147.
San Blas, 151.
San Damaso, 146.
San Domingo, 18, 32, 38, 42, 76, 99, 102, 104, 118, 121, 126-128, 135.
San Fiorenzo, 119.
San Fiorenzo Bay, 101, 102.
San Fiorenzo, ship, 50, 68, 69, 119, 128.
San Francisco, ship, 146.

San Hermenegildo, 149.
San Josef, ship, 83, 146, 149.
San Leon, ship, 147.
San Nicolas, ship, 146.
San Pio, ship, 145.
San Vincente, ship, 146.
San Vincente, ship, 146.
San Ysidro, ship, 146.
Sanders, James, 66, 147.
Sandfly, ship, 130.
Sandoval, ship, 148.
Sandwich Islands, 152.
Sandy Hook, 13.
Sangaar, Strait of, 152, 153.
Sans Culotte, ship, 119, 124.
Sans Pareille, ship, 120, 138.
Sans Quartier, ship, 134.
Sanspareille, ship, 84.
Santa Brigida, ship, 73, 148.
Santa Cazilda, ship, 56.
Santa Cecilia, ship, 146.
Santa Cruz, 104, 129.
Santa Dorotea, ship, 56, 57, 92, 147.
Santa Elena, ship, 51, 146.
Santa Margarita, ship, 25, 30, 39, 40, 96, 123, 126, 146.
Santa Maria, ship, 85.
Santa Sabina, ship, 146.
Santa Teresa, ship, 66, 147.
Santa Teresa, ship, 66, 147.
Santander, 90.
Sardine, ship, 125.
Sardinia, 16, 54, 138.
Sardinian, 118.
Saumarez, James, 15, 16, 23-25, 92, 96, 118, 139, 149.
Saunier, Captain, 86, 87.
Sause, Robert, 115.
Savage, Henry, 104.
Sawyer, Charles, 35.

Scarborough, ship, 154.
Sceptre, ship, 110.
Scevola, ship, 23, 127.
Scharhorn Eiff, 65.
Schiermonnikoog, 69.
Scillies, the, 24.
Scilly, Isle of, 126, 128, 130.
Scipio, ship, 154.
Scipion, ship, 98, 118, 122, 130.
Scotch Brigade, 68.
Scott, James, 114.
Scott, Matthew Henry, 99.
Scourge, ship, 10, 101, 125.
Scout, ship, 34, 100, 114, 116.
Seahorse, ship, 55, 96, 131, 132, 145.
Searle, John Clarke, 46, 110, 139.
Searle, Thomas, 69.
Seaton, George, 101.
Seduisant, ship, 127.
Seine, ship, 24, 45, 46, 55, 56, 81, 82, 96, 100, 131, 137.
Semillante, ship, 11, 12, 68.
Senegal, 138.
Senegal, River, 84.
Senegal, ship, 84, 138.
Sensible, ship, 55, 115, 131.
Sept Isles, 78.
Serapis, ship, 64.
Sercey, Pierre Cesar Charles Guillaume de, 35, 45, 46, 49, 67, 97.
Serieuse, ship, 131.
Serocold, Walter, 99.
Severn, ship, 130.
Seychelle Islands, 91, 139.
Seymour, Hugh, 134, 143.
Seymour, Michael, 128, 133.
Seymour, Stephen, 102.
Shannon, River, 104.

Shark, ship, 101.
Shaw, Charles, 72.
Sheerness, 62.
Sheriff, D., ship master, 113.
Shetland Islands, 100, 112, 121.
Shingles, the, 114.
Shippard, Alexander, 99.
Short, John Ides, 109.
Shortland, Thomas George, 132.
Sibylle, ship, 24, 53, 67, 68, 91, 93, 95, 96, 121, 133, 139, 145.
Sicily, 100, 107, 121, 131.
Sierra Leone, 54.
Simon's Bay, 140.
Sincere, ship, 118.
Sinclair, James, 64, 90.
Sinclair, Patrick, 18, 119.
Sir Thomas Pasley, ship, 112.
Siren, ship, 31.
Sirene, ship, 77, 102, 121, 142.
Sirius, ship, 62, 63, 85, 138, 143, 154.
Sjoelland, ship, 150.
Skipsey, William, 137.
Skynner, Lancelot, 109, 125.
Smith, Charles, 99.
Smith, Francis, 139.
Smith, Lieutenant, 112.
Smith, Matthew, 26, 27, 101.
Smith, Matthew (2nd), 83.
Smith, William Sidney, 25, 34, 35, 37, 124, 125, 133, 134.
Smyrna, 101.
Soehesten, ship, 150.
Solebay, ship, 76, 135.
Sotheby, Thomas, 103, 112.
Souris, ship, 130.
South Africa, 71.
South America, 81, 85, 113.
South Carolina, 19.

THE ROYAL NAVY 195

South Sunda, 121.
Southampton, ship, 34, 40, 41, 126, 145.
Souverain Peuple, ship, 131.
Spain, 66, 90, 88, 149.
Spanish (Spaniard), 17, 47, 48, 49, 51, 53, 56, 66, 69, 73-76, 79, 82, 83, 85, 87-90, 94, 95, 102, 106-109, 112, 117, 118, 122.
Spanish Royal Navy, 94, 95, 145.
Spartiate, ship, 131.
Speedy, ship, 54, 75, 88, 89, 99, 114, 122, 149.
Spencer Gulf, 157.
Spencer, ship, 38, 39, 126.
Sphinx, ship, 119.
Spider, ship, 102.
Spilsby, 158.
Spitfire, ship, 99, 128, 133.
Spithead, 31, 101, 157, 158.
Spread, John Mathias, 149.
Sprightly, ship, 113.
Spy, ship, 122.
Stackpoole, Hassard, 115.
Stag, ship, 33, 63, 111, 133, 140.
Stap, William, 101.
Stephens, Philip, 152.
Ster, ship, 140.
Steuart, Don Jacob, 48.
Stewart, George (Lord Garlies), 29.
Stirling, Charles, 55, 56, 107, 130, 131.
Stopford, Robert, 54, 72, 124, 125, 135.
Stovin, George Samuel, 112.
Strachan, Richard John, 20, 31, 83, 120, 123, 128.
Stromboli, ship, 147.

Stuart, William, 140.
Succes, ship, 140.
Success, ship, 69, 113, 137, 140.
Suffisant, ship, 119.
Suffisante, ship, 34, 39, 124.
Suffren, ship, 128.
Sumatra, 45, 57.
Superbe, ship, 35, 122, 124.
Supply, ship, 153, 154.
Surcouf, Robert, 82.
Surinam, 134, 143.
Surinam, ship, 134.
Surprise, ship, 37, 74, 125, 148.
Surridge, Thomas, 120.
Surveillante, ship, 128.
Sutton, John, 125.
Sutton, Robert Manners, 99.
Svoerdfisken, ship, 150.
Sweden, 54.
Swedish (Swede), 53, 82, 84, 114.
Swift, ship, 105.
Swiftsure, ship, 22, 23, 78, 114, 120, 132.
Swin, the (a passage), 103, 104.
Swiney, William (2nd), 60.
Sydney, 151, 154.
Sylph, ship, 44, 51, 52, 90, 130, 133, 141, 147.
Symonds, Jermyn John, 103.
Syria, 69, 108, 109, 133, 134.

T.

Tagus River, 103.
Tahiti, 151, 154.
Tahitians, 152.
Tamar, ship, 70, 71, 134.
Tamise, ship, 36, 39, 40, 95, 126.
Tarleton, ship, 118.
Tartar, ship, 104.

Tartary, Gulf of, 152, 153.
Tartu, Captain, 17.
Tartu, ship, 18, 49.
Tasmania, 156, 158.
Taylor, (unknown) a
    midshipman, 158.
Taylor, Bridges Watkinson, 60,
    111.
Telegraph, ship, 113, 133.
Temeraire, ship, 122.
Temple, John, 103.
Temple, the Paris, 37.
Tenerife, 57, 95, 129.
Termagant, ship, 137.
Ternate, ship, 143.
Terpsichore, ship, 47, 48, 127,
    145, 147.
Tetuan Bay, 113.
Texel, ship, 144.
Texel, the, 34, 39, 62, 109, 124,
    141, 143, 144.
Thalia, ship, 29, 122, 129.
Thames, ship, 17, 18, 40, 98,
    126, 138.
Themistocle, ship, 119.
Therese, ship, 79, 137.
Thetis, ship, 32, 73, 123, 141,
    148.
Thevenard, Captain H.A., 25.
Thistle Island, 157.
Thistle, John, 157, 158.
Tholen, ship, 141.
Thomond, Murrough, Marquis
    of, 58.
Thompson, (unknown), painter,
    75.
Thompson, Thomas Boulden,
    59-62, 107.
Thorn, ship, 32, 123.
Thulen, ship, 141.
Thunderer, ship, 128.
Tiburon, Cape, 76.

Tigre, ship, 123, 139.
Tiller, John, 114.
Timoleon, ship, 131.
Todd, Andrew, 110.
Tokio, Bay of, 152.
Tom Thumb, ship, 155.
Tonnant, ship, 131.
Topaze, ship, 45, 118.
Torres Strait, 158, 160.
Torride, ship, 108, 132, 134.
Tortue, ship, 18, 49, 128.
Totty, Thomas, 114, 130.
Toulon, 19, 20, 40, 55, 98, 99,
    118, 119, 136.
Tourtelet, Captain, 38.
Tourterelle, ship, 29, 30, 122.
Towry, George Henry, 32, 33,
    122.
Trafalgar, 160.
Treguier, 124.
Trehouart, Captain, 26.
Tremendous, ship, 76, 135.
Trent, ship, 88.
Tresahar, John, 103.
Triangles, the, 114.
Tribune, ship, 39, 40, 105, 126.
Tricolor, ship, 119.
Trieste, 61.
Trincomale, 101.
Trincomale, ship, 73, 109, 135.
Trinidad, 111, 146.
Triomphant, ship, 119.
Tripp, George, 109.
Triton, ship, 50, 52, 73, 134,
    135, 148.
Trois Couleurs, ship, 41, 126.
Trois Rivieres, 84.
Trollope, Henry, 42, 43.
Trompeuse, ship, 102, 111, 119.
Trondhjem, 124.
Troubridge, Thomas, 23.
Trusty, ship, 25.

THE ROYAL NAVY 197

Tucker, Tudor, 105.
Tunis, 125.
Turkey, 140.
Turks, 62, 133.
Turquand, William, 78.
Turquand, William James, 112.
Twysden, Thomas, 72, 100.
Tyler, Charles, 106, 129.
Typing Island (Myako-sima), 153.
Tyrrel, Edward, 98.

U.

Undaunted, ship, 102, 118, 119, 143.
Unicorn, ship, 39, 40, 96, 126, 128, 140.
Unie, ship, 144.
Union, ship, 98.
Unite, ship, 36, 37, 99, 125, 129.
Urania, ship, 18, 49.
Uranie, ship, 17, 18, 89, 139.
Urca Cargadora, ship, 147.
Urchin, ship, 113.
Ushant, 19, 25, 110, 119, 120, 122, 126, 128, 134.
Utile, ship, 40, 41, 115, 126.
Utrecht, ship, 144.

V.

Vado, 140.
Vaillant, ship, 127.
Vaillante, ship, 47, 59, 111, 132.
Valetta, 137.
Valiant, ship, 128.
Valiente, ship, 147.
Valk, ship, 144.
Valkyrien, ship, 150.
Valteau, Captain, 43.

Van Tromp, ship, 142.
Vancouver, George, 157, 160.
Vandongen, Captain, 11.
Vanguard, ship, 35, 96, 123, 124.
Vanneau, ship, 103, 117.
Vansittart, Henry, 148.
Variante, ship, 36.
Vashon, James Giles, 151, 152, 160.
Vautour, ship, 50.
Vedette, ship, 135.
Velosa Aragonesa, ship, 147.
Veloz, ship, 149.
Venetian, 140.
Venezuela, 74.
Vengeance, ship, 44, 45, 50, 68, 69, 81, 82, 96, 137.
Vengeur, ship, 20, 37, 76, 117, 119, 120, 135.
Venice, Gulf of, 139.
Venturier, ship, 129.
Venus, Point, 152.
Venus, ship, 11, 83, 138, 144.
Vera Cruz, 151.
Vertu, ship, 45, 54, 57, 58.
Verwachting, ship, 143.
Vestal, ship, 33, 128, 140.
Vestale, ship, 34, 47, 48, 69, 70, 95, 103, 127, 134.
Vesuve, ship, 123.
Victor, ship, 91, 92, 140.
Victorieuse, ship, 34, 63, 119, 124.
Victorious, ship, 45.
Vigilante, ship, 98, 124.
Vigo, 149.
Vigo Bay, 111.
Villaret de Joyeuse, Louis Thomas , 27.
Ville de Lorient, ship, 128.
Ville de Marseille, ship, 135.

Villeneuve, Jean, 59, 62.
Villeon, Captain P., 20.
Vincejo, ship, 147.
Vindictive, ship, 142.
Viper, ship, 80, 137.
Vipere, ship, 99, 104, 119.
Virginia, 105.
Virginie, ship, 37, 38, 126, 143.
Vivo, ship, 149.
Vizagapatam, 128.
Vlie, 144.
Vlieland, 109.
Vlieter, ship, 144.
Vlieter, the, 144.
Vlugheid, ship, 33, 141.
Volcan, ship, 38, 126.
Volontaire, ship, 25, 121.
Vriesland, 141.
Vrijheid, ship, 142.
Vrouw Maria, ship, 142.
Vulcan, ship, 98.
Vyvian, William, 84.

W.

Waakzaamheid, 62, 63, 143.
Waikiki Bay, 152.
Wakker, ship, 143.
Waller, Thomas Moutray, 79.
Wallis, Henry, 90.
Wallis, James, 65, 108.
Wallis, Provo William Parry, 160.
Warberg, 114.
Warre, Henry, 35.
Warren, John Borlase, 20, 25, 35, 36, 44, 51, 52, 54, 79, 119, 120, 122-125, 127, 129, 132, 136.
Warren, Robert, 90.
Washington, ship, 144.
Wasp, ship, 80, 111.

Wassenaar, ship, 142.
Watson, James, 110.
Watson, Joshua Rowley, 102.
Watson, Lieutenant, 101.
Watson, Robert, 33.
Weazel, ship, 108.
Weerwraak, ship, 143.
Wells, Thomas, 20.
Welsh, 50.
West Indies, 11, 19, 24, 30, 32, 35, 46, 47, 63, 70, 98, 100, 101, 103-106, 112, 115, 117, 119, 121-125, 127, 130, 136, 147-, 151, 154.
Westcott, George Blagden, 146.
Western, Thomas, 70, 134.
Weymouth, 25.
Weymouth, ship, 110.
White, Charles, 33, 128.
White, John Chambers, 44, 52, 133, 141.
White, Thomas, 108.
Whittle, Lieutenant, 107.
Wight, Isle of, 109, 114.
Wilding, ship, 133.
Wilhelmina, ship, 63, 143.
Willemstad, ship, 140.
William Pitt, ship, 20, 109.
Williams, Thomas (4th), 39, 126, 140, 146.
Wilson, George, 122.
Wilson, Henry Smith, 109.
Winthrop, Robert, 102, 111, 126, 145.
Wodehouse, Philip, 105.
Wolley, Thomas, 51, 129.
Wolverine, ship, 65, 71, 94, 144.
Wood, James Athol, 106.
Woodford, ship, 49.
Woodley, John, 101.
Wooldridge, Francis, 140.

THE ROYAL NAVY

Wooldridge, William, 90, 109.
Worth, James Andrew, 133.
Wrench, Matthew, 104.
Wright, John Wesley, 37.

X.

Xenophon, ship, 157.

Y.

Yames, Lieutenant J., 114.
Yarmouth, 110.
Yesso Island, 152, 153.
Yonge Frans, ship, 143.
Yonge Lansier, ship, 143.

York, ship, 148.
Yorke, Joseph Sidney, 33.
Young, George Forbes
          Freeman, 151.
Young, James (2nd), 73, 148.

Z.

Zealand, ship, 141.
Zealous, ship, 134.
Zebra, ship, 121, 124.
Zeeland, ship, 141.
Zeemeeuw, ship, 141.
Zefir, ship, 141.
Zephyr, ship, 63.
Zuijder Zee, 144.

LONDON: PRINTED BY WILLIAM CLOWES AND SONS,
LIMITED, STAMFORD STREET AND CHARING CROSS

INDEX OF AVAILABLE BOOKS

Chronicon Books is dedicated to the production of inexpensive high-quality editions of neglected, out-of-print history books and documents which are in the public domain. Below is a list of titles currently available. Ordering information can be found at chroniconbooks.com

A HISTORY OF THE ART OF WAR IN THE MIDDLE AGES by Charles Oman

>Volume I
>Volume II

A HISTORY OF THE ROMAN REPUBLIC by Cyril E. Robinson

A PHILOSOPHICAL ESSAY ON PROBABILITIES by Pierre Simon Laplace.

CHURCH HISTORY FROM NERO TO CONSTANTINE by C.P.S. Clarke.

ETRUSCAN RESEARCHES by Isaac Taylor

FIREARMS IN AMERICAN HISTORY — 1600 TO 1800 by Charles Winthrop Sawyer

HISTORY OF SWITZERLAND by Wilhelm Oechsli

HISTORY OF THE GATLING GUN DETACHMENT by John Parker

HISTORY OF THE INDIAN NAVY by Charles Rathbone Low.
>Volume I - 1613 to 1816.
>Volume II - 1811 to 1830.
>Volume III - 1831 to 1853.
>Volume IV 1852 to 1863.

HISTORY OF THE THIRTY YEARS WAR IN GERMANY by Friedrich Schiller

ORDER OF BATTLE — THE UNITED STATES ARMY GROUND FORCES IN WORLD WAR II — PACIFIC THEATER OF OPERATIONS by the Office of the Chief of Military History

RAILROADS, THEIR ORIGINS AND PROBLEMS by Charles Francis Adams

ROGER OF SICILY by Edmund Curtis

SKETCHES OF BUTTE by George Wesley Davis

STUDIES, MILITARY AND DIPLOMATIC by Charles Francis Adams

THE ART OF WAR IN THE MIDDLE AGES by Charles Oman

THE AUXILIA OF THE ROMAN IMPERIAL ARMY by G.L. Cheesman

THE CRISIS OF THE NAVAL WAR by John Rushworth Jellicoe

THE GRAND FLEET — 1914-1916 by John Rushworth Jellicoe

THE HISTORY OF ATLANTIS by Lewis Spence

THE HISTORY OF CHIVALRY by G.P.R. James

THE HISTORY OF ENGLAND by David Hume

> Volume I — Julius Caesar to King John
> Volume II — King Henry III to King Richard III
> Volume III — King Henry VII to Queen Mary I
> Volume IV — Queen Elizabeth I and King James I
> Volume V — King Charles I to the Commonwealth.
> Volume VI — Kings Charles II and James II.

THE HISTORY OF FRANCE by John Gifford

    Volume I — the Roman, Merovingian, and Carolingian periods
    Volume II — the Capetian period
    Volume III — The early Valois period
    Volume IV — The continuation of the Valois period. The reigns
        of Charles VII and Louis XI
    Volume V — The later Valois period
    Volume VI — The Bourbon period

THE HISTORY OF THE REIGN OF THE EMPEROR CHARLES V by
    William Robertson

    Volume I
    Volume II
    Volume III

THE HOLY ROMAN EMPIRE by James Bryce

THE LATIN KINGDOM OF JERUSALEM by C.R. Conder.

THE LOMBARD COMMUNES by W.F. Butler

THE MAJOR OPERATIONS OF THE NAVIES IN THE AMERICAN
    WAR OF INDEPENDENCE by Alfred Thayer Mahan

THE MEDIEVAL EMPIRE by Herbert Fisher

    Volume I
    Volume II

THE ORIGINS OF THE ISLAMIC STATE by Abu al Abbas al
    Baladhuri

THE RISE OF THE DUTCH REPUBLIC by John Lothrop Motley

    Volume I — 1555 to 1567
    Volume II — 1567 to 1577
    Volume III — 1577 to 1584

THE ROYAL NAVY

THE ROYAL NAVY by William Laird Clowes

    Volume 1A — Earliest Times to 1399
    Volume 1B — 1399 to 1603
    Volume 2A — 1603 to 1660
    Volume 2B — 1660 to 1714
    Volume 3A — 1714 to 1763
    Volume 3B — 1763 to 1792
    Volume 4A — 1792 to 1802: Administration and
        Major Operations
    Volume 4B — 1792 to 1802: Minor Operations and Exploration
    Additional volumes to 1900 in progress

THE VENETIAN REPUBLIC by J. Carew Hazlitt

    Volume One — AD 407 to AD 1205
    Volume Two — AD 1205 to AD 1365
    Volume Three — AD 1365 to AD 1457
    Volumes Four — AD 1457 to AD 1797
    Volume Five — Culture and Government
    Volume Six — Culture and Government

WE THE PEOPLE — The Founding Documents

Printed in Great Britain
by Amazon